CONTENTS

FOREWORD

Book: *The Rising AI Mind from Globally Correlated Big Data Center Entity* (ISBN: 9781654255275)

Amazon's free banana and robotics as co-workers; Apple, Facebook, Google, LinkedIn (Microsoft) and their Astromega luxury touring coaches for employee commute: stainless steel body frame, dramatic upper-deck sky view rooftop, dual-deck entertainment system, individual lighting and ventilation, integrated heating and air conditioning systems, provide a state of the art moving center and comfortable environment for all the passengers. Hi-speed Wi-Fi on board and business VPN enable you to connect into the company meeting at your figure tips, once on-board, you are considered working in your office, for the timed employee, the time riding on the bus is counting into your 8-hour work day —

There are on-site ginormous snacks, beverages, liquors, food, over ten-thousand-dollar commercial grade expresso maker (self-served) and staffed coffee house, as well as manor type furniture: branded, comfortable, and durable. Massage chair, sleeping pod, meditation rooms plus full serve massage services. GYM, pools, bowling alley and the dance floors —

Green Plants and beautiful flowers by the sides of

every cubical aisle or decorated on the wall. There even has a duck-tube-slide (from top floor serpentines to the first floor though layers of wall-to-wall room-to-room) inside the mountain view building (MTV 1950). An indoor climbing wall in tech Conner building (TC3). Numerical decorated meeting rooms and collaborating areas; secrets chambers for on-site (alcohol) parties, secretive entrance from a wall-like-bookshelf, beer dispenser on floor, and what you want more —

You may think these employees are high there in the meetings and talking about sophisticate algorithms, like I was interviewed in the Google New York office: simply put, to write the code in C++ on white board for the shortest steps to reach the center square of the array from an external starting square all at once, aha? not always. There was an infamous case of a "special" diet (veg) lady filed the high priority ticket for the missing pistachio (for rotation, pistachio went to next floor, lol). And an email marked "Important" to all employee, one lady lost her ring during her on-site shower (~10s am) and urged every one for this emergency: found back in no time — while Google's sacking on its employees had been labeled as chopping off its traditional absolute freedom, speculating the cause of Larry and Sergey's stepping down —

Amazon is so good, that If you can work in Amazon, you'll find easy to work anywhere! Because it's damn stressfully with so many robotics around you. Still less than Apple, which neither provides enough restroom places for their shuttle bus drivers nor lets them rest enough: less than 20 minutes for their meals. While you are on the sick bed, you will get your share of due document delivered to you, must finish before the nurse pull the needle off your a$$. Facebook is good, once you finish up your internship, you may hear the project that you have worked you're a$$ off the whole summer is just a piece of garbage no reason to start in the beginning, plus luck ones may need help your director for the laundry, albeit his wife's dirty undies together —

Ladies behave badly, while a busy employee found all the laundry room driers were occupied and done without removing clothes: with only one piece of small patties with size of a nosenet (word coined in the book, English words were inadequacy as the first step of IAAD, the reverse course of AI together with the Python coding language: see book for detail) in one of the driers —

∞   ∞   ∞   ∞   ∞   ∞   ∞   ∞   ∞   ∞   ∞

Although patient H.M. (Henry Molaison, 1926 – 2008) was the most famous case in the history of neuroscience, Clive Wearing (1938 –) is a stupefying case alive. Henry could not form new memory while Clive Wearing is the living manifesto of the truth that connectivity and integrity are of paramount importance for the homo sapiens' elevated intelligence and shrewd creativity —

When Hellen Keller was not capable of language, she was not able to form thoughts simply because there is nothingness in there and there is nothing to form. On Clive Wearing side, he has ample of elements and building resources, however, the digitization and disassociation expeditiously rob the thoughts and meaningfulness of the life —

It is not hard to say that the language elements and their associated connectivity are among the essential resources for the cognitive intelligent activities to function and sustain —

∞ ∞ ∞ ∞ ∞ ∞ ∞ ∞ ∞ ∞ ∞

After switching his advisor (in his freshman summer 1901), Einstein's mind was still an indecision. One year later, Einstein was conceiving (no! No! NO! I know what you are thinking, not that) — to withdraw the tiresome damn PhD course, he said, "the whole comedy has become tiresome for me." ... and Einstein could not stop doing "That Thing You Do" until he was finally stuck on a so-called unified theory and successfully drove himself into (so far) "a dead corner." —

∞ ∞ ∞ ∞ ∞ ∞ ∞ ∞ ∞ ∞ ∞

Not only in Bible and Science, but also in NBA, people are declaring the perfection too. Kevin Durant told the Wall Street Journal while doing "for billionaire" headspace: "So me? Shit, how you going to rehabilitate me? What you going to teach me? How can you alter anything in my basketball life? I got an MVP already. I got scoring titles" (vs GSW) —

∞ ∞ ∞ ∞ ∞ ∞ ∞ ∞ ∞ ∞ ∞

The homo sapiens, had achieved more than any peer so far in the universe. The obvious differences between human's ability of inherent and other creatures enable the species to pass through the expertise over external channels on top of the biological genetic limit. That, by far, is the driving force for all the great human achievements. Some other creatures, for example, octopuses, which are capable of learning through simple observation, among others, is at excel on the problem solving and issue resolving. However, it may be a bit challenge for octopuses to write down words in water: not only the paper always gets wet, but also the fact that the sea water simply bleaches the ink away, not mentioning the regulations requiring these octopuses have to submit a copy of their book to the congress library —

To the "dirt" limit, human cannot see anything or smell anything to enter the territory boundaries of the circle of the lion pride, albeit that circle had been marked with the pride's chief's pee-pee, golden standard of code of conduct, which has been always well received and respected by the creatures —

∞ ∞ ∞ ∞ ∞ ∞ ∞ ∞ ∞ ∞ ∞

Quantum computing aside, the huge leap of world wide web during the past quarter of century orchestrated the master stroke of the IAAD epoch, which spans from the beginning of homo sapiens all the way to current generation civilization —

Taking only Google's hardware infrastructure, through its worldwide-allocated data centers, in terms of amount of per-capita-resource, Google now offers a whopping >200MB RAM, >700MB (SSD storage), >5 GB (Hard Disk), with a computing power akin to an Clay-2 supercomputer, for each person of the 7 billion population on the planet earth. Aggregating with Microsoft, IBM, Facebook, Twitter, Instagram, Amazon, ... and many more, such like gaming data-center-services, navigating, weather forecasting, and many more, plus government and military agencies, the number will be astonishedly huge —

∞ ∞ ∞ ∞ ∞ ∞ ∞ ∞ ∞ ∞ ∞

It is much worse for watching the phone or the monitor screens than watching TVs, which was an old school argument between the parents and the children. Now the parents shall pray that their children to watch TV instead of watching on the closer and smaller screens —

∞ ∞ ∞ ∞ ∞ ∞ ∞ ∞ ∞ ∞ ∞

In this case, if Taylor Swift is with GF, what does she need to put in the email user name field is: taylor.swift-@globalfoundries.com as the Gmail user name — her password is omitted here to protect her personal credential —

∞ ∞ ∞ ∞ ∞ ∞ ∞ ∞ ∞ ∞ ∞

(F-35 Joint Strike Fighter) the sensor fusion software has been described as one of the most difficult parts of the program. The difficulty of integrity, which is the primary function of DAAI process. The final Block 3 software was planned to have 8.6 million lines of code. General Norton Schwartz has said that the software was the biggest factor that might delay the USAF's initial operational capability. US congress described this software suite as complicated as anything on earth on the wake of a serial of software bug related issues —

∞ ∞ ∞ ∞ ∞ ∞ ∞ ∞ ∞ ∞ ∞

With all the issues from intrinsic flaws and limitations, what are the outlook on this self-driving car thing anyway? Although there are not as good as one may expected, they are still silver lines out there —

There the inauguration of autonomous high-speed train in Asia: the fast, dizzy, glamorous, and comfortable autonomous train has become a new breed of national luxury display. The old school play book to fool the general population: You have this and I have this, so you must have copied from us! At this point, the US does not have anything on that level, so that play book cannot be applied —

Here the S*** hits the fan: another deadly self-driving car accident in US. The National Highway Traffic Safety Administration is investigating the crash of a speeding Tesla that killed two people in a Los Angeles suburb. The black Tesla Model S had run a red light before the killing; it was noticed that the Tesla has broad appetite: including fire trucks and police cruising vehicles (by crashing into). The National Transportation Safety Board referred to it as "automation complacency." —

∞ ∞ ∞ ∞ ∞ ∞ ∞ ∞ ∞ ∞ ∞

When everything done and fitted into their roles,

an integrity of DAAI, the global scale artificial intelligent entity collectively forms. That is what we called rudiment mind of the earth brain (MOTEB) takes into form in the heat of culminating big data processing power, increasingly distributed artificial intelligence, and seamlessly interconnected global network information highway channeling. The flow of information creates communications; the competing and gating of these streams are representations of the natural selections of survival of the fittest; finally, global consciousness comes into existence in the form of the integrity of the distributed entire assembly (IDEA).

∞　∞　∞　∞　∞　∞　∞　∞　∞　∞　∞

For the best benifit for the US auto industry, albeit already left behind, and the "oil" business, the US will continue surpressing the high-speed rail and advocating freedom of automible and boosting oil industry, such as the leakingKeystone Pipeline and the offshore oil spilling Deepwater Horizon thus to stimulate the endorphin secretion in the 1% population's nucleus accumbens.

Errata:

This book had been drafted in MS Word and edited in Kindle Create, which is error prone and lacking features, tables, inline images, bullets, and many more cannot be edited once imported. The table of contents has been generated by randomly chopping off the original texts and resulting some out-of-context piles in the "Contents" list, while the original page is correct and there was no way to manually edit the content list. An example of the awkwardness of DAAI deployment, the core tune of this book's plot, "Once approaching natural reality, the AI always shows inabilities for the fullness, smoothness, and sufficiency for the objects.

CHAPTER 0: JUMPSTART IN THE ERA OF ARTIFICIAL INTELLIGENCE (AI)

§ 0.0 REPRESENTATIONS OF GLOBAL CONSCIOUSNESS

Rudiment mind of the earth brain (MOTEB) takes into form in the heat of culminating big data processing power, increasingly distributed artificial intelligence (AI), and seamlessly interconnected global network channelling through information highway. The flow of information creates communications; the competing and gating of these streams are representations of the natural selections of survival of the fittest; finally, global consciousness comes into existence in the form of the integrity of the distributed entire assembly (IDEA).

The invention of modern programmable computers in the early of twenty century creates the primary discrete point particles of zero-degree localized numerical data process entity: atomic machinery unit (AMU). At the moment the then AMU is considered no structural describer needed: the flow of inputs and outputs does not impact any other AMU, near or far.

AMU grows and thrives with the computing power,

storage capacity, and of course, driven by the complexities of problems to be solved. All these information attributes are dyed in totally different dimensions: these dimensions are not to be absorbed easily and naturally by human beings, which have been accustomed to the true tSpace system of the external physical world (tSpace to be used for this):

In which, eyes are to see, ears to hear, nose to smell, tongue to taste, together with sensations of temperature, mechanical (touch, pressure, vibration, proprioception, etc), pain/itch, emotions, and so on. A bliss and sweet experience generates waves of striking pulse through the expanse existing in the internal universe of mind like in topological space. The visual, auditorial, emotion, plus any other dimensional manifolds, together, anchor the event as traces of memory, a key element in the global conscious awareness, naturally without conscious interference. To denoted the expanse of the internal world of mind uniquely and conveniently, we put forward a word of enSpace, which is not only in cadence with in(ner)-space, but also connoting enclosure space within the skull.

Now that the expansion of information in the space of computational dimensional manifolds (under the same token and also for a more general representation, we put forward a word of iSpace, denoting information space entity, retreating from "dispace: digital space" for obvious linguistic reason) had grown into a stage beyond the common awareness can absorb and digest without special training and orientation.

§ 0.1 CREATIONS OF INTERNET, YAHOO! AND GOOGLE

§ 0.1.1 The Human Invention of World Wide Web by Tim Berners-Lee

"Well, I found it frustrating that in those days, there was different information on different computers, but you had to log on to different computers to get at it. Also, sometimes you had to learn a different program on each computer. So, finding out how things worked was really difficult. Often it was just easier to go and ask people when they were having coffee.

"Because people at CERN came from universities all over the world, they brought with them all types of computers. Not just Unix, Mac and PC: there were all kinds of big mainframe computer and medium sized computers running all sorts of software.

"I actually wrote some programs to take information from one system and convert it so it could be inserted into another system. More than once. And when you are a programmer, and you solve one problem and then you solve one that's very similar, you often think, 'Isn't there a better way? Can't we just fix this problem for good?' That became 'Can't we convert every information system so that it looks like part of some imaginary information system which everyone can read?' And that became the World Wide Web (W3)."

As CERN (European Organization for Nuclear Research. "CERN" is derived from the acronym for the French Conseil Européen pour la Recherche Nucléaire) scientist Tim Berners-Lee said. The pushing forward to fulfill his idea became the birth synonym of world wide web in 1990.

§ 0.1.2 Introduction to Tim Berners-Lee's Network Resources: Jerry and David's guide to the World Wide Web

With the infrastructural hardware foundation, added on top of the no-volume iSpace limited AMUs, the seeds of core information immediately found their way out of the confinements, infiltrated into the distance nodes (computer cluster, LANs: local area networks, we will not be detailing these conceptions here) and distributed inside the iSpace like growing weeds. In an era, everybody was used to get information and knowledge from content indexed and published materials, such as books, brochures, magazines/journals, and newspapers, etc (aside from entertainment TV channels) plus directory-listed phone books, The data and information as the result of Tim's network were not easy to peep and accept except for the computer network experts during these days. A web-based "phone book" with organized directory lists was thus born: "Jerry and David's guide to the World Wide Web" in January 1994 (Jerry Yang and David Filo were electrical engineering graduate students at Stanford University). The initial success of the guide inspired their fascinations of "Yet Another Hierarchically Organized Oracle", the Yahoo! Information listing engine, which denoted layer-arranged subcategory databases and authentic information sources.

People accepted and enjoyed Jerry and David's wonderful work naturally: layback, not much thinking to browse through. Same as picking up a magazine and browsing through. You do not need know what you want beforehand, just browsing through the Yahoo! Portal, all the doors are opened to you... You absorbed the knowledge already half cooked and visually organized. You have a clear trajectory with these structured data of information. Traces of reading memory were clearly printed into your enSpace. Yes, Yahoo! The home page, the subdirectories, and even the page contents all had a "form" to let you to cling on, you had a visual clue to integrate the information into your enSpace index. For example, at that time, if you want to get the information regarding Stanford University, as I now can "play it out" from my memory: you would start from http://www.yahoo.com (at that time, no virus, no hacking, no need for the https://), then click the left column "Education" -> "Universities" -> "State" -> "CA"

->"Stanford University". For the none-US universities, they can be selected after click into "Universities". There were countries entry there). Showing below is a typical Yahoo home page in the later 1990s.

§ 0.1.3 WWW "Phonebook" with depth: Here are the early Yahoo! Homepages

23

Showing above was the type of vivid "impression" in my memory: the Yahoo! Homepage in later 1990s. By then, it was a wonderful one-stop encyclopaedia.

More specifically, on the Yahoo! site, the data indexing with Yahoo! approaches, had not been totally submerged without a trace of printed matter, a half way between tSpace (physical world) and enSpace (human mind), leaves you with a comfortable traceable physical (layer-arranged subcategory) dimensional manifold to label the representations of the information from iSpace data into enSpace.

Yahoo

[What's New? | What's Cool? | What's Popular? | A Random Link]

| Yahoo | Up | Search | Suggest | Add | Help |

- Art *(619)* [new]
- Business *(8546)* [new]
- Computers *(3266)* [new]
- Economy *(898)* [new]
- Education *(1839)* [new]
- Entertainment *(8814)* [new]
- Environment and Nature *(268)* [new]
- Events *(64)* [new]
- Government *(1226)* [new]
- Health *(548)* [new]
- Humanities *(226)* [new]
- Law *(221)* [new]
- News *(301)* [new]
- Politics *(184)* [new]
- Reference *(495)* [new]
- Regional Information *(4597)* [new]
- Science *(3289)* [new]
- Social Science *(115)* [new]
- Society and Culture *(933)* [new]

There are currently 31897 entries in the Yahoo database

At the time of Yahoo! thriving, the world wide web had a handful millions of pages (in the era of the homepage look like the one provided above), Yahoo (when it was not Yahoo!) indexed specific 31897 entries in this 1994 (funding year) Yahoo homepage. Importantly, most of the websites by then were created and maintained within government agencies or academic-orientated organizations. The knowledge of internet was limited in these small group of people with expertise and needs. The MTV (Music TV) and Hollywood movies created louder shockwaves and higher brightness. And the popular thinking patterns were more traditional, people were still in the distancing cold war mindset. The technology revolution showing of force to dethrone the industry revolution were still in their last glories (before the society striding into the internet and information era): industry revolution -> technology revolution -> information revolution.

§ 0.2 INNOVATION, AMBITION, VISIONARY, MANAGEMENT, SUCCESS, OR NOT, IT'S COMPLICATED

§ 0.2.1 Larry Page, Sergey, and Susan Wojcicki's Garage

For all the good and proper as Yahoo! could be, Yahoo! was overtaken by Google, which was founded in Sept 4, 1998 by Larry Page (Google parent company Alphabet CEO), and Sergey Brin (President of Alphabet) in Susan Wojcicki's (CEO of YouTube) garage at 232 Santa margarita Ave. Menlo park, California 94025 (When Google was erected, Yahoo! homepage was like the first one of those two screenshots aforementioned, Yahoo! and Yahoo homepages). Curiosity? Here is a short YouTube video on it (https://www.blog.google/products/maps/inside-googles-original-garage-1998-style/). You can take a virtual tour with it as well, here is an image of the preserved "garage" internal view.

Inside Google World Wide Headquarter original location: 232 Santa margarita Ave. Menlo Park, California 94025. AKA Susan Wojcicki's garage. A wise invest for Susan, readily qualified her for YouTube CEO. YouTube brings in more than 20 billion per year for Alphabet (Google's parent company). Be remined, Susan was head of Google Video sector, which had ultimately failed to its competitors, including YouTube. While cannot compete, bought it, and became their CEO, and Susan's job is immortal. In the picture, the far distance is the door of the garage, the bright low right towards the side door, while behind the camera there is another door leading to hallway to the house. Today, the whole house is spared and kept. If you earned 500 million because of your garage, you cannot care less on it.

Upon now, Larry and Sergey have announced stepping down from their posts, the venture they founded. Leaving Sundar Pichai the only centralized power figure in the whole business. Throughout the book, sometimes, they were still treated as in the posts for continuity and easy for readers to connect their amazing success.

The Google's emerging might have been be all the other way as a sweet flavour for one of Yahoo! subdivisions; provided that the strategic mindset of business management was a little different in David Filo. David warmly turned down the knocking at the door $1 million opportunity to acquire the intelligence property (there has been no Google yet) and kindly guided the golden duck to find its paradise today, thrives in the never land, as some notes told later.

§ 0.2.2 Larry Page: "enSpace representation of iSpace world wide web is a graph"

As children from both mathematician/computer parents and Jewish origins, Larry and Sergey converged into Stanford university to pursue their PhD educations after colleges from University of Michigan (1995) and University of Maryland (1993), respectively. They met in the future potential student's campus tour in Stanford guided by Sergey who was a second-year grad in the computer science department in the summer of 1995.

Sergey was a recognized math prodigy in middle school and enrolled into college one year earlier. At Stanford, Sergey focused his intellectual energies on interesting projects rather than actual course work with full loading none-academic classes - sailing, swimming, scuba diving etc. Academically, Sergey had jumped from project to project without settling on a thesis topic, "I talked to lots of research groups" around the school.

The enSpace representation of iSpace world wide web is a graph. A lot of algorithm problems are graph related. A picture of graph in Larry's brain was the spark that would evenly ignite the whole world. After entering Stanford University, Larry quickly settled his doctoral topic on world wide web (w3): each computer was a node (AMU), web page hyperlinks were connections between these AMUs - a structure of graph. The W3 World Wide Web, Page theorized, may have been the largest graph ever created, and it was growing in fast pace: Larry set about pondering the link structure of the Web. Grown up in academic oriented family, Larry knew the importance of scientific citations, a special ranking on the academic publications. An established term SCI (Science Citation Index) is still the official ranking criteria for an academic article today. Recently, Google scholar citation is seeing increasing influence because of simplicity and accessibilities. i.e. if you go to the SCI site: http://mjl.clarivate.com/cgi-bin/jrnlst/jloptions.cgi?PC=K, you will end up a sign-in page. Cannot get what you want. And if you search in Google, i.e. "scholar citation Einstein" or "scholar citation Hong-Ying Zhai" you will get pretty quick access to the publications for these profiles.

For any scholar to be promoted, the person's SCI ranking are of paramount importance. The new papers these will cite your publications are the key players. As for this, it was a tedious work to future-live-tracking the dynamic and growing entity. Larry's idea graph on the w3 was largely nurtured in this nest, matured (together with Sergey) in Googleplex and is still thriving in the current social society of information technology.

§ 0.2.3 Ask Larry: The BackRub Should Have Been Called FutureCit?!

So, Page's project was on the implantation idea related to the "interconnections" on the w3, so called Back-Rub. Larry reasoned that if he could divine a method to count and qualify each growing link on the w3, "the Web would become a more valuable place."

The idea's complexity and scale lured Brin to the job. While Sergey was still hunting for project to anchor his doctoral dissertation on, he found the premise behind BackRub was fascinating. After talking to lots of research groups, Sergey found "this was the most exciting project, both because it tackled the Web, which represents human knowledge, and because I liked Larry."

Larry and Sergey worked diligently for all the detail to the core, of:

Google.

§ 0.2.4 Google's Success was by Harnessing Your Intelligence and —?

With the suggestion from Jon Kleinberg at IBM's Al-maden, Larry and Sergey published a paper titled "*The Anatomy of a Large-Scale Hypertextual Web Search Engine*"

Provided these backgrounds, it was still a wonder that

Google can be the Google of today (of course, Alphabeta inc.):

1. Google succeeded in driving people from lay-back observers to active participants, this is by far the most radical and dictatorial, set profound models for the late successors to follow.

   In the traditional social norm, people are stationary and passive, the publishers have been taking full responsibilities to bring information to the readers like (sort of) feeding ducks. The publishers had already pickup what the common people can read and reach. As a result of this traditional pattern from whole history, the readers are less involving into which to read. Yes, they can pick up different themes from all the publications. In that pattern, the diligent readers had pretty good grips on the whole knowledge library with physical forms and know the dimensional manifold pretty well. For anyone to read, before browse a journal, s/he can be blank in the brain, started by cuing in the covers or the table of contents ... everything flows in without having to find way through and navigating through a channel of decision-dependent-outcome. While the answer in a published book may not be the best, but you accepted its credibility and felt much more at ease. The unnoticed truth is the materials that had been not put in to publications are far more immense that these in physical carriers. But the general populations do not doubt these published answers because of the discrepancies from the unpublished knowledge. However, when you get the total stranger answer from Google search, you are not so sure about it. There are huge portion of the knowledge chunk in dark (you know their existence, albeit low ranks in Google's search list), you are not that comfortable to accept and feel easy, before accessing to a couple of resources and gaining the confidence into yourself.

Google's algorithm counting common users' activities and mining huge common features out of them: the key is the links and connections. Just like its original idea: assembling the forward links and nodes; using Google has totally changed every person's thinking pattern or even life style: forward thinking. In the beginning, a text box is displaying before you. Now at "Google" portal, you have more or less uncertainty and panic in the beginning: an ordinary people don't know what to do with it: an empty text box with "Google" on top of it, no place to chime in by clicking. What does all this about? You have to know what you want and distilled it into key words or string, i.e. "First televised presidential debate" once you are here, Google does the next. However, the job that you have done is the most extraordinary part, not Google. In fact, Google has forced you to chime in its machinery input, from which any automation can be made possible, and this part, is by far the key obstacle for all the artificial intelligence to put into execution. Now, they use ways of "training" process.

Google takes your intelligence as their fundamental entry condition for their algorithm to work, and Google so far so good. This is remarkable. Thanks to Wall Street business running model and US society's openness.

2. The big reason that Google had surpassed Yahoo! was the design model: Yahoo! was still half traditional. The mission of it was to harvest knowledge and bring them into "physically structural" forms and provide readers with information services.

   Searching the Web is immensely useful. But is it a profitable business? For a decade, the answer was "no." Web search was a perennial money loser. For engines like Lycos, Ask-Jeeves, and later AltaVista and Google, banner ads brought income, but not profits.

   The "Searching for Profit" had been grown out from the infamous "Banners and Pop-Ups", which was later very enthused by Yahoo! That is still the patterns Yahoo! follows today. Yahoo! has been pretty awkward in this situation: some of the videos of their email portal are so resource depleting, that the users are hardly able to click or enter user name or passwords (especially in the early days when the computers were not powerful enough for these resources-depleted video rendering).

   There was an online site "GoTo.com" starting a

model of search-based advertising. GoTo.com pioneered the mechanism that Google later bet its revenue on: advertisers paying to place links near search results related to particular keywords. Then, in 2000 Google turned itself—and the search industry—into the iconic Web triumph by refining GoTo.com's insight: advertisers would pay to place links near search results where keywords appeared, an old-school auction feature let advertisers bid on keywords. AdWords, Google's revenue generator, was born.

Google's biggest success was for profits thinking and exploring the digital advertisements in the whole scale for the first time and succeeded. Because Google has every one participated and counted into the weight for advertisements while Yahoo! had not fully explored how to turned the huge number of usership into money. For them, sometime, more users might be a burden (for the servers). Google had been born as one of the Wall Street's Gooden duck, they had never let it loose in the beginning.

In the digital society, the interconnected world can only have one winner for every field, thus Google won, and won big.

The takeaway, Google was born as Wall Street's Golden duck. Google had successfully turned the visiting count into a creditable criterion for AdWords and claimed the mechanism would be proportional to the business

profits for these advertisers, importantly, it is true and accepted. That is the innate skill for Wall street. Google and Wallstreet have accomplished this well together.

3. All other factors are less important. Smart management, wise vision, not only Google employs "smartest people on the planet", but also snatches good consultants for business investing, as well as the chefs ..., plus, once in such position, keep cruising is not extremely challenging. Successes are opportunities arising in different stages of the business execution in the human society. The leading role from all the participating parties looms large as a general rule just because most of its gears snapped into the nature and society developing engine in precise time, location, and social demanding, which are largely games of chances. For all that, inspecting the Google product grave yard: more than 200 projects have been failed so far: instead of crying over the spilled milk like Yahoo! Google never mind overdoing that acquisitions. Of course, diligence, hardworking, and visionary etc are the basic requirements for anything coming into play in this society: i.e. even the R*s*i*n meddling US election was not without greatness in every aspect.

*This book has been written in MS Word and imported into Amazon Kindle Create, whcih cannot accept changes and editing for certain elements. As a consequence, the above "table", actually bulletin in MS Word, cannot be editted during proofreading, these software bugs have left some rough places. I feel deeply disturbed... I also feel balanced: because I had enough saying on the inanity of sofrware and AI, from their creation. Key theme in this book.

§ 0.2.5 Yahoo! A directory Service Contrasting to a Search Engine

By early 1998, Yahoo had added email, shopping, classifieds, personals, games, travel, weather, maps, people search, celebrity chats, a kid-oriented version called Yahooligans, and an online magazine. At the time, it was competing with search portals like Excite, InfoSeek, and Lycos to provide everything on the net in one place. Although there were a lot of shortcomings that can be seen today, one of the greatest features then in Yahoo! site, was that these services were fully recorded and free! Now, the internet pool has grown thousands and millions of folds; however, everybody is becoming a fishing target. The websites are profits-driven and neither information nor the flow of information experiences free treading. The freedom of information flow is one of the key driving factors for the human civilization and should be espoused instead of protected and subject to exploit. In fact, the key common information resources availabilities have been becoming scarcity: who wants to work for others for free! The original entertainment-based mindsets have been bent to the nickel or copper, such like, even the YouTube visiting number can be exploited.

Yahoo! started with an information hosting website called "Jerry and David's guide to the World Wide Web." The site was never intended to include searchable pages per original design, as it can be seen in the Yahoo! homepages in § 0.1.3. It was more of an information service directory platform that included some of their favourite websites from across the web (think about Lee's initial sparks on the internet: was intending to provide the access to the resources in other computers. Yahoo! was just gathering these key resources in one organized site: www.yahoo.com). Their name wasn't exactly short (36 characters). They needed something catchy–something people would remember. In March 1994, they changed their name to Yahoo! and registered the domain on January 18, 1995. Remember Yahoo! Yang and Filo added the exclamation point to the end of Yahoo! because "Yahoo" was already trademarked by a company that produced BBQ sauce. And they also engineered backronym as "Yet Another Hierarchical Officious Oracle" (or Yet Another Hierarchically Organized Oracle); the term "hierarchical" described how the Yahoo database was arranged in layers of subcategories while the term 'oracle' was intended to mean 'source of truth and wisdom and 'officious' described the many office workers who would use the Yahoo! database while surfing from work." With their code sources and information hierarchies so wise and refined, mostly, so successfully, any extra "ado" was supernumerary, better making strides without further ado!

§ 0.2.6 Should Larry Page Have Been Larry Turn— Leave It To David Filo

In the prime time of Yahoo! prosperity, along came a start-up called Google. Back in 1998, two individuals, Larry Page and Sergei Brin, who were unknown to the technology company offered to sell their little start-up to AltaVista for $1 million so they could resume their studies at Stanford (both suspended their PhD studies for perusing Google). But no luck. With the Stanford Alumni advantages and Sergey's social skill, he made a bold call to David Filo. The outcome, of course, as you know already, not as Sergey's plan, worse or better! Instead of Yahoo! to license the emerging new search algorithm, David Filo convinced Sergey Brin and Larry Page to strike out on their own, and introduced them to one of Google's earliest investors, Michael Moritz of Sequoia Capital. From the all-round Yahoo! point of view, Yahoo! was an art creation with refines and curations, the little tricks here and there used to extract information by machine is a minimal necessary function to have as the engineers' basic skills for coding. On top of all these, remember Yang and Filo had remove their name from the company original name, here, Google's technique entity called: PageRank, named after Larry Page, although this was often overlooked, should Larry Page have a surname Larry "Turn", they would have been much "lucky" and secured the deal.

Yahoo! and Google had the opportunity to work hand-in-hand. It would have been a better service today if they had worked out well. As we had annotated, Yahoo! was a nature discourse on the information in its primitive first time for the digital format, just as another version of a phonebook with depth, inheriting the tradition and custom. In the meantime, Yahoo! adding entertainment and resource components to the lodge for users to enjoy everything the host provided, tailored and selected specially on the menu. For many in the 1990s, this spunky little start-up with the funny name was the internet. It began life as a web directory, manually curated and categorized by humans, who were known simply as "the surfers." Yahoo was the first site to add news, sports, and finance feeds to its web directory.

At the end of the day, Yahoo! had shed $3.7 billion to acquire GeoCities, a web hosting website. Ultimately, David Filo was reluctant to spill a little $1 million on Google)

§ 0.2.7 It Took Extreme Perseverance to Fail Yahoo!

Of course, the Yahoo! misses on business strategic acquisitions so much, the list can go on and on: In 2002, Yahoo! again could acquire Google for a raised bid of their offer $3 billion (Brin and Page were waiting for a higher price targeting around $5 billion or so) then Yahoo Chief Terry Semel refused to raise the offer as it looked to again build its own search engine to compete with Google.

In July 2006, Yahoo! tried and let go another business

acquisition, Facebook, for $1.1 billion. Yahoo! also had opportunities to acquire eBay and YouTube, and even entertained making an offer for Apple two years before the iPhone was unveiled (The Apple idea didn't get much traction inside Yahoo!). The last "table" "turn" might be in 2008, this time Yahoo! was on the selling side. Yahoo! spurned offers—most famously when then CEO Jerry Yang aggressively rejected Microsoft's attempts to buy Yahoo for $44.6 billion in 2008.

Yahoo! had many high-profile business acquisitions, we just use their $3.7 billion purchase of GeoCities as a specimen here: in 1999 acquisition, GeoCities, which let millions of people build their own websites. Just remember Yand and Filo started their business as a website hosting, a very addicted toy for then internet enthusiastic crowd. A tip of telling that Yang and Filo were not on top of the business strategic visions. Borrowed their lessons, Google had Eric Schmidt built the corporate infrastructure needed to maintain its rapid growth as a company and on ensuring that quality remains high while the product development cycle times were kept to a minimum.

CHAPTER 1: CULTURES IN MORDEN HIGH TECH FIRMS: LIVES AND BALANCE

§ 1.1 CASUAL OR UNCEREMONIOUS: A NEW BREED OF BUSINESS ETHICS

ork It was casual on a college level in Yahoo! David Filo didn't wear shoes. You could wear shorts and flip-flops to work. It was super entrepreneurial, which is now kind of a cliché. In the beginning, Yahoos (Yahoo employee) didn't care the outside business weather too much. Furthermore, they had made Yahoo! A stock "casino": Yahoos were known to wager on whether the company's stock price would go up or down. A tease on the markets. One loser had his head shaved in front of the entire staff; others ended up at tattoo parlors to have the company logo permanently enshrined on their posteriors. It was prank and very punk rock, kind of making the technology up as we went. And things started getting crazy.

Casual and comfort can also go to a degree. Either lads or lasses. May be because too much emphasis on the casual, there were a lot of dressing styles would be considered unceremonious, with the under shirts sticking outside the overcoat. Let's use here as the basic start point *When and How to Tuck in Your shirt?* (https://www.artofmanliness.com/articles/how-tuck-in-shirt/):

"Shirts that are made with a flat bottom hem are meant to be worn untucked. But if the shirt has visible 'tails' — that is to say, the hem varies in length, rather than being even all the way around — it should always be tucked in.

"Wearing a shirt with tails untucked is not a forbidden look. But it is a juvenile one. With nothing else on the upper body, it makes you look like a teen rebel at a grown-up wedding. Under a jacket or with a suit, being untucked makes you look like you're trying too hard to be stylishly rumpled."

May be that was exactly they want.

Equipped with adjustable office desk (from 20s to 50 inches) give everyone opportunity to work tall. Some gals preferred more ("less"). While people used to wear flip-flops, some lady wear bare feet: Alfonso gave Dianna a floor mat such like the cashier in grocery store standing on. That was I made aware when the charming Dianna one day slipped besides me and talked to Alfonso, with whom I was lunching together.

Here was one of the kind scenario: There was a charming dude fooling around whole time, very active in the chat room for the unfunny jokes and memes. In the meantime, attracting a lot of people to stop by and perform long conversations with bursts of loud laughing. We were in a training, which was scheduled to start at

12:30pm. In the same team, everyone knew there was no projects in queue, aka, the team was in idling status. Even the normally lazy layback guy was able to get an early luncheon (remember, in their work place, free food: starting from 11:30am all the way to 4pm). The dude was noticed in shopping web sites whole morning or "working" on his small screen (phone). Two minutes into the training, with a couple of remote teleconference parties joined, this guy rushed into the main training room with a whole pie of small boxed pizza in hand and apologized for bringing food into the room, very sincerely and politely: because of his busy schedule... If things stopped just there — no; during the course of meeting, there were at least 3 times the pizza issue had been brought up again either by the instructor or the remote attendees, praised the good smell, at the end of the event, the guy earned an impression of busy, polite, and fun to mingle with — he is projected not far away from promotion.

More? That will be another whole volume of book to cover the various scenarios and events for what are happening and had happened for "general populations."

§ 1.2 NEW POPULAR CULTURES IN ERA OF INTERNET SOCIAL MEDIA

We know the basic facts: wide spreading does not warrant a wholesome entity. Like the flu or measles. However, these "bacteria" or "virus" have found paradise in the social media platforms.

On a technique point of view, in most of the cases, nobody knows for sure for a "thing", which can be anything from an acronym to a system protocol. (it seems it is the current norm in all the business). The "LGTM" is one of the acronyms used, in addition to "afaik" and so on. These are the real obstacles I had met while I was having conversations (via chatting) with the members around the world. I was so rejecting on these "**C**omputer **R**aster **A**nd **P**rogram" systems (please read this phrase as acronym, which was the name given by the current Director for Neutron Scattering Division in Oak Ridge National Lab, HMC, who was my buddy when I was there. The system was his brainchild, hand built together with me, automated program coded by me in LabView platform. The system had been built for US

Department of Energy the Coated conducting program with materials of High-Temperature superconductors, such like $YBa_2Cu_3O_{7-x}$ or $Bi_2Sr_2Ca_{n-1}Cu_nO_{2n+4+x}$ [x<=1, n=1,2,3]. The system was automated for multiple-target raster for sophisticated many-element material compound, creating heterostructures for research on exotic properties on these man-made new materials, to just brief as is.), and refused to look up for them with the expense of anguish in the understanding. Whoever has curiosity please Google yourself: Yep, I am tirelessly writing these out and affording no my time to these "Computer Raster And Program" as they were used in an official business document here: "First, that system trusts you to write stylistically correct code which reflects these best practices. Having readability allows you to submit CLs without explicit "readability approval" from a reviewer (though you still must have an LGTM from a reviewer)". In the quoted context two unnecessary acronyms I do not know and I have not bothered to look up.

There are certain specific and technique-based glossary, may be necessary; however, the madness of such kind of social media platforms creeps into the high-tech companies and becomes a fashion. It is a sad thing, only adding unnecessary obstacles for the already faded human communications. On that, the meeting can go to extreme.

You may think these employees are high there in the meetings and talking about sophisticate algorithms, like I was interviewed in the Google New York office: simply put, to write the code in C++ on board for the shortest steps to reach the center square of the array from an external starting square all at once, aha? not always. Instead, after half of the planned time spending on greeting, jokes, meme around the world different sites, "We do not have a agenda today, Thanks every one!" which was yesterday's planned hour-long meeting. Ice-cream machine broken, parking spaces, all can be meeting themes.

And GVC (Google Video Conference) has been used extensively: Two people (can neither use only men nor only women in this case, so I put gender neutral there) were seen using GVC and talked passionately, if only you know that their cubicles were next each other!

§ 1.3 "OFFICE TO GO," THE UBER VERSION

Help Me Understand The Uber Cancelation Scam?

(further detail can be read: https://onemile-atatime.com/uber-scam/)

Uber Passenger (Upx): Ben Schlappig

Uber Driver (Udx): Alejandro

Location Miami Airport.

Upx was a travel consultant, so, expert. With pretty confidence to handle in different situations and to advise.

After a long trip Upx stuck with Udx. Who accepted Upx request.

"I waited... after 10 minutes the car still hadn't moved, so I called the driver. He didn't answer. So then I messaged him: 'Hello are you on your way?' The message showed as 'Read,' but he didn't respond.

"I waited another five minutes, and then I called him. He didn't answer.

"Then after another five minutes I figured I'd practice some reverse psychology. I assumed he wanted me to just give up and cancel the ride, so I messaged him telling him to take his time. He also read that: 'Please take your time, I can wait all evening if need be!'

"I wasn't about to cancel the ride, so I kept the ride 'live,' and in the meantime got in a taxi---

"Finally after over 30 minutes I decided to cancel the ride. There was a $10 fee, though I disputed it and it was immediately refunded. Sorry you had to "drive" 31 minutes for me. Alejandro!

"Surprisingly this guy had a good Uber score and literally thousands of rides behind him. So I can't say with 100% certainty that he was a scammer, in the sense that I'm not convinced he was trying to make a 'living' through cancelation fees.

"So that's why I'm curious about the inner-workings of Uber. Do drivers always get to keep the cancelation fee, even if it's refunded? Are they just banking on people not requesting a refund? Is there some point at which drivers can be in trouble for having an unusually high number of cancelations/disputes?"

There were many comments (here are these that will serve for our plot):

"How long have you lived in Miami, Lucky? That response is typical of any and every cab driver down here, they're the absolute worst scam artists out there."

Another,

"This is hardly limited to Miami. I've had this happen to me in D.C., Toronto, Austin, Chicago, Stockholm, etc . . . all over the place. "

+2

"Yeah, this happens a huge amount in Saudi and especially Egypt."

+3

"Huge issue with that in Romania (Bucharest airport, to be precise)"

And there was other kind of story, by Dan C.

"I have experienced this several times with Uber drivers. Recently, I was trying to get TO the airport. I requested a ride, the app said the driver was 9 minutes away. A quick check of the map showed the driver needed to exit the highway and come back one exit, etc. so all seemed reasonable. I made my way to the pickup location 8 minutes after the original request, looked at the app....12 minutes away, The driver was now on a different highway, moving further away, quickly. I called, no answer. I messaged, no response. The app now shows 15 minutes ETA, for a 25 min trip to the airport, after waiting 10+ minutes already. Now at risk of missing my flight, I called once more, no answer. I cancelled the trip."

Finally there was this guy, from a different point of view, by Pete nantista:

"As a former driver in las vegas, sometimes the cancellation fee pays more than doing the trip which here ends almost the same way everytime 5 stars no tip. As far as leaving the trip open to screw the driver. The driver is probably already on a lyft ride while your playing with his uber account. Now personally don't don't have it in me to screw people over or play games so don't do not agree with drivers doing this, but with it being reported by several news outlets that 90 percent of you low life passengers don't tip, but do complain you get what you give" [sic]

As these pretty much had answered the Upx's question, here are some untold truth directly related to Upx's questions:

1. In Dan C. story, Dan's Uber driver was driving for Lyft at the moment of "acceptance" Dan's request. Fact: The current drivers are on multiple platforms simultaneously. To ensure they can max their income.

2. For Upx Ben's case, his "receiver" with Uber account might be simply placed in the airport waiting lot. While the Udx was on another platform or really idling.

3. The Upx's paid amount is not directly linked to the Udx received amount. In certain cases, Udx can get more than Upx's payment.

   For a $5 minimum payment city. Driver gets $3.99 for Lyft and $ 3.66 for Uber, Lyft/Uber take all the booking fee, drivers take all the tips. Lyft claims taking 20% of the payment plus booking fee while Uber takes 25% and booking fee. Although people claimed they take more than that

   In Uber there is a promotion called ### trips guarantee for ####$, if the driver can finish certain trips in designed time frame, the driver can get certain amount of money. If the drivers real earnings are less, Uber will fill the gap. Uber also offers hour-guarantee.

Lyft competes fiercely with Uber, to "glue" the drivers to the Lyft platform. Lyft offers # rides ##$ bonus. In a minimum $5 city, Lyft offers $15 for 3 continue trips: the driver must finish all 3 trips without break to earn the bonus. However, in this case, the totally payment from the passengers for the platform is: $3x5= $15. The driver gets $(15+3x3.99)=$26.7. The extra $12.7 is paid by Lyft.

4. The drivers have the obligation to answer any request that the system dispatches to their phone, if they do not accept, they will be subject to certain regulations.

As the dissection above, the two platform are in fiercely competing and so far, neither of them is profitable.

With this facts-based story, we are going to do some dissections on why and how people converge together like the case in the ride-hail platforms.

§ 1.4 CONNECTED BUT INVISIBLE: NETWORK PLATFORMS AS CURTAINS FOR VILLAINS

It is obvious the § 1.3 Udx was mean and filthy. Regardless the motivations. Think about the case of a passenger to catch a tight schedule or emergency—; on the hand, the Upx was not that all grace. He played and tricked his way through anyway.

The Udx would never lose because Udx had nothing to lose; the Upx felt good because Upx thought he got an upper hand: Should somebody told him that Uber driver would get nothing, Upx would have felt much better, I guess.

In a lot of scenarios, I had people on spot and they talked very sweet and promising for a deal, but they never showed up later. The "face-time" and public visualization had formatted them in someway of decency while on spot for day-to-day lives. However, the network connected platform does not embrace a visualizing scenario.

As the results of the connected but invisible working or living platforms, it is a very good curtain for these villains to set on act.

No matter it is email fishing, password hacking, or inter-government elections meddling, plus all kind of data breaching.

Today, almost all the high-tech companies are working on the network platforms. Thus, their employees sometimes can behaviour in their native color.

§ 1.5 PROFESS OF SHAM FROM THE CORPORATE EMAIL SCAMS

Texting to this end, it does not hurt to utter another annoying "profess of sham" on corporate email scam.

Everyday a lot of people are busy husting. It seems their only job is answering the likely or unlikely curious events. For the very email chain of the "Congratulations!" below, which had gone on and on for many days. All the corporate identities and information had been eliminated: the 3 vertical lines are columns in which whole block contents had been removed, in addition to the line-by-line redacted areas.

	Re:	new venture - Congratulations , best wishes	9:29 AM
	Re:	new venture - Good Luck I will miss workin	9:19 AM
	Re:	new venture - Best wishes for your new adventure	9:14 AM
	Re:	new venture - Congratulations on the new role Ya	9:06 AM
	Re:	new venture - Congratulations on your new role &	9:05 AM
	Re:	new venture - Congrats Yang! Myself and the rest	8:56 AM
	Re:	new venture - Congrats and best wishes in your n	8:48 AM
	Re:	new venture - Glad worked with you and grew with	8:44 AM
	Re:	new venture - Good luck and thanks and co	8:42 AM
	Re:	new venture - Congrats and best of luck ! Or	8:39 AM
	Re:	m] OoO Sick - Feel better soon! On Thu, Dec 5, 20	8:32 AM
	Isst	Create new option in	8:21 AM
	Re:	new venture - Congratulations and best of luck Ya	8:14 AM
	Re:	new venture - Good luck ' ! We'll miss you! On	8:11 AM
	Re:	new venture - Youtube will be lucky to have you, c	8:07 AM
	Re:	m] OoO Sick - Be sure to do nothing. On Thu, Dec	8:02 AM
	Re:	new venture - Best of luck, ! Here's hoping hi	7:36 AM
	Re:	new venture - Best wishes on your new role! I'll de	7:31 AM
	Re:	new venture - Congratulations again We ap	5:42 AM
	Isst	Fix server ·	4:34 AM
	[Cai	OoO Sick - I am not feeling well so I am going to s	4:29 AM
	Jus	hours left to save 40% - Last chance for this grea	12:37 AM
	[Cai	Automation (based) 2	12:02 AM
	[Cai	Automation (S based) 2019	12:02 AM
	Re:	new venture - Congrats and best wishes!! On Wec	11:52 PM
	Re:	new venture - Congrats and best wishes in your n	9:52 PM
	Re:	new venture - Certainly some amazing contributic	9:30 PM
	Re:	new venture - We will miss you, Best of luck	4
	Re:	new venture - Thanks for everything, ! Best v	4
	Re:	new venture - Good luck in the new role Yang! On	4
	Re:	new venture - All the best ! On Wed, Dec 4, 2	4
	Re:	new venture - We spent all of that time talking toc	4
	Re:	new venture - Good luck ' We will miss your	4
	Re:	new venture - All the best, ! On Wed, Dec 4, 2	4
	Isst	[2761 ju2.chs09-1 data \	4
	Re:	new venture - Best of luck, ! On Wed, Dec 4	4
	Re:	new venture - Yang, we will miss you a lot!!! Cong	4
	Re:	new venture - Best of luck in your new role	4
	Re:	new venture - Good luck on your next adventure Y	4
	Re:	new venture - You will be missed for sure. Best w	4
	Re:	new venture - Best of luck in your new position, Y	4
	Re:	new venture - Best of luck ! On Wed, Dec 4, 2	4
	Re:	new venture - good luck, ! – arun On Wed, De	4
	Re:	new venture - Thank you for all your contrib	4
		/ venture - Hello all, With mixed emotions, I'm plea	4

Similar situation can go to the "Welcome!" new member emails, which is so often in a big organization. Tons of emails day in and day out are flowing on top of the network email system.

But that is not the worst.

The worst case is the sick email relay. "OOOs." TBF (to be frank, learned from chatting), as it is crystal clear in everyone's mind (most of the sick OOOs are—), however, why so many good well profess of sham emails as scam. There are several OOOs every day, more on Friday and Monday, piling up the most on these days before major holidays and days after holidays. There was a fresh OOO case after new year. One's Grandma passing away: my guy said "He had 3 grandmas at least! (in US)" while another adding, his friend said, that guy had another two grandmas in Indina (passed away during his tenure here).

My lunch colleagues complained to me a few times, one of his small enclosed officemates had been sick for days, still hanging around, she was a contract and paid by hours. However, on the first day returning to work after christmas, I over heard one person asked another "why not work from home?", "because there is no body at home ..." So, the "OOO" and "WFH" (work from home as they were shown on the calendar) because they can do this, if they will be chopped off their $, they would never do it, working in office while sick. The good intention "OOO" for not passing virus to others never stands a point in that situation.

If removing these "congrats," "Welcome", and "OOOs", there is really not much and the email is a much better place to read and response the important messages.

We are human and we would really appreciate a warm-hearted message in the sick bed. However, this is a work place and most of the messages can go to a specific person instead of going to all: the replier just to show s/he was working by sending the messages around.

For the same token, the short meeting minutes of a few lines have been frequently sent later night or earlier morning. Instead, it could have been finished in a minute if she was in office. As a 14hr/6day office resident, I do not see her the whole day, except after 5 pm, sitting or standing by the supervisor's office and chatting with her supervisor. I am not sure if this is one kind of work flexibility.

§ 1.6 PEOPLE BEHAVE BADLY ON AND BEHIND THE NET

In Google, the Googlers played the many category of pranks.

The old school pranks, such as in "the Office" either UK version or US edition have well evolved into the new era iSpace edition: Connected but invisible. There are expressed in many ways.

Here is a way of Google current inter-colleague prank. Should one of them leave the desk without locking the screen for a bathroom break or snack/coffee trip, boys or girls next door would jump into the keyboard and do quite a few things, among them, the most unharmful is party invitation: Furby party, Ninja Warriors' tournaments, and many more.

The following heavily redacted screenshot (all business info removed) is one of the kinds. But that is not the top amuse moment, the one that could not go further is the following thread as it had happed in the serial pictures.

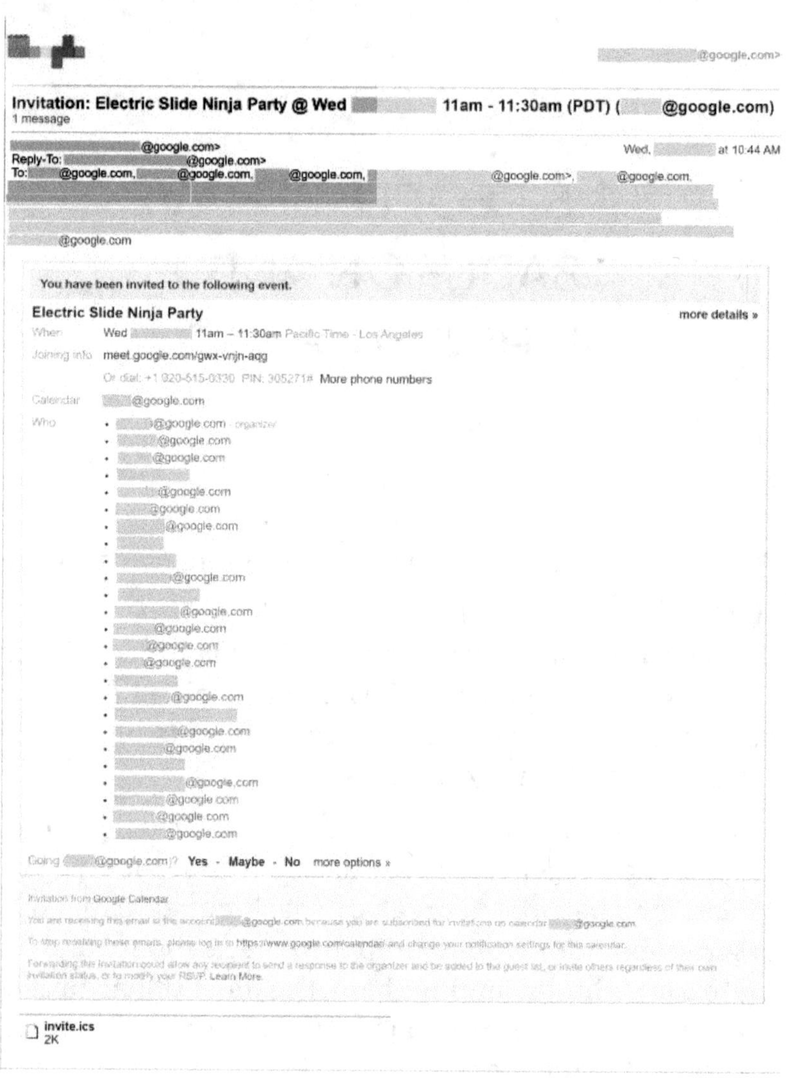

@google.com>

Invitation: Electric Slide Ninja Party @ Wed ▮▮▮ **11am - 11:30am (PDT) (** ▮▮▮ **@google.com)**
1 message

▮▮▮ @google.com>   Wed, ▮▮▮ at 10:44 AM
Reply-To: ▮▮▮ @google.com>
To: ▮▮▮ @google.com, ▮▮▮ @google.com, ▮▮▮ @google.com, ▮▮▮ @google.com>, ▮▮▮ @google.com,

▮▮▮ @google.com

You have been invited to the following event.

Electric Slide Ninja Party   more details »

When   Wed ▮▮▮ 11am – 11:30am Pacific Time - Los Angeles

Joining info   meet.google.com/gwx-vnjn-aqg

            Or dial: +1 920-515-0330 PIN: 305271# More phone numbers

Calendar   ▮▮▮ @google.com

Who
- ▮▮▮ @google.com - organizer
- ▮▮▮ @google.com
- ▮▮▮ @google.com
- ▮▮▮
- ▮▮▮ @google.com
- ▮▮▮ @google.com
- ▮▮▮ @google.com
- ▮▮▮
- ▮▮▮
- ▮▮▮ @google.com
- ▮▮▮
- ▮▮▮ @google.com
- ▮▮▮ @google.com
- ▮▮▮ @google.com
- ▮▮▮ @google.com
- ▮▮▮
- ▮▮▮ @google.com
- ▮▮▮
- ▮▮▮ @google.com
- ▮▮▮ @google.com
- ▮▮▮
- ▮▮▮ @google.com
- ▮▮▮ @google.com
- ▮▮▮ @google.com
- ▮▮▮ @google.com

Going ▮▮▮ @google.com? **Yes** - **Maybe** - **No**   more options »

Invitation from Google Calendar

You are receiving this email at the account ▮▮▮ @google.com because you are subscribed for invitations on calendar ▮▮▮ @google.com.

To stop receiving these emails, please log in to https://www.google.com/calendar/ and change your notification settings for this calendar.

Forwarding this invitation could allow any recipient to send a response to the organizer and be added to the guest list, or invite others regardless of their own invitation status, or to modify your RSVP. Learn More.

invite.ics
2K

This office desk picture serves as a lead-in, as it happened.

The dude was getting a cup of hot (set at 203 F) H_2O in MK (Google's MicroKitchen, beverage, snack, fresh produces etc.), not far, every floor has MK. With a lot of things going on (virtually in iSpace), illustrated on multiple screens, (except the 17" laptop screen was just showing the location of Qatar). When the dude came back, the dude did not know one of the computers, actually, the desktop PC beneath the desk (which powers the top 3 screens while the middle screen was shared with laptop), had been hacked for a moment, until many meeting responses came in, accepting or absent the meeting, with one of them featured with two wide-open Furby eyes.

This is not extraordinary, not until another "gentle-dude" chiming in:

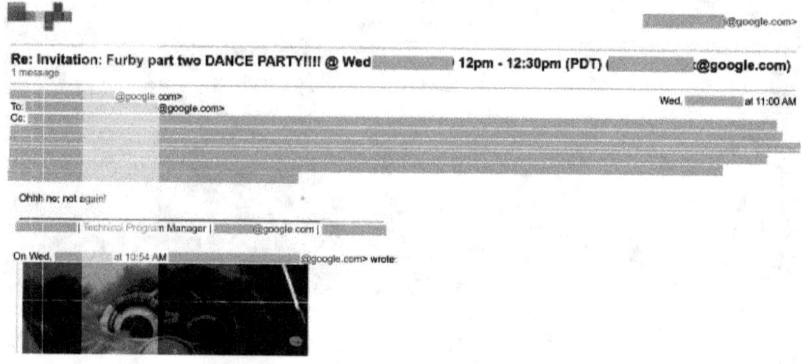

It was not surprised because this dude was a technique program manager, seemed always on the right side whenever others were in situations of mistakes, thus uttered (in writing), "Ohhh no; not again!", why needed 3 "h" for oh? Why there was an "again!"?

For others, just let it go! He didn't; now he got his share:

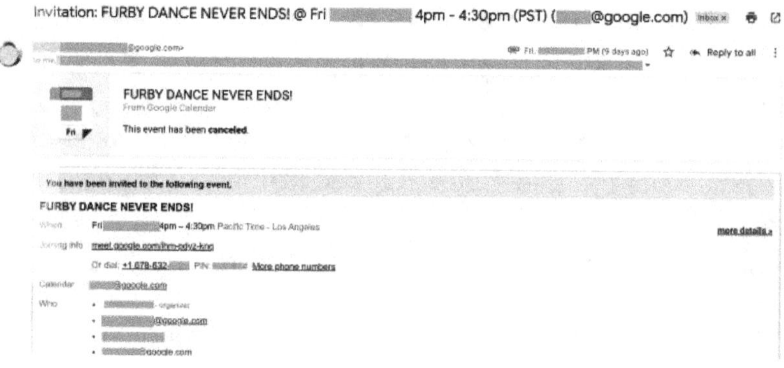

Some dudes had taken care that "gentle-dude," manager, from whom a "FURBY DANE NEVER ENDS!" torment invitation was sent out to all the members of that department as the picture showed above.

That can be properly ended there and then. Not as a

dude always showed the different aspect, the dude, decided to send out another global message. This time, was a note of cancelling the event. As the message header screen shot showed below. Even in this scenario, showed a little difference than others. Pretty cool staff.

This is one kind of last straw to sick the email system with more scams.

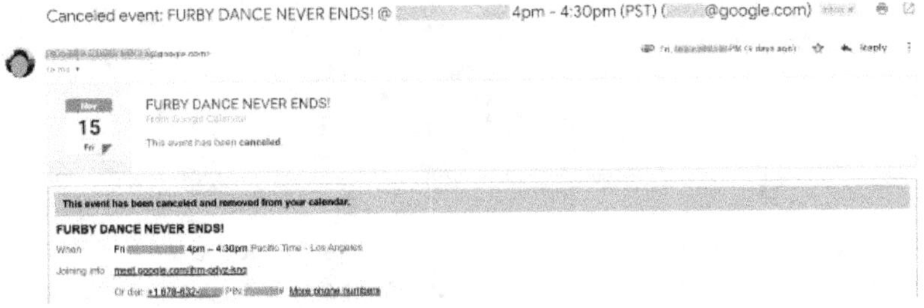

In the old days, with skills of all the nuts and bolts in computers and coding, Googlers would change the authentication process of their co-workers and/ or with total remote web portal control, the victims would suddenly experience erratic behaviours. After victims reached the thresholds of password attempts (their interface had been remotely controlled by the prankers) they lost their Google portal access ... you know what that would bring to them in current cloud-based business, they even cannot get IT help (need accessing IT resource portal). They would have to "report" a ticket (in Google "a bug") with the help of other people (often the disguised prankers, although the victims did not know), all a sudden, they would have to work with IT team to figure out what was going on and how to get out of the mess (the prankers might have never revealed themselves).

The above was not from Pablo Picasso's Les Demoiselles d'Avignon during great depression, although the scene was depressed because charming people behaved badly: this was from a "gotcha" photo captured a pair's fun time: while the lad (behind the lass) was hacking a coworker's computer, the lassie was turned excitedly and thrilledly on.

§ 1.6½ LASSIES BEHAVE BADLY

I could not leave the section without this ½ contributed from lassies, who always claim they are equally important and have been treated unfairly, here they get the equal share.

Equipped with adjustable height office desk (20s ~ 50 inches) give everyone opportunity to work tall. Some gals preferred less than more. While people used to wear flip-flops, and one lady wear her bare feet out: For that, A.S. (my buddy) gave Dianna a floor mat such like used in the grocery store by the cashiers (standing on). I was made aware when the charming Dianna one day slipped besides me and talked to A.S., with who I was lunching with.
Two people (can neither use only men nor only women in this case, so I put gender neutral there) were seen using GVC (Google Video Conference) and talked passionately, if only you know that their cubicles were next each other!
The one work day between Christmas weekend and New Year was unique because it was considered a short and "slow" day. P.K. planed a sport play event with me since our scheduled days fallen into holidays. I was freshly relocated my residence and I was planning to have my wearing overcoat washed while we were playing. When I was rushing out the change room before our

play and greeting to my partner, who was just entering the building, I noticed a charming lady, who actually was A.S. "likes" girl "Megan" (mistakenly called by A.S., did not know her real name) siting and playing on her laptop in the lobby.

While my partner was there waiting for me, I was thinking like, going in, putting my over clothes (coat, jeans, while I was in sport gears) in the washer quickly. However, I noticed all the washers (6-8 total I guess) were in used: finished but nobody removed the washed clothes. After walking several laps down the aisle, I decided to empty one washer: I wrote a note to the sticker on the washer door with arrow marker pointed to the drier: "Your clothes is in the drier with medium T set." Once I proceeded the moving, I noticed only very few items, less than a quarter of the normal washer capacity of lady's clothes. I got my business going in no time and left without a second thought.

The sport play was good, and after quite a while, I was excusing to put my clothes in the driers. To my surprised, this time, the driers were occupied: all finished but without removing from the drier and no people claiming the responsibility, simply only me. Same scenario as I was trying to wash.

I decided to follow the footstep as the washing. I opened a drier and found it was empty, I was thinking somebody might just run an empty cycle. More surprisedly, with careful search (sticking head in), a tiny lady pantie (trust me, I went to JC Penny dot com to get the name right) was there, akin to a nosenet (I have to coined this word to describe what I was seeing. Shakespeare had to created more than 1000 new words for his writing to be completed, and I found the English library was short of resource for this case: a perfect example for our later discussion of the AI awkwardness: the AI process: DAAI vs the human languages + computer languages developments and digitizing: IAAD, detailed in "Chapter 16 The Inside-Out of the AI: From IAAD to DAAI").

When I was rushing back to the sport play, I noticed that "Megan" walking elegantly… Upon this writing, I am thinking maybe "Megan" was the one behind my laundry difficulties.

§ 1.7 WHEN LARRY PAGE FLIPPED THE BIRD TO THE WALLSTREET AND NET BUSINESS IS A UNICORN

The modern specious and officious enterprises do not root on solid rocks. Their real infrastructure is in the iSpace (cyber space), they are quick in expansion and integration in the markets and de fact no-franchised global presence.

It has been a bewildering phenomenon for a lot of people, why the second of the kind business cannot be prosperous alongside the successfully one. Yahoo! couldn't find their luck once Google erected. Microsoft's great Bing design had met the same fate; unlike its "success" story of a wild showdown with Windows' bundled Internet Explorer over Netscape Navigator. Now after many attempts, Microsoft joined Google's Chrome, akin NBA's Kevin Durant Jointed Warriors, "If I cannot conquer you, join you!" When Walmart was starting, there were century-old stores like K-Mart, Sears, Target, JC Penny, and many more local brands. After Walmart finally won out of the total war, the globalized market had been formed. If interconnected flat global market had played a role in Walmart's success, Amazon's success has been largely solo and singular. After eBay's success, now, every on-line market has "used" products. Google, Amazon, Facebook (was starting in time of MySpace), Twitter, …

Net business is a unicorn type, there is normally only one winner: the internet renders all the world wide places as one globalized market, which is transparent and flat to all the consumers. The regional protected barriers do not exist anymore. Business competing becomes barebone real value based and smart technology preferred.

We have introduced some inside story about Uber and Lyft, which had been fiercely catching up before Uber growing strong enough. In this special case, the result, they have been on a suicide mission, neither of them has so far profitable.

In the modern interconnected world, all the businesses rising to a near-burst bulge were pumped by Wall street flooding funds, they were often illumining but as thin as air internally. Yahoo! Google! Facebook, Twitter, Instagram, on and on. They were different than Apply and pioneer Microsoft, which began as a parasite within IBM machines. The sneak Elon Musk had quick sacrificed his PayPal for exchanging materialized businesses Tesla, SpaceX, etc. They are all touchable solid based, reflecting his uninhibited void enSpace (in business entity point of view, his mind must be well funded) and eager stepping on the traditional firm ground. His recent revealing "Cybertruck" was exact the example of his mindset: taking the advantages of both the specious cyber fantasy together with tough bodybuilder. Google have tried pretty much every breath to secure the peace of mind by expending to hardware businesses, same as Amazon, Facebook, etc. Easy come easy go! It is hard to be on the up and up.

Of course, when Larry Page flipped the bird to the concerns from Wallstreet's weather during the Google executive meeting, he was not realizing both internet and Wallstreet had contributed greatly to his enterprise.

Today, Google has been more complying with all Wallstreet weather, as well as government, state and social regulations. For example, they would set a quiet period: "These weeks immediately before Google's Quarterly earnings release." To eliminate any misleading or malpractice on the stock market. Google knows now, they have to work with Wallstreet and the public.

§ 1.8 ABSOLUTE FREEDOM IN GOOGLE, WAS SORT OF

"The Wind of Freedom Blows" the Stanford University motto heavily tinted Google's company culture. These business mindsets have been well reflected in the individual employee: we just take one close look with one of the aforementioned enterprises. Picking one of the current news on Google news site, and select the source of BBC instead of bias inside US. Here is the title, "'Thanksgiving Four' say Google is punishing them."

"Story of Google firing four employees while those employees claimed they were being punished for 'speaking out', in what activists within the company describe as an attempt to 'crush' workers' attempts to organise. This is explicitly condoned in Google's Code of Conduct, which ends: 'And remember... don't be evil, and if you see something that you think isn't right – speak up'.

"Staff inside Google were told via an internal memo that the firings were related to data security and employee safety.

"End of an open era: Observers see the move as heralding the end of Google's famously open working culture. Executives have locked down the degree to which employees can access information on projects they are not involved with, while earlier this month Google's chief executive Sundar Pichai told staff its weekly 'all-hands' meeting would no longer take place.

"They think this will crush our efforts, but it won't," the Google workers statement distributed on Monday added. For every one they retaliate against, there are hundreds of us who will fight, and together we will win. One of the most powerful companies in the world wouldn't be retaliating against us if collective action didn't work."

There are tons of firings and lay-offs events around world. Normally the external audience or media may not care these individual events (comparing with large scale lay-offs), why does this matter? It does because of a lot of news reports, in which the emphasis is that the Google's employees have been traditionally vocal and actively participated movements to orient Google's business in an absolute free land. As claimed, true or false, one of the workers fired was connected to a petition condemning Google for working with the US customs and border patrol agency, which had been involved in President Donald Trump's crackdown on illegal immigration. A year ago, Google employees poured out of premises at its Mountain View campus and around the world to protest the company's handling of sexual misconduct allegations. Like Facebook and Twitter, Google also stands accused of turning a blind eye to political disinformation on its platforms.

They are all sound Googley, which is a world used quite often inside Google from cyberspace to the space on the "Loo". The phase "Don't be evil" has been gossiped in its full length (https://gizmodo.com/google-removes-nearly-all-mentions-of-dont-be-evil-from-1826153393) and I am not repeat here.

For a while, they had embraced a kind of absolute freedom at least in some Googlers' dream world. Now, the reality shows differently: there isn't any real absolute freedom anywhere in the world. These had overlooked the simple truth.

§ 1.8.1 Google's "Traditional" Culture Is Special One Kind with a "Cost"

So why Google firing a few individual employees matters? Let's first look at the company's view: In the memo, Google said the fired employees had repeatedly searched for, looked through and distributed information "outside the scope of their jobs." One of the workers set up notifications to receive emails detailing the work and whereabouts of other employees without their knowledge or consent, the memo said.

From a view of blank start, the company's statement does not give anyone a cue of attention. But not you, a witness of the story unfolding within this book.

Once anything is tinted in a political color, the truth has been decoupled with the entity and people do not care anymore. Embracing an attitude of above politics, Google has only found self-trapped. To tune in the mindset of these "rebel" individual, an outside will need some facts and samples to get a comprehension.

§ 1.8.2 Exposing the Real Nature of the People Akin to Releasing Genie from the Bottle

One day I was fetching a cup of hot water from MK, as normally the only the one (or a few) left in office after hours (around 7pm). I noticed a lady was sitting there having some fruit salad. At the moment, the dinner was serving and why eating there, so I asked her what she was eating? She signalled me she had made that by mixing the fruit from the fruit bowl and the yogurt from the fridge. I said to her why not went to the cafeteria to get the dinner—turned out she does not understand English. She gave me a phone, I typed in—she expressed thanks, must be. Although I did not understand what she had said. That was last Friday. Last evening (Monday) I was on the same trip (I do try to drink a lot of water), and noticed she was opening the janitor's storage room—"Hola!" (prounce "OO-La", I knew that from TV program "Dora, the Explorer!") She greeted me. In the meantime, she signalled the two full "to-go" boxes of food, these boxes are used in the cafeteria to take the meal to go.

I hadn't been in the same culture and I do not feel comfortable to simply witness when people take to-go boxes (here used plural) of food barely in hands and board the GBus, the luxury double deck coaches, and leave the boxes on the seat. I am not saying the facts their boxes are always taking one or two passenger's space, I cannot bear the odours of the food and I even cannot bear these "odours" leaked out from their souls.

In the last picking up station of my daily GBus in campus before getting on the highway for distant city. There is such a dark skin person of south Asian sub-continent, he always carries more than one meal-to-go boxes, these boxes are always heavily smelling; thanks Google offering all kind of foods. This akin stinky curry-some smell kills the whole bus. I am not sure I am super sensitive—since nobody complains, as a new comer, I have not said a word. Every evening, the contracted Gbus driver greeted to the "smell" guy enthusiastically, nothing less than his greeting to me. Although I did feel special because we exchange more words, if you read my acquittance with him later.

There is a very "sweet" lass who sometimes rides skateboard, even her moderate manner of carrying the skateboard quietly all the way to the back of the coach will earn a respect. Most importantly, she nods me sometimes that my stop is coming since she had experienced that the bus drivers had failed my stop. One day, she boarded the GBus with a pot of plant, Google has many plants and flowers in the office and they are well maintained; another day, she was boarding the bus with a few leaves of salad in a humongous glass bowl, and silverware. She finished her salad in no time—

The wonderful plants inside the the building ....

Now, I really appreciate these with "demeanor" who pack their to-go boxes in their bag or they drive to work, I do not care how they store in their Tesla, a popular vehicle because google offers charging your vehicle for free.

In the food trucks for the lunch, there are more drama. Because food trucks are in the open campus, no gating like the cafeterias inside the building. With contracting food vendors can key-in the pickup orders themselves, they are not checking who come for the meals. No matter he or she, a habit of getting the second box is common. It is not surprising if you see a charming girl is shouting, "I am still Hungary!" after a regular lunch box. She is just on her way to get the second one. These are perfectly normal. The lunch is becoming "lean" and in Google's climate, they will all downgrade a little, with the same dollar number that they can collect form Google.

The dramas are definitely not from them, which are the "norm." I had one colleague, who drives Tesla, very decent. Although I might be the closest person in touch with him, but I am hardly able to sit down and have a meal with him. Anytime I try to recruit him to lunch, he'd answer busy or prefer later. Seconds I am in line in front of the food truck, he is there in other lines. I mean lines, he'd be seen in a line, disappears a while then in another line. When I pass their office after lunch and lunch break (always chatting with colleagues in the lunch site before getting back to office), I end up finding him having lunch going at his desk. The decency goes without gossip and prying into others. We go on well, and during our game break in the one of the weekend, he said, "I like work here, we almost do not cook at home—", he has one wife works at apple, and one son at high school, these are the partial knowledge from his words.

That is perfectly legit.

There is an old man, carrying a recycling grocery shopping bag like, one day I was queuing behind him in a drizzle rain. I noticed he already had two lunch boxes in his bag, from his age (>60s) and wearing flip-flops, now I am thinking he cannot be a google employee—

Now the old couple every Friday at dinner table in that Google campus, with paper visiting labels in their "white meat", seem all right and acceptable.

§ 1.8.3 The "Be Yourself" vs "Be at Home" Take Kids/ Dogs to Work with Alcohol at Your Finger Tips

Even this title sentence seems conflict of "interest:" how the kids and alcohol are balanced, but that is the life at Google: "Consumption of alcohol is not banned, but use good judgement and never drink in a way that leads to impaired performance or inappropriate behaviour, endangers the safety of others or violates the law."

"Google's affection for our canine friends is an integral facet of our corporate culture. We like cats, but we are a dog company, so as a general rule we feel cats visiting our offices would be fairly stressed out."

So, it is pretty common but I feel it is pretty distracted from the barks next to you, it is common there are a few in the same area, they are excited, they are fighting, under your desk. People are treating this friendly, I, for one, still do not know how they can be so happy or fake so perfectly.

On a Sunday around noon, when we were on a sport break and sitting in the MK (the game room opens to Micro Kitchen), my colleague told me he observed groups of people party in the office every Saturday, now I can see the scattered snacks and unreturned supposedly refrigerated beverages, such like the whole box of (do not know how many bottles) "Dannon DanActive Probiotic Dailies", lactose free milk and so on; set aside organic brand teas and soda, which does not decay and is not a big deal.

With all the chair and table in a mess and the floor was littered with snack wraps, scattered nuts and crumbs, we were sighing on what we were seeing. My friend told me, this is Google's culture, nobody tells a thing. When I was leaving the office on Sunday evening at around 8 pm, I noticed all had been tided up. Google contracts third parties for the maintenance and kitchen food suppliers, the connection might have been lost in the middle.

A person's mind is an integrity of all the things in that mini world. Trivial or significant is not by the event but by this person's capacity of judgement at the moment.

In another scenario, if you are absolutely stripped the freedom, what you will be? Many Googlers bring as many and as often of their family and friends to enjoy the corporate dining fest (I mean on the daily based or daily menu based, yes, they are spoiled and picky, more like to rush in for the sea food, steak, etc.)

§ 1.8.4 Google Does Have the Code for the Right Conduct Regarding Firing "Thanksgiving-four"

When the outsides are trying to seek explosive news, they always link an event with political and make the boundary murky. As in any company, Google also have the "Code of Conduct" in place, do not take apart and isolate it out, anything has a balanced counterpart.

"Privacy, Security, and Freedom of Expression

"Always remember that we are asking users to trust us with their personal information. Preserving that trust requires that each of us respect and protect the privacy and security of that information. Our security procedures strictly limit access to and use of users' personal information, and require that each of us take measures to protect user data from unauthorized access. Know your responsibilities under these procedures, and collect, use, and access user personal information only as authorized by our Security Policies, our Privacy Policies and applicable data protection laws.

"Google is committed to advancing privacy and freedom of expression for our users around the world. Where user privacy and freedom of expression face government challenges, we seek to implement internationally recognized standards that respect those rights as we develop products, do business in diverse markets, and respond to government requests to access user information or remove user content. Contact Legal or Ethics & Compliance if you have questions on implementing these standards in connection with what you do at Google.

"Responsiveness

"Part of being useful and honest is being responsive: We recognize relevant user feedback when we see it, and we do something about it. We take pride in responding to communications from our users, whether questions, problems or compliments. If something is broken, fix it.

"Take Action

"Any time you feel our users aren't being well-served, don't be bashful - let someone in the company know about it. Continually improving our products and services takes all of us, and we're proud that Googlers champion our users and take the initiative to step forward when the interests of our users are at stake."

Google already lost some edges comparing with Amazon, Microsoft, etc on the cloud as a service, globally. Google also left behind in the connection with bank and transactions, not as good as Apple, who had famously "tricked" the kids to spend with their parent's credit cards. The recent US government/military project JEDI (Joined Enterprise Defense Infrastructure) awarded to Microsoft, while Amazon fires a lawsuit against the US government, Google had already left far behind (please see the later discussion with full Gartner reports). In reality, Google had upper hand in terms of protocol and algorithms; however, it was Google self-inflated guideline of none government involvement that hurt Google's bid for a government project.

§ 1.8.5 Social Cultural Heroes or Spoiled-Brats?

As the GBike ending in Burning-Man Google's gentle reminder(please refer to § 7.3), plus those many layers of childish behaviors or exposed natures, Google has ultimately tolerated. However, for whatever the purposes, connected but invisible, and did spooky things —that was not like the Uber case's Upx vs Udx, you were performing these filthy things to your next table colleagues, and as everybody knows, there is a system in place (software layers) to monitor these activities. That was so called warning message, well served. Spoiled brat to a certain degree, the options left for the company to choose are not that many.

An often seems trivial thing sometimes reflects the deep personality and the resultant consequence is often out of proposition. If we do not consider that trojan war was started by a playboy dude's harassment inappropriately to a charming girl in a different party, we may start with "the Pig War" of 1859, if the people in this land do not care the lands outside Columbus's view field. The war was between US and UK, with US Army dispatched George Pickett—later a Confederate general, to lead the troops. The aptly named Pig War nearly saw an argument over a slaughtered swine lead to a full-scale conflict between the United States and Great Britain. Albeit the US command-in-chief now seems on war with every soul in the planet, like Russell Westbrook one-against-all in NBA games. People are normally very generous in an all well situation, like in the super bowl, you can tackle others without (normally) being blamed to pick a fight. The following observations are the otherwise. Sitting in front of the second deck of the coaches in busy 101 road of San Francisco will give you a good opportunity to observe, say the motorcyclists. All started from an observation one day, a motorcyclist gave his middle finger by extra striding in front of our coach, I had no idea how the coach driver managed to agitated this flammable motorcyclist; days later, from a rare view, I noticed a motorcyclist waved friendly to these cars he passed. Not every car, but these leaned to the left side of the leftmost lane. From the association I suddenly realized these motorcyclists had taken the ways of other vehicle drivers' style (some of them driving close to the left side, some to the right; these are totally random to other observers) as the attitudes toward to them (motorcyclists): they must have thought that the left swinging of driving was a way to give them space, since the motorcyclists drove between two adjacent lanes, which must be a traffic violation for themselves. How subtle is that, many of the road rages might have a similar root: when you are on your "businesses", you are inclining to categorize the others in the same mindset, regardless the real thoughts in others.

These officious dwellers in these elite companies elaborate or eschew. If you have read the preceded pages, you know that they are busy and idle in the same time; they are bored and stressed in the same time. Reasons for their twisted emotions lie in the tedious work, the way deal with the machines' inputs and outputs, in their words, the paperwork and the documentations. You may also hear those physicians' stressed and bored work of obligations, they have to enter all the routine "data" to the system. If you are in one of these officious dwellers' chatting rooms, you may notice they are paying attentions to everything residing outside of their working domain, and elaborating beyond the juiceless. The dull and ostentatious vigor is going to pulp anyone's candor out of shape in no time. On the other hand, what are the functions of these never ended meeting pranks anyway?

Nonetheless, these corporate fun seeking brain resources sweep and hover over and go beyond their campuses, make their presences known and loudly. They are in 100% readiness for the outside flashing points. To comment or to show the 100% correctness as the mindset of the motorcyclist's "business"-on-the-wheel. Should they have enough work on their plate or they have real passions and interests on their "things," not saying to be totally blind to the outside world, they probably would have found plenty to anchor their vigor on and care less.

§ 1.8.6 What in Facebook

The easy come resource paves the attractive work environment, free and comfort sometimes return fussiness and arrogance instead of creation and innovation. Once one is in, s/he often finds that the career path forward is not very well defined and actually labyrinthine — the one prompted fast is often the one who is not going into the engineering due diligence. Put it this way, once inside the company, one's promotion is not proportional to the "diligence" of one's work. The criteria become murky and a lot of attitudes involves. In this point, the "success pizza training" in § 1.1 serves a good "role model" for these aiming for fast promtion.

In Facebook, which was looking at Google, too hard, sometimes. "The complete lack of focus", such like, "On the last day of an internship, the team decided that it was not worth completely rewriting the project," which was the work the intern 100% had devoted on. And just because you're working for a cool company

Facebook still means you're working, does not means that you are filled with satisfaction and having your dream come true. Although Facebook is also looking for their version of prank, however, their prank is totally losing its original any amusement "I was asked to complete really inappropriate tasks." One anonymous former employee of Facebook confessed, "The team treated me like garbage and I was asked to [do] really inappropriate tasks (i.e. separating the director's laundry complete with his wife's dirty undies still attached)."[sic]

§ 1.8.7 Apple Implements Much Strict Rules

My sport partner told me he had never able to visit Apply "spaceship" albeit his wife is an apple employee. Apple controls what you talk about with your spouse. One user interface designer called Justin Maxwell said: "The measures that Apple takes to protect its creative and intellectual environment are unparalleled in the valley, and it's been a disappointing experience since leaving there. Apple's security policy extends to blogs, to speaking engagements, to what we talk about with our spouses. Most people get it and respect it. The ones who don't -- the ones who need to put Apple under their name so they can get a speaking gig at SxSW -- are kindly ushered to move on. If I was still at Apple, I would not be responding to this question, nor would I feel wronged for not being able to."[sic]

Apple makes characteristic grammar and punctuation changes in its internal documents in order to track leaks. After Business Insider obtained a couple of leaked memos from retail chief Angela Ahrendts, the company began making changes to its internal communications to help it figure out where the leaks came from. It now sends differently worded memos to different sections of the company in hopes of tracking leaks back to the source when those memos are quoted in the media.

And for the workload and stressfulness, there is a serious risk of burnout. "You don't work at Apple unless you are seriously motivated to work there. The ones who are there for a check, or stock, are the ones who burn out first and fastest," which will satisfy everyone's curiosity in this planet if they s/he still does not understand the real reasons of these "Thanksgiving four" fired by Google. While in Apple, even in your sickbed, they will email you in hospital. "In recent weeks I contracted a nasty incapacitating mosquito born virus and was hospitalised for a short time. However, rather than receiving support, I was emailed a presentation to my hospital bed with a note that it needed to be completed 'urgently'. Even on the very morning of my wedding I was still being harassed by phone and email to send a report someone had lost." This is exactly the opposite case what we have just brought up in the case of Profess of Sham emails in Google (I definitely don't endorse the none responding, but not the way of "reply to all" and in one of another cases, the reply was three days later). Clearly Apple is in an extreme end; however, the Google is on the other end.

§ 1.8.8 Don't Satisfy at Your Company, Come to Amazon: If you can work in Amazon, you'll find easy to work anywhere!

A lot of people might not have the experiences of working in multiple companies, especially with these latest high-tech companies, besides these who are really good on technologies or those who are apt to changes. Working in Amazon can be easy and, in the meantime, challenging, here are some inside out intelligent advices.

Pros:

1. Very easy to get hired. You may impress bar-raiser by solving FooBar, and can get hired. Sometime they even hire you by just a single hacker rank round.

2. Good initial compensation. Free Banana (Amazon has this "free bananas stand" — available to anyone).

3. It's good only if you have plan to leave within a year.

4. Perks and the possibility to get a better job. If you can work in Amazon, you'll find easy to work anywhere!

Cons:

1. Very easy to get fired.

2. Bad promotion process. Lucky ones get promotion within a year, unlucky ones get 4+ years

3. 0-5% increment. Almost discouraging for you.

4. Leadership leaves team very frequently, and so SDEs

(Software Development Engineer) effort get waisted.

5. You will always hear that this is VP level project, you work 7-8 months on the project, and suddenly project gets de-prioritized.

6. Worst hiring practices followed. Leaders don't know how to hire people; they always compromise quality to accomplish their goal and latter fire.

7. It's kind of ego issue with Amazon. they have completely forgotten their value and now not innovating anything rather than just doing useless thing to remain in the market.

8. Amazon will disappear in the coming decade, so not good for long term.

9. Every morning a few mandatory questions prompt in the system to gather employees' feedback about managers, co-workers, any intention to quit the job or rate the company coolness.

10. Employees must state weaknesses of their colleagues in their performance reviews. These are taken to build up cases against other employees.

11. The 9-10 combination (along with the fact that there is rarely room for promotion) encourages an unhealthy company culture of distrust among employees.

12. In two years that I was there, I had the impression I didn't know the people in my team and I learnt myself to mind my own businesses only.

13. Questions and pushing back changes are not normally welcome. Employees must abide by any rapid changes and tenet "show a backbone" would not really

work.

14. Some marketplaces (e.g. India) get larger work-loads. Noticeably, they are expected to be available am and pm, in meetings at indecent times!

15. More on-boarding training before new employees are thrown in the fire. The first couple of weeks can be very confusing on where to find the information you need that pertains to your job.

16. You have to be self-motivated. NO ONE will hold your hand and tell you that you're doing a great job. If you need constant affirmations from management, this company isn't for you.

17. It would be more human to make staff redundant instead of bullying them with Performance Improvement Plans (PIPs) until they resign. Employees deem 'Success stories' meetings superficial and unproductive. It gets people's motivation down and takes their time. Nice perks do not really retain employees, it was a pity to see talent leaving all the time...

[sic]

§ 1.8.9 Keeping Busy Is One Kinda Approach to Ground Those enSpace Hovering Energy

Now, if you look at Google's employee, their freedom and workload are amazingly cheerful, which is the source and power of their "Don't be evil" and "speak up". A step further, for the academic scholars in college campuses, I often saw them in their office from very early in the morning of the weekends, some time before 6am. While the topic of parking issue is one of the constant threads in the chatting room, when I drive off from home around 6am, I always find I am the only one in the parking lot once arrive. Do not blame the employees for their later appearing because of they are not required to do so. In the meantime, in the corporate environments, employees hardly overdo. Why shall they!

If everything can be obtained in a comfortable way, people will not spend effort for it. For all the good and generosity Google provided so far, the insiders might not even realize what they have. When I stopped by our department's another office (same building), I was just catching the complains between these two (very good colleagues of mine). They were talking the better meals like in LinkedIn. I was made aware that the india lady's dissatisfactions were multiple, First, the "La Palace" cafeteria provides less options (as far as I know, they only serve for snack like light foods and beverages, because we had other two cafeterias in next buildings one of which also serves dinner. Not all buildings serve dinner, since there are less people stay that later. We have a cafeteria starting 5:30pm, another starting 6:30pm); second, she said, "some of these days, I want vegetation, all I can find is Tofu based—," I was joking, "Are you going to have your lunch with me or in LinkedIn today —;" off we went.

Engineering is full of dull details and tedious repeats, there is no depth: you know it or you do not know it. Before you know it, everything is mystery, once you know the unknows, it will suddenly pale and tasteless. If whatever you are doing will be buried under the mountains of data and documentations in iSpace, you will not as motivated as you were after a while. For the same standing, if one works on research, it is different. The unknows and mysteries will always capture the motivation. The richness and interests of the projects are often enhanced by the depth of dig. You are not working for machine or process anymore, now you are working for your own drive of problem solving. So, you are turned on by the what you are doing and thinking on the deep mechanisms of the things, the process of sorting out the issue becomes part of your conscious mind. You are not part of a business process or iSpace janitor, like these tech engineers and technicians. You overlook the project unfolding and evolving, naturally take the responsibilities, thus, you are self-motivated and you are not just conveying a sectional motion without an identity.

The internet and modern tech-company's network-based businesses have created the connected and invisible realities: the tSpace business practices thus have transcoded into iSpace big data manipulations. The digital iSpace's activities are not that closely monitored and regulated as the work in the traditional tSpace real world. The consequence of this society and business evolutions has created the opportunities and environments for the enSpace souls to show the real colors. Spooky actions at the hidden space; in the meantime, malicious exercises behind the network curtains.

To these new era University grads and prodigies, John

Henry Newman had some words for you, from more one and half centuries ago, "it is well to have a cultivated intellect, a delicate taste, a candid, equitable, dispassionate mind, a noble and courteous bearing in the conduct of life", regarding on "Knowledge its Own End", please use knowledge wisely, act on the up and up, not do the spooky actions at iSpace distance.

CHAPTER 2: PRIVATE DATA COLLECTION AT DAWN OF INFORMATION SOCIETY

§ 2.1 YODA AS A GURU AND GEEK

A step closer "you", on the Google private data collections: here are some humble advices on "viewers discretions". Let use DudeYoda as subject, shortened as DY, on Urban Dictionary — Guess what, don't worry about it. And all the followings are the deeds and thoughts of DY. It turned out, DY is an alpha geek who started with his career in science but had been heavily doped with fundamental fuels from digital society: penned quite a few articles on computer program coding and algorithm in the same year of Yahoo! starting and had been continuing, i.e. freshly finished a book titled "Cognitive Big Data Analysis on the Mind", ISBN-13: 978-1085867863/ ISBN-10: 1085867862. Available in print (in book-stores) around the world and in eBook (online); with another book under review plus this very line that you are reading here while it was still being written and poured out during the plot developing (actually, was in the final polishing process). So DY knows "a little". i.e. After "feeling" something might have been evolving regarding DY's content in DY's Gmail communications, DY fully downloaded and deployed the whole Gmail content to his local storage and created localized Gmail read-out interfaces, including but not limited to, all Gmail accounts, Yahoo Mail accounts. Went on thoroughly flushing out all the contents in these online email accounts. It took a while for this action to be completed (the server side had caches and backups, however, after a while: days to months, they would be synched and refreshed, old version would not be active anymore. Provided the practice that the email contents have traditionally not been always backed up and kept permanently). Of course, that was totally irrelevant with Google's private data collecting. DY's none residence on social platform is totally on personal choice or candor. Just does not have that type of hobby. These lines are just to say, DY is a crackerjack on these "things" and knows how to act accordingly. Now back to the Google's private affair collections.

§ 2.2 SOFTWARE CAN BE "BRAND" OR "GENERIC"

S tarting from the "generic" vs "brand" analysis on software vs hardware. DOS (Disk Operation System) is a generic software, generally speaking (at least up to the C:\> prompt, means not running any specific command or software, only from BIOS -> IO.SYS -> MSDOS.SYS -> COMMAND.COM). Simply because DOS can be run on almost all the PCs, all the virtual PCs, and so on. Android and iOS are not generic, they are hardware-bundled none-general-purposed software suites. Android, has a specific package for every hardware manufacturer, simply because their hardware I/O needs specific driver packages known internally and written by their developers within their organization. A Pixel provided Android OS does not functional fully or at all on a Galaxy device. This is enough for this layer of understanding purpose.

As the dissection on the *Star Wars: The Mandalorian* in the later sections, the toy-like "AI" creations for the Yoda's soup sipping is a "generic" "thing" because this Yoda, or the "Y" in the "DY" (lol), does not requires any specific I/O for the specific functionality to work flexibly. DY had not even "opened" the mouth for the sipping (if you check carefully on the frame-by-frame images), and we have no idea if the soup was too spicy or sweet, hot or cold, and so on. The "creations" had delta nothing.

§ 2.3 THE FANCIER THE IOT, THE CLOSER TO THE PRIVACY

However, if you want to monitor your camera installed at your door bell, that task cannot be generic. It would have to know its specific IP, online/offline status. Once you are connected with the camera, your location, devices used, and the camera location and many more data have been used. That layer of information is much closer to you than that of DY. Another example, if you fly a drone in virtual reality, you do not have much real world parameters to match: such as, battery status, environment, wind, the theatre space dimension etc.

If we sit back and think it again, the current AI services have been deployed closer and closer to your life, in your bedroom, in your bathroom, and even under or on your skin (the wearing gadgets). You probably do not want the wearings suddenly shoot paint balls or failed to response your situations. At such an intimating distance, eye on the timely and comfortable service, the gadgets are exploring all kind of sensible information to feedback for their design and services.

§ 2.4 YODA'S ACCOUNT ON GOOGLE'S PRIVACY ACCESSING: IT HELPS

DY had day to day work to perform with multiple computers. Without Microsoft Office suite installed on DY's business desktop and laptop. Sometime, DY has to use the software installed in the home computer (workstation). DY had tried to use Microsoft Windows bundled Remote Desktop software to start, but not success: one of the many information that DY did not have was a static public IP to start, of course there were ways to bypass but there were still a lot of configurations these were too tedious to satisfy all. In a Chrome-based remote desktop software: http://remotedesktop.google.com/ as the starting URL address, with a Google account, all the aforementioned issues naturally do not exist anymore. This is a generic type (in the eyes of end-users) of connections based on Google cloud. And the Microsoft Windows based software is hardware-layer based. While this is all Good then the private is kicking in, at least in some people's eye. Since DY routinely connected to the home PC to use the functions only found in the Microsoft office and not provided in Google office suite. Sometime DY turned the home computer off. At that scenario, when DY was trying to connect, DY was surprised to see the interface showing, that DY's intended connections was not available with note of the last "online" date and time, which is a bit surprising, it looks like Google (Chrome this time) pried into DY private life.

This kind of privacy "spying" is appreciated in DY's humble view.

§ 2.5 BE A GOOGLER AND BEING GOOGLEY

H ere are some high or low "samples" for some facets of the "Googlers":

§ 2.5.1 Google's Technologists

Sample [1] John M. Martinis, who joined Google in 2014, his role at Google is Chief Scientist Quantum Hardware. "Out of Office today" (lol: back the day after tomorrow: Friday).

Basic "Bio": UC Berkeley Grad (B.S. - PhD).

In 2010, awarded "Science breakthrough of the year" for the first demonstration of the quantum ground state in a mechanical oscillator system with collaborator Andrew Cleland.

In 2014, awarded the London Prize for low-temperature physics research on superconducting quantum bits.

A NIST Fellow, and Fellow of the American Physical Society*.

*Note: to clear the confusion: The Fellow of the APS is not a member or fellow of the American Academy of the Arts and Sciences, which serves the nation as a champion of scholarship, civil dialogue, and useful knowledge. Among the Academy's Fellows are more than 250 Nobel laureates and 60 Pulitzer Prize winners. For example, one of my papers' co-author: Ward Plummer is the member, elected 2014; and elected Fellow of the American Physical Society in 1981, 33 years earlier. (Our paper source: https://journals.aps.org/prl/abstract/10.1103/PhysRev-Lett.97.167201#fulltext).

What Martinis's best work so far is the "Quantum Supremacy" paper published in Nature magazine. We have some detail discussions in the chapters followed.

§ 2.5.2 Sample [2 to n-3]

We Skip Those

§ 2.5.3 Sample [n-2]

The align class instructors, YES, you are right, talking about the gals who were on the massage group in the Google's wellness team. Here is my comment when I was asked to give a feedback for their class: "The classes are very effective if you really do it following the instructors. And I was surprised to know that these instructors are so knowledgeable. They have pretty amazing deep understanding on the mind-body issue and some even can go certain depth. As a scholar on neurology, I am thinking Google has done a good job in terms of picking up team members. Greatly appreciated the classes offered." When I was attending the first classes, I was thinking the amazing lecture content that lady had given might happened singularly just because that lady was a good learner (I had asked where she gotten those knowledges as I had mentioned in the context in the booked later); not until I attended the second similar class from another instructor, from who I had a short class of "refinement" first without much attention on talking; Once she started talking about the "mechanism" of human body in her second class: "Foundation", I was awed this time by, not one individual instructor, but by all of them as a team.

§ 2.5.4 Sample [n-1]

The Google bus drivers. Using more of these day-to-day dudes, will close the gaps of the Googlers vs you the reader.

§ 2.5.4.1

The dude my buddy. Who was the fixed driver for that Van Hool TDX double-deck tour coach for the latest home bound trip. On my first day, I was sitting behind him, as a stranger, not very sure about the stops and the running style in the GBus system. Once I felt the

Dude passed my stop without pulling over, I, almost like talking to myself, "This is my stop". The driver immediately drew up (a few dozen yards passed) and apologized to me although I was not upset at all. Next day, the dude turned the inside light on before my stop while talking (to me, of course, sitting in the middle of the coach) "I am not forgetting your stop!" It was clear, my stop had no passenger before my arriving. It needs some time for him to get used to it: this was why the dude missed (the second and the last time) my stop again one of these days. I was kind of drifting in the mind so I was not realizing till some distance has been passed, I said (I was normally sitting in the middle seats with table) "missed stop", what happened next, kinda moving, the dude immediately expressed sorry, I replied, "no worry, I can do some exercises". However, the dude said, "Just stay there, I'll turn back after next stop"; he did loop the bus back by navigating a pretty narrow route back to my stop (the bus was too big to make U-turns). We became friends.

§ 2.5.4.2

The Morning picking up is a different bus, the driver is same good in terms of driving and business conduct. He drives really fast and aggressive, because in San Francisco bay area, if you do not drive aggressively, you will have hard time to just merge all way to the innermost HOV/express lane. However, while pulling over, the vehicle is very slow and gentle, and the bus was really slow at any turn. The quality of riding comes from the combinations of driving skills and bearing of care, to which, I even felt it goes too far: at our morning picking up stop, there were always a Mom and a boy with age for the elemental school (with school bag, normally carried by his Mom). The Google employees crowd at the stop are sometimes confusing the city bus drivers (well, in that extend, they are not very like anything of the GBus drivers), that city bus, #77, pulled way over the correct location, and before the pair of people approaching the door, the bus left. I felt sorry for them, naturally. Especially for an elemental school pupil. I asked them if they could ride school bus, the Mom replied "No!" This short conversation was spot by the arriving Google bus driver. I am thinking he must have mistaken these two, boy and Mom, are related with me. While I was boarding the bus, he asked me what had happened. Next morning, after the Google team boarding the bus, the driver asked me, did they (the boy and the mom) missed the bus again, "I don't think so!" my reply (Their bus had not arrived yet). The bus driver went off the bus and talked to the kid and the Mom ... I have not seen them ever since ... I just hoped they had not done some extra service for them on my behalf, an ordinary commuting rider.

§ 2.5.4.3

For these who were used to driving and not riding bus, provided that so many Google buses in the busy hours:

The crowded GBus Queue

People will be confused whether the schedule bus passed or not. They will never have trouble: there is a "staff" (from the transport team, I guess) at each of the major boarding station during rush hours (3-7PM). One of the days, after visiting Larry Page's office, I came out of the building, kinda being confused with the chain of more than a dozen of these Van Hool buses. I went to the desk on spot, the lady (with a iPad and paper note book on her desk) succinctly told me that my bus would arrive in a minute and the "head sign" was yada yada. In the meantime, she showed me her log book that the bus schedule check box was still empty, while reporting loudly to the crowd the arriving bus "head sign" and destination … showing nothing missing nor incapable of handling. These, are the scenarios, that make you feel proud to be part of the organization and energize the souls to thrive together. At another occasion, on the station besides my office building, the bus was missing the schedule and I was arriving with one of the buses of the same route leaving, based on my reading on the schedule, on-the-fly, I was not rushing to board that specific bus (because time not matching). While I was asking this station "crew member" (same duty as the one I just mentioned), she told me the buses were delayed and the one I had seen passing was the previous run (20 minutes earlier) thus I had to wait a bit longer (the one I was targeting also delayed). She was frequently coming back to check with me and reported to me the status: and expressed her sorry to me many times.

§ 2.5.4.4

I had many conversations with the drivers of the "campus connectors". One of drivers was from Apple. She related Google vs Apple akin to day vs night. At apple, she had difficulty to find place to "pee" except some designed buildings in Apple campus. She had literal 10 minutes as lunch break. Apple! Listen: these drivers are actually driving the lives around, regardless the type of passengers, their lives are the same. The drivers' alertness and mental status are directly linked to the life or death of the people, not mentioning they are your employees. For special "Apple culture" for internal regulations, we get that! To squeeze the last drop of mental alertness from shuttle drivers is not a wise management for the safety. Another driver has just freshly joined from Yahoo! Which also offers the food and stuff, when I gave him a brief on Google, he "likes" equally.

§ 2.5.5 Sample [n]

The food team.

This is a story itself worth a volume of a book, so I am just using the two ladies who were managing the Food Trucks (luncheon). They were shying away in the beginning, after we initialized the conversation, we learned that they had kinda college degrees either in computer languages or in music! The interaction with us makes them understand their customers and I could tell their confidence and ease at home ever since, which I have conveyed to my colleague on the observable changes on them. We became friends. The food crew likes our suggestions or "demanding", and we are glad to know them with great information regarding our luncheon and stuff behind in addition to get earlier or exclusive news for coming events or parties: such like, the BBQ event, when and where, and "appreciation cookies" day and so on. This noon, I was sitting there having my luncheon myself (BBQ Chicken Udon), one of the girls approached me and talked for a while till my colleagues came. In the mean time she was offering cookies and (from my judgement) she was thinking I might feel along. Yes, it was these kinds of "Googley" makes you feel at home and appreciation, they are very warm and friendly to all the people there. I appreciate people are showing their best at this daily stage.

§ 2.5.6 Sample [n+]

Of Course There Are Others and Here Is One of a Kind

I did have this experience with one kind of Googler: while my colleague and me were sitting at table having dinner together, I saw there is only one person at the salad bar, so I was expressing excuse for a short leaving to retrieve one strawberry. From instinct, I was standing behind the only person and waiting for her to finish. Just the moment the lady leaving, a guy cut in front of me with two to-go dinner boxes. I cannot mind less for his cutting in line. Nonetheless, I was feeling kinda necessary for a genital reminder, again not because of the cutting in line (only me) but because that person spent 5 long-minutes to fill his boxes, why that long? He flipped over all the strawberry in the pantry, it looked like he was weighting or evaluating each strawberry by examining every side of each strawberry ... and upon my word "Sir, there is still people waiting behind you! (not mentioning his cutting in)" His response was even outmatching his action, at the top of his voice, akin the devil's rejects while grieved as if he had just lost his parents, with words like "I don't understand ... ", yes, he would never understands how to act decently and humanly, regardless his qualification for certain acrobats of coding languages — I frequently meet this guy, he does pose a exist-being-thing appearance for me anymore.

§ 2.6 WHO YOU CAN KEEP UP WITH KARDASHIANS OR TRUMP: WHEN SCANDALS BECOME FEVER PITCHES

Google's data process, analysis, and mining are typical and bearing more representing characteristics than current other platforms, such as, Facebook, Twitter, LinkedIn …, even further, the Amazon, eBay, and so on. All these are targeting account-authenticated specific set of data management, redirecting, and utilizations; above all, these entities had not been designed for freely distributing purpose. they require stricter rules to distribute their flow, you can say they were "wisely" developped or for-profit purpose. The cornerstone element of their strict requirements is the registration and login: because they are harvesting the resources closer to you and more subjective. Ironically, it was their Trump Called Trudeau 'two-faced' after NATO video goes viral (https://youtu.be/b-1l-Am555Y):

Same as the social platforms, political platforms are also two faced.

Those "two-faced" social platforms' ersatz claim (of the privacy protecting) that had set you up in the first place to give up the control of your personal private matter to them; instead of protecting your privacy, they have been tirelessly exploiting all the facets of your texts, pictures, memes, and many more to distribute in their interests, mostly on the business profits-driven. Even selling to the third parties, and so on. Their original "consents" agreement (only serves a purpose to let users agree) was worth nothing to them only to disguise the end-users into their trap. Politicians also uses this as a disguise to subtly express their real motivations in an often-confusing manner, Donald T. started this, Donald T. (Tusk) cashed in on it, no matter who is who, eats his own salt (same trick on same platform):

Donald T. Tweeted "@donaldtusk Despite seasonal turbulences our transatlantic friendship must last #Trump #NATO" with the above photo. It was Donald T. Introducing this kind of "just for kidding" excuses for escaping his awkward scandals: he got himself "shot" the same way.

The old philosophical master had said "To be fond of knowledge is to be near to pandit. To dedicate with vigor is to be near to magnanimity. To process the feeling of shame is to be near to energy"

Today, the "process crime" has been no longer a crime; shameless is practised as kinds brave:

Oath of Office (US Senate):

"I do solemnly swear (or affirm) that I will support and defend the Constitution of the United States against all enemies, foreign and domestic; that I will bear true faith and allegiance to the same; that I take this obligation freely, without any mental reservation or purpose of evasion; and that I will well and faithfully discharge the duties of the

office on which I am about to enter: So help me God."

As the Senate Majority Leader Mitch McConnell bluntly acknowledged, "I'm not an impartial juror," and he must have perceived such loyalty demonstration for White House could gain the political advancement; he broke the fundamental constitutional oath when he swore in.

With all these in play, the result of "shameless is practised as kinds brave", they can be in fever pitch, but no energy, physically.

CHAPTER 3: COMPUTER OF THINGS AS AMU

No matter Berners-Lee's world wide web or the variety current social media platforms, they have been all made possible from these data/information process units. Those can be traditional computers, Android devices, iOS devices, as well the emerging quantum computers (which are subject to disputing). These are the Atomic Machine Units. In this part, we mainly focus on the AMUs those are from Si-based transistor chips.

§ 3.1 INTEL HAS BEEN UNABLE TO KEEP UP WITH THE CODE OF THE INTEL'S OWN TRADITION

Hardware-wise, the "point particle" prototype individual entity AMUs had been matured with so called "Moore's law". Moore's law is the observation that the number of transistors in a dense integrated circuit doubles about every two years. The observation is named after chemist Gordon Moore in his only-one-authored paper published in *Electronics* on April 19, 1965, titled, *Cramming more components onto integrated circuits*. Gordon Moore was the pioneer of Fairchild Semiconductor (by Nobel Laureate William Shockley, Oct. 01, 1957), co-founder (with Robert Noyce, physicist) of Intel (in July 18, 1968).

There is no physical restriction and mandate on the speed of problem solving down the road on the technology nodes. Although the mobile platforms have enjoyed fast speed growth, Intel had seen increasing challenges to keep the pace from 22nm technology since

2012. Two years earlier than that, in an internal meeting in IBM, I learned from a model appeared in a short orientational brief by IBM vice president, in an easily understood statements, the vertical (depth) projecting power had reached the limit and saturated, the next possible developmental direction would be toward horizontal (width). This is really the truth of the moment: clock speed had not been increased much after stepping into GHz. And the hardware manufactures have put more and more cores into a single chip. While perspectives along the 3-D design had not been very successful.

§ 3.2 LIMITATION OF THE COMPUTATIONAL HARDWARE: WHY THE CLOCK SPEED OF SI PROCESSORS STALLS AT GHZ

The "point particle" AMUs had indeed reached a state of extreme potential: the clock speed, and the packing density of the cores. In clean physics conception, here to let you get a general idea of the limit, regardless the technologies.

§ 3.2.1 New High-End Gadgets Come with Performance Cores and Efficiency Cores.

The CPU clock signal is generated by oscillator crystals, which has a characterizing frequency so called the clock rate. Using another crystal at half the frequency makes the CPU run at half speed thus low the performance, which are why the new generations of phones and other gadgets equipped with high and low speed cores (taking the Apple most advanced processor: Apple A13 Bionic-Third-generation Neural Engine, 64-bit ARM-based SoC. Hexa-core/6-core: 2 performance Lightning + 4 high efficiency Thunder). On the other hand by replacing a higher frequency crystal ("overclocking" vs "underclocking" for reduced frequency) will enhance the process performance. However, there is certainly a limit to do this and the clock speed was not by selection of crystal but by the processor capability. For a given CPU, the clock rates are determined at the end of the manufacturing process through actual testing of each processor. While transistors are reliably getting smaller, they're not operating more rapidly. The reason transistors have gotten faster because their gates (the center tiny spot that really modulates the on/off in response to current) have thinned out. The current gate thickness has already reached the rock bottom the size a single layer of silicon. Of course, as a "gate" it needs to be an insulator (thus gating the carriers: electrons or holes. Picture this as critical as the aortic valves in the artery close to the heart, a very important part). The following "Fashion" shows why the gate is important.

§ 3.2.2 Trad-In Fashion of Gadgets: Those Rare Metals US Doesn't Have

Once the gate could not get any thinner, alternative ways to increase the clock speed had been exploring: research found different gate materials can allow different gate operating speed. Traditionally, this was silicon oxide. Now, as I had worked on, especially in the FinFET RMG technology which is the case in the Apple A13 Bionic, the silicon oxide has been modulated by Replacement-Metal-Gate (RMG), and this is the key process to use rare earth metals: Hafnium (Hf), Tantalum (Ta) - not rare earth, together with Eu, Tb, Dy, and so on. On this part the US does not have much leverages to pick a war with China, which has the rich nature resources on rare earth metals in this planet. Before the trade war, China had abolished the quota of rare earth materials exporting, a very positive policy for US. The difficult of obtaining rare earth metal is a key driving factor why you can Trade-in of your phone: to recycle the rare earth metals. However, they only offer higher price for the the pretty late generations (the technologies with rare-earth metals are mostly from 16/14-nm technology and below, such as iPhone 6S, rarely in 20s-nm technology).

Today, with the shrinking size of the features inside the chip, so do the wires connecting them. The smaller the wires, the greater the impedance and lower the current. Smart routing can help reduce travel time and heat production, but a dramatic speed increase might require a change to the laws of physics.

§ 3.2.3 "FinFET RMG Gate-at-1-Atomic Thickness?" No problem! Here Is an Intuitive Way Why Processors' Speed Stalls at about 3GHz

Trained as a physicist, I often use a very intuitive way to understand the nature phenomena. We had the above detailing on the clock speed: oscillator crystal, the FinFET, the RMG, single atomic layered gate, and why the rare-earth metal depletion has led to the trade-in wave of the phones. However, at the end of such elaborations, we still find the "Hz" of clock speed has to be determined by actual measurement. Nothing close to our puzzle: why the process speed is stalled at GHz (1,000,000,000 Hz), of course, from GHz to anywhere a single digit GHz, and centered around 3 GHz, if I have to give you a single number (I have this in my mind all the time).

The latest Apple A13 Bionic to power the iPhone 11 Pro Max runs at a maximum clock speed at: 2.42-2.96 GHz (the performance cores) and 1.78 GHz (efficient cores); the latest Qualcomm Snapdragon 855 (the latest Samsung Galaxy Note+, better the Galaxy 10 Plus) sets a similar range with 2.42-2.84 GHz and 1.8 GHz. In retrospective, during the Intel x86 family infancy, the CPU clock speed grows like rocket. Here is the timeline of the processor speed.

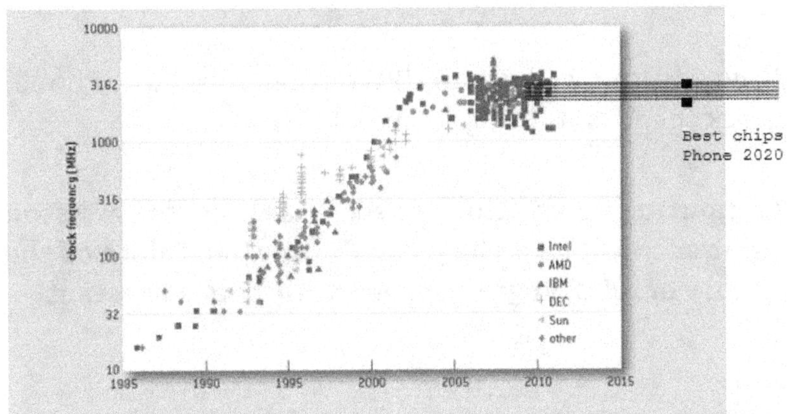

CPU clock speed timeline, The black lines and square dots denoted the latest chip speeds in the newest 2020 phones. (image sources: http://deliveryimages.acm.org/10.1145/2190000/2181798/horowitz_fig7.png)

Actually, it is a very simple case for the first-degree estimation, in physics, fundamental physical conceptions always play in the universe. Let's give it a try in this case.

Given the chip (integrated circuit unit: die is the term in use) size (end-to-end, in multiple cores CPU, referring the single individual core): 5 cm (~ 2 inches).

The speed of electromagnetic wave is 300,000 km/s.

Clock speed of a CPU is the cycle time of a complete logical process. We will make the running distance as 5x2 (it can be bigger or smaller: the chip can be roughly considered as 2-dimention of 5 x 5 = 25 square centimeters. The perimeter is 20 cm) as a fair number, which is 0.1 m. and here is the limit of the clock speed of this chip:

f = (300,000 km/s) / 0.1 m = 300,000,000 / 0.1 Hz = 3 GHz

Now you know why your CPU (either your PC or Phone) clock speed is sticking around 3 GHz.

Computing speed (clock speed wise) has its hard stop limit according to the corner stone/postulate of the theory of relativity: the speed of light is a constant.

§ 3.2.4 New or Old: These AMUs at the Finger Tips Frequencies Are All Sitting at GHz

The day-to-day gadgets and professional "machines" are spanning across five years (it is a long time if you are using the same gadgets in that time period):

- Sony Cell Phone Chip (System 2GB Ram Android 6.0)
    - Released June, 150.3 x 77.4 x 7.9 mm (5.92 x 3.05 x 0.31 in)
    - Chipset Mediatek MT6752 (28 nm)
    - CPU Octa-core 1.7 GHz Cortex-A53

- Laptop Chip (System 32GB Ram on Windows 10 64-bit 17763.720):
    - Intel® Core™ i7-7820HQ Processor
    - # of Cores: 4
    - # of Threads: 8
    - Package size: 42mm x 28mm
    - Lithography: 14 nm
    - Processor Base Frequency: 2.90 GHz

- Max Turbo Frequency: 3.90 GHz

- Desktop Chip (System 64GB Ram on Windows 10 64-bit 17763.720)
    - Intel® Xeon® W Processor
    - # of Cores: 6
    - # of Threads: 12
    - Package size: 45mm x 52.5mm
    - Lithography: 14 nm
    - Processor Base Frequency: 2.90 GHz
    - Max Turbo Frequency: 4.50 GHz

Without worrying about the sophistications of process and complications of the technology, in a simple first-degree model, it is pretty clear that the "point particle" AMU, the dimensionless computing unit has reached its nature threshold.

§ 3.3 EXAMINING DIFFERENT TIERS OF BANDWIDTH IN AND OUT A AMU/COMPUTER

In a limited system, when all the AMUs are collectively executing in a correlated well configurated entity, which forms supercomputer. For example, the current World No.1 Superconductor "Summit" is located in Oak Ridge National Laboratory, with Rmax (The highest score measured using the LINPACK benchmarks suite) = 148,600,000,000,000,000 FLOPS (floating point operations per second) and Rpeak (This is the theoretical peak performance of the system) ~ 200.795 x 10^15. CPU is based on IBM POWER9 (14 nm FinFET) and GPU is based on Nvidia Tesla V100 (12 nm FinFET).

CPU Cluster: 9,216 POWER9 22-core CPUs

GPU Cluster: 27,648 Nvidia Tesla V100 GPUs

As seen from the "summit" configuration data, it employs $2^{13} + 2^{10}$ CPUs and $2^{14} + 2^{13} + 2^{11} + 2^{10}$ GPUs. We are trying to emphasis the importance of one element here: the visualization, picturization, or any kind of illustration on the context.

The importance of "conceptualizing the context takes big stage": once you need make the result into a meaningful representation, the infrastructure will have to scale up.

This supercomputer, albeit same scale of a single "cluster" in a global cloud computing (there are in the range of hundreds to thousand or more at this moment of writing). However, represents another level of strongly correlated computing. The infrastructure demanding is on a totally different level.

Before we move to the network infrastructure and protocols. Let's take a look at the data flows inside a computer.

All these discussions are serving for the purposes of conveying the information across the system spot on: promptly and distributionally. The realization for this is by bus alternations, with the conceptions of 32-bit vs 64-bit computing.

we are focusing on information distributing evenly across the system on-demand.

§ 3.3.1 Hundreds GBps to Hundreds Bps: Data Processing vs Networking

Level 0: CPU/Chip level (all these Bs here are bytes, i.e. GB, MB, are gig- meg- bytes)

CPU will come with 3 tiers of cache (usually labelled L1, L2, L3). Theoretical data transfer rate bandwidth for L3 cache is a monstrous 175 GB per second (or 175,000 MB/s.

Specially, in multiple core chips, such as AMD's Ryzen 7 2700X, the "Infinity Fabric" design starts 30 GB/s and hits the heady heights of 512 GB/s (512,000 MB/s) at its upper bound. Essentially, this is how AMD manages to share cache over its 4 CPU clusters so efficiently.

Level 1: RAM level (RAM: Random access memory)

DDR4 RAM speed is around 25,600 MB/s while GDDR5X VRAM has a data transfer rate of 45,640 MB/s

Level 2: Motherboard PCI lanes: ranging from 1GB/s to 16GB/s

Level 3: VRAM and Display ports 1.x GB/s VRAM and 2.25GB HDMI to 5GB thunderbolt

Level 4: Storage HDD 560 MB/s to 750MB/s while M.2 SSD can go 3.6 GB/s

Level 5: USB 3.2 can go 2.5 GB/s

Level 6: Networking and network Port.

In this category the speed varies a lot: forget about the dial-up speed at 7 KB/s (56 kbps). The current network speed ranges from KB/s (wireless) to hundreds of GB/s optical fiber (100 Gb/s b: bit) is common in advanced datacenters.

Networks are by far the most important and exotic. 5G "protocol" strategies are practically in a war of greedy and grabs. We are not making fuss on the political but we will have to address it from its scientific and fundamental nature.

Level 7: Bluetooth with distance 10m – 400m and speed 2.0 Mb/s (AKA 250KB/s, version 5.0). Essentially, Bluetooth and Wi-Fil are running the same protocol in different market branding.

Level 8: Parallel port (150 Kb/s-250Kb/s), serial port (50 bit/s – 128Kb/s), joy stick (game port via serial port). These old school connecting protocols have been replaced by USB port and wireless.

Level 9: analog port microphone and audio (HD autio using USB or other ports, including HDMI, Bluetooth, Wi-Fi, etc). These are really depending on the digital processing: sampling. Ranging from 8 Kb/s to a few hundreds.

Now we go back to the level 6, networking and data links, our theme of topic.

Supercomputers, clusters, datacenters, and so on, are all the levels of big data and information process entities.

§ 3.3.2 The Datacenter as a Computer

We will use Google's newest system, as an example without going into technical details, which, the architecture, had been detailed elsewhere in *The Datacenter as a Computer*. (ISBN: 9781681734330 print, 9881681734337 eBook. © 2019 by Morgan and Claypool.)

The Container Datacenter Displayed in one of the Google Campus around the Bay.

The infrastructure of large-scale networking is very important. Many tech companies are working on the cloud computing and data storage. Amazon, Microsoft, Google, etc., to just name a few.

However, people are normally thinking clouds as storage places, only a few forward-thinking companies had the vision that they can use clouds for purposes beyond simple storage. Amazon comes the first then Microsoft, and so on.

The datacenters are the latest and advanced hubs for the data processing and distributing.

From the lengthy narrative connotations, based on the information distribution and infrastructure on the planet earth: the intuitive understanding in a comprehensible view can be articulated by tuning in the organism's basic functionalities. From discrete AMU devices (servers, workstations, common computers, phones, tabs, and any other IoTs) to inner integrated " supercomputers", they are not the entities built for the information distribution and intercommunication. The cloud-based datacenters are the primitive general distributing purposed hubs, for information storage, process, and distribution. Cluster is the basic unit of computing allocation. A cluster is a group of machines that share a namespace, a specific set of networking gear, a physical location, and a range of IP addresses. In general, computing tasks are allocated within a cluster. Machines are organized into racks. A "rack" is a set of machines connected to the same (rack) switch and all in the same physical encloser. Rack switches then connect to the "cluster fabric," which provides connectivity between rack switches. Clusters are also connected to the next layer up in the network, usually the Cluster Aggregation layer. Relatively speaking, communication within a rack offers the highest amount of bandwidth per machine. Cluster fabrics, cluster aggregation fabrics, and backbones provide less and less bandwidth in that order.

Within Rack (a collective of dozens of servers within the same encloser. Occupying about square meters area with a bit less 2 meters high for a full 42U rack. U: rack unit, is a unit of measure defined as 1 3/4 inches ~ 44.45 mm), the data transfer full speed can be 5-12.5 GB/s. However, the speed in the cluster fabric (within same cluster) will see a 5:1 oversubscription with 1-2.5 GB/s. Moving on the external layers, cluster aggregation fabrics, and backbones provide less and least bandwidths. (Google Cloud's global network serves 20 regions, 61 zones, and 134 points of presence). The speed of data between end users to the points of presence, of course is much lower, but not necessary in a reduction of time (traffic is normally low).

The relatively low bandwidth of the cluster fabric is currently the barriers holding back the cluster's performance as a supercomputer. So, the datacenter is not quite the same as a supercomputer yet. As a result, the supercomputers are still far superior and more powerful in many ways over the current datacenters.

In a general conception, both from design and implementation, the datacenters have erected similar with supercomputers around the world. As in Larry Page's original imaginary graph of world wide web: the datacenters are bulging out in the network distribution fabric resembling the ganglions in the nervous system. With the latest technologies (please refer to *the Datacenter as a Computer*), either cable wire with Cu or optical fiber, the bandwidth within cluster (the independent entity to serve) is about 1 GB/s, which is two more grades lower than a normal computer (~ hundreds GB/s or higher). In the future, the bandwidth will be surely much higher. The lowest speeds grades exist between end users to the points of presence (POPs are the outmost boundaries of the enterprise centralized clouds). The speed can range from below 1 KB/s (dial-ups, if still exist, it does; 1G cellular system has a speed of 2.4 kb/s, which is 300 B/s, 300 letters per second; etc.) to hundreds of MB/s for corporate network. However, it is not the speed that matters, what matters the most is the protocol that specific entity employs. In some way, may be the token the information has been converted. i.e. any king of language formulation on the nature objects has already largely simplified the object and tokenized it in a specific glossary.

Hardware, software, networking, plus any other treasure-like intellectual properties are the important elements to snatch, these "material" accumulations still cry for a distillation and beyond: fissions and fusions type, that really transcode these symbolic resources into the information blocks in a way that can be channeled and nurtured into a self-sustainable "life" form. The importance of that is it can survive, self-consistent, with "virtual" metabolic mechanism, to ensure its "life" validation, justification, and existence in cadence with that environment around him.

The thriving social networks lay the ground work for it.

§ 3.3.3 The Protocol is the key

While there will be in-depth discussion later on the role of the protocols in the AI development. Here, in the network layer of data manipulation, it is already showing the importance of methodology.

In leap for quantum computing via entanglement, work from Princeton university utilizing silicon quantum bits establish a long-distance relationship. As we have a large portion for the quantum computing and their hardware vulnerabilities, which hindering the real applications but random, not even a real random though.

Group from Princeton University, might have been stimulated by Google's Quantum Supremacy in Nature magazine, also published a paper on quantum long-haul teleportation (LHT: a term in Datecenter technology for long-haul transportation, a borrowed term) in Nature, freshly.

The mechanism they were using is called spintronics semiconductor: using trapped spin (carried by electron, electron spin, of course) in double quantum dots. The spintronics, comparing with electronics, is a pioneer branch in condensed matter physics. The recent decease of Stanford professor Shoucheng Zhang was a pioneer on that.

To realize quantum computing's promise, these futuristic computers will require tens of thousands of qubits that can communicate with each other. Today's prototype quantum computers from Google, IBM and other companies contain tens of qubits made from a technology involving superconducting circuits, but many technologists view silicon-based qubits as more promising in the long run.

Silicon spin qubits have several advantages over superconducting qubits. The silicon spin qubits retain their quantum state longer than competing qubit technologies. The widespread use of silicon for everyday computers means that silicon-based qubits could be manufactured at low cost.

Princeton team connected the qubits via a optic fiber, which is the main hardware links for data transferring in the datacenters these I am working on, in this case, however, the wire is actually a narrow cavity containing a single particle of light, or photon, that picks up the message from one qubit and transmits it to the next qubit. The two qubits were located about half a centimeter (4 mm, to be exact) apart. This is a large distance in the VLSI integrated chips.

The key:

To synchronize or in other saying, find the protocol to communicate between these two spins (electrons).

The team succeeded in tuning both qubits independently of each other while still coupling them to the photon.

With that in their pocket, they can do some deep analysis and systematic work.

For our elucidation: the protocol is the key and it can be explored via out-of-box thinking manner.

CHAPTER 4: THE RAW VS FORMATTED INFORMATION AS A VALUE ASSET FOR BIG DATA MACHINERY

§ 4.1 THE ENTRANCE TO THE ARTIFICIAL INTELLIGENCE PARADISE HAS NOT BEEN FOUND IN CERTAIN LEVELS

We are going to use some examples to elucidate the basic conceptions. Let's just pick right now, this very moment in the Google's portal. The one that is not seen by the external world, but the Google internal population. Google's internal search portal called: "Moma" (And according to "Google Internal Glossary": Moma Search, Google's internal search engine. Moma searches internal documentation sources like Drives, Sites, and g3doc. It's based on the websearch stack, and the front end is a GWS plugin. "Moma" is not itself a Google acronym. It is named after Google's old main intranet file server, which itself was named after San Francisco's Museum of Modern Art, as all Linux servers at the time were named after city landmarks. It was given the nickname by Craig Silverstein, Google's first employee.) The ambiguous lines in above statement in the parentheses had been authenticated with a bona fide nano mistake: a signature line in company email account (@google.com, from the end-user interface point of view, not much different from @gmail.com) with personal phone number, merely a few days later. The internet-stranger phone number had been searchable with full email contexts preceded within Moma. In Google, everything the employee writes, if not solely stored in Windows or Mac based hard drives, it is automatically publicized; and Google is working very hard to make chrome book the only OS for both their employees and users around the world, on that devices, everything is cloud based —.

In the homepage of Moma portal, unlike a bare "Google" in front of you, there are some concise briefs with pictures on the emerging topics. They are more "Yahoo!" like than "Google" like, if you just pull the current Yahoo! homepage and take a close look: comparing with the following screenshot, which was a recent the Moma portal homepage (see screenshot).

Forget these on the top left either Beefsteak or poached shrimp and so on, those were the Googlers menu for luncheon, which serves at no cost for them as the whole world know. Let's focus on the right side on the current topics: among these 12 topics (not including menu please), there were three topics, as listed below: (1) Accelerating social good with artificial intelligence

https://www.blog.google/outreach-initiatives/google-org/2602-uses-ai-social-good-and-what-we-learned-them/

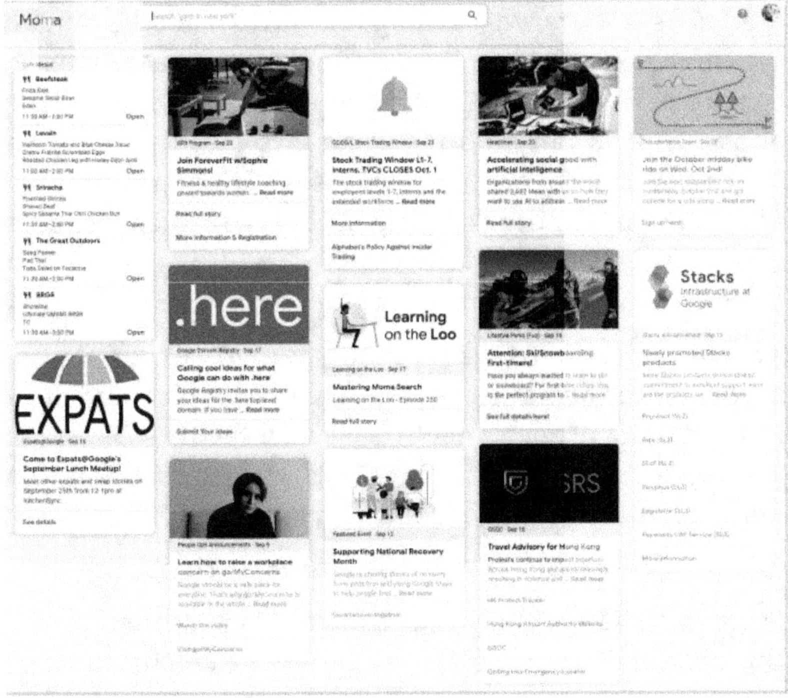

The Google internal home portal: Moma

This topic is on the Google's effort to utilize AI to tackle some practical international issues. Here AI is the major approach for the problem solving. The link above is public accessible on google blog site. "Forecasting floods", "protecting whales", "predicting famine", etc. were the ongoing projects, to just name a few.

They were involving how to channel the projects' inquiries into the AI input stream; thus the "system" could understand and tackle them.

(2) Stacks Infrastructure at Google

https://goto.google.com/stacks?utm_source=Moma+Now&utm_campaign=moma_now_card&utm_medium=stacksannouncement

Stacks is a curated catalog of infrastructure which organizes Google's product development resources so they're accessible and useful to Google engineers (the above link is not public). Products are divided into domains, each of which is overseen by a group of senior Googlers known as "Eng Elders." Products are also assigned a support level, which reflects the degree to which a product provides support to its users.

As you can see here, again, that was a process of how to manipulate the data and resources, in a quick and non-redundant sentence, **machine search feeding. Humans are working on the information stacks to prepare a half cooked digestible "food" for "system".**

(3) Mastering Moma Search (learning on the Loo)

(http://go/lotl-250) The site snap view is provided as the screenshot. This item is more specific, even in the Google, the engineer crowd of elite, they still need this kind of "brainwash" to accustom them to user the right approach, right input, to provide the lead-in for chiming in a stream, the Google search algorithm. Furthermore, as the Moma entry titled, "Learning on the Loo ", not only the red top blue jean brown skin Googler was sitting awkwardly as seen (don't you think the human legs were needed to balance the seat and the desk, bearing huge amount of force, according the dynamic and force analysis), actually, for annotation purpose, "Loo" is toilet within Google community (Google is brainwashing Googlers when they in their cognitively vulnerable status: "psychological warfare" in use for the fitting for the software machinary, lol). Now you get an inside of the critical role on the "shaping" the raw data into the minimum machinery understandable context.

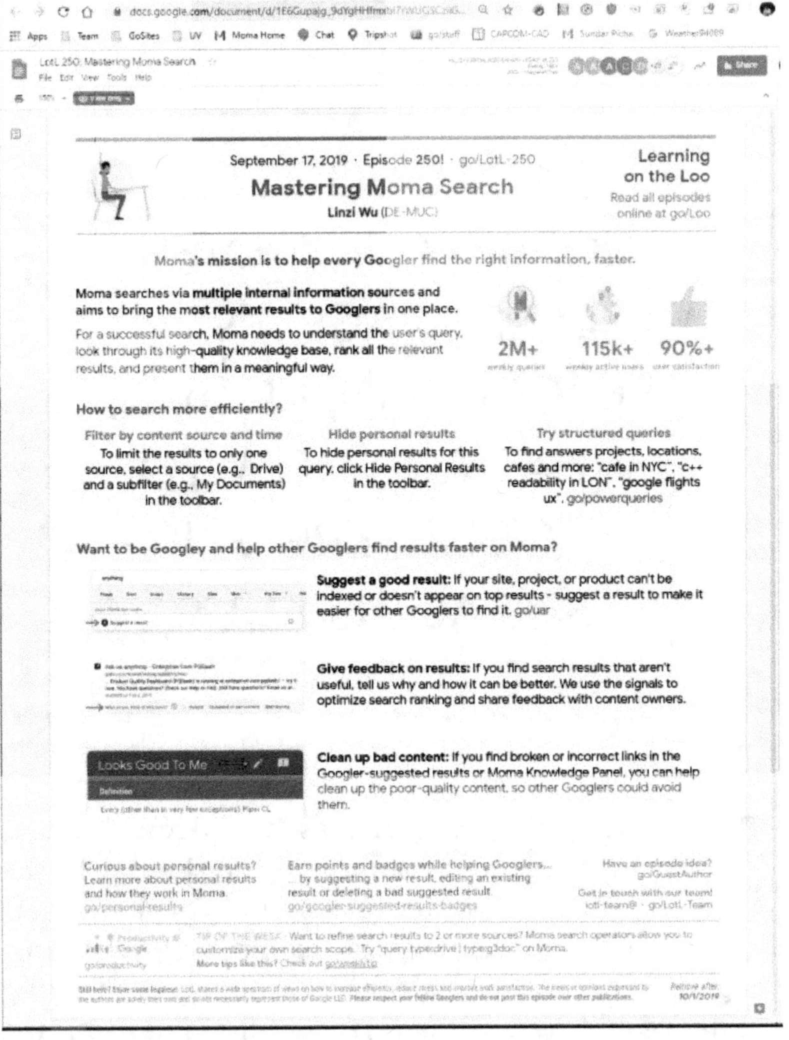

Learning on the Loo: the above print-out posted all over Google campuses on, above, or beside the loo, about which if you are confused, please read the context to learn what is the loo inside the Google.

§ 4.2 IN GOOGLE, NOBODY, NOT EVEN LARRY PAGE AND SERGEY BRIN, KNOWS WHAT AND HOW TO "GOOGLE", ERGO NO-SAY AS DEFAULT

In a brief, the Googlers, as a collective team, from beefsteak/poached shrimp all the way to the "Loo," (Did we just run across a loop of eco?!) their big share of functions are sourcing, cleaning, remixing, preparing, processing, stir-frying, cooking, … feeding the data gobbling machinery, … outputting, examining — Google feeds them — they feed the machines, the information and data processing beasts.

From the born of Googleplex, Larry and Sergey, requiring Google users to proceed searching with their high intelligent cognitive process at play for selecting the proper keywords, as the default skill without explicitly specifying. In Google, nobody, not even Larry Page and Sergey Brin, know what to feed or how to feed their search box algorithmically; or they even have not realized that they had not known this as an issue and left at large. There are software generated criteria as an intermediate databased somewhere; but not explicitly expressed anywhere accessible to either internal or external users. It can be said, Larry and Sergey had left the biggest indecision to the end users, subtly. Now, when we are talking about and working on artificial intelligence, that indecision is by far the paramount mountain that is lying and blocking the entrance to the heaven of Artificial intelligence.

there are known knowns; there are known unknowns; there are also unknown unknowns — it is the latter category that tend to be the difficult ones

§ 4.3 THE BIGGEST ENEMY OF F-35 IS ITS SOUL — ALONG COMES BOEING 737 MAX (WHILE BOEING'S STARLINER IS A PLUS)

There are challenges on demanding and crying for the breakthrough. Another easy over looked scenarios are deeply hidden in any nature entity. Let's annotate it in concise examples: The current companies are seeing increasingly challenges to accommodate all the big data structure and information projectile. To accustom all the collected data, these companies gradually generate characterized and specialized glossary, culture, and executing mechanism. To some degree, there are so many information and data to harness, the supposedly autonomous solutions in a company are often as many as or even more than the issues to be resolved. This is the problem for any autonomous project. F-35 Fighter Aircraft is a good example in this category. As for this strategic national project, neither human brain power nor material resource had been spared to achieve the goal. However, at the end of the day, F-35's biggest enemy is itself. The sophisticated software could not handle all the possible situations by design. Simply because the AI is not there yet or the protocol is not right. No company, in now a day, could have a clear awareness of itself on the flow and integrity. Too many directions have been pursued while address different issues. Every issue has a special trajectory and they, as a whole, cannot integrate themselves in a self-consistent way.

FAA predicted Boeing 737 Max, facing more delays, would crash 15 times over its lifetime. As the process of recertifying the Boeing 737 Max has already stretched into 2020, a House committee released documents showing the Federal Aviation Administration predicted the troubled jet had the potential of being involved in 15 crashes over its service life if changes weren't made.

The Maneuvering Characteristics Augmentation System (MCAS) is a flight control software system developed for the Boeing 737 MAX to provide handling qualities similar to the Boeing 737 NG, especially in low-speed and high angle of attack (AoA) flight. It lowers the nose without pilot action when it determines the aircraft is too nose-high, based on input from airspeed, altitude and angle of attack sensors. However, it is susceptible to erroneous activation, as evidenced in the deadly crashes of Lion Air Flight 610 and Ethiopian Airlines Flight 302. The 737 MAX is indefinitely grounded until regulators decide the aircraft is airworthy, pending software and instrumentation updates and revisions to information for flight crews. They may also be required to undergo MCAS training sessions in flight simulators.

As we also know, that the software was as complicated as anything on the earth, the words by US congress on the F-35 sensor integration. Boeing 737 Max has failed in the same suite. Most strikingly, were they both rooted in the failed integration from the sensors' inputs into their "soul." While F-35, in once case, can render the in-chamber oxygen too dangerous for the pilots; the Boeing 737 Max a step forward; the company simply left the brain tumor there in its brain: crazily nose-diving regardless what the plane has seen or been warned. When the 737 Max stubbornly sinks itself, Boeing company ultimately decided they could shield this information from alerting the pilot. Do we have Volkswagen, not long ago, made their Dassel vehicles "know" whether they were in test mode or on the road, and achieve "clean air" high standards.

Automation difficulties are popping up everywhere. There will be a great dissection on the driver less car later and the latest instance was in space, the Boeing Starliner, which was being propagandized to deliver a huge shockwave to American during the Christmas time both on earth and in space (international space station), failed to dock (to achieve the correct orbit) and had to terminated its voyage early by returning to earth (successfully touched down).

"featured wireless internet and tablet technology for crew interfaces," the starliner capsule's main engine not to fire as scheduled to push it onto a path to rendezvous with the space station. But suspicion immediately fell on the capsule's software, which was directing the spacecraft's operations after launch. Many a time, you will read the advertisements from Ford and Chevrolet on unnecessary gadgets while their main target of driven as a vehicle failed miserably behind the competitors, the "..." reflects Boeing in the same mind set. Also, the reason why they had lost the bid for the F-35 program to Lockheed Martin (Boeing was riskily using radical c-fiber body design).

§ 4.4 AUTONOMOUS VEHICLES/SELF-DRIVING CARS AS EMERGING TECHNOLOGY ARE ON AN UPHILL PATH

For the current autonomous vehicles, these are the opinions from the technical masterminds. One of them said, "I'm confident we can make cars that will never hit anyone, I'm less confident we can make cars that will never ever get lost." While another claimed for the foreseeable future these cars will operate only in defined areas in good weather — even moderate rain challenges today's sensors and algorithms. "we have no solutions for winter." John Krafcik, CEO of Waymo, told the Wall Street Journal recently that in his view, "autonomy always will have some constraints," and doesn't see a day that any car could be "fully autonomous" under all weather and driving conditions. "It's really, really hard...you don't know what you don't know until you're actually in there and trying to do things." John is on the frontlines for these advanced technologies, his mindset echoes former

United States Secretary of Defense Donald Rumsfeld, "as we know, there are known knowns; there are things we know we know. We also know there are known unknowns; that is to say we know there are some things we do not know. But there are also unknown unknowns —the ones we don't know we don't know. And it is the latter category that tend to be the difficult ones."

All the current solutions are on the track of continue the trajectory that was not born for this task. (no worry, you will understand this after my following example.) The car was originally designed as a toy on a 2-D manifold with 2 free degrees of movements. Of course, on flat surface. Before the first repeated human path of movement, the total nature animals were on a 3-D manifold with 3 free degrees of movement (if including flying and swimming creatures etc.). For a car (thus to represent all vehicles), which was designed to move not to "respect", it was well on its mission. Only later on, people realize in a popular area, it was worth to construct a pavement path — later the roads, the streets, and the highways. Before car (vehicles), people walk on the earth surface, that's the basic picture to realize. Autonomous car may not able to run on it perfectly, even not in a totally wildness field. Since the infrastructure are not for the autonomous car from the very first day. It is a great challenge from an error prone methodology to a universal driverless car, the price of the bug catch and debug are paid by human lives. The sophistication and complexity are not solutions for perfection and flawless.

A perfect crystal (your diamond, for example) grows natively, never by sintering with amorphous mater-

ials and defects removing (such as, charcoal).

The human life is on the line with driverless cars, so it should have been designed with perfection, not from an approach, starting from everything at large and then through a refining process, which can improves, but in this case, an alternative brand-new design on the infrastructure might be a wiser solution, instead of sharing the resources with the current system that was paved for constant adjustment and steering.

Do we have a good example for positive development, yes, we have, the railway system? Now we have high-speed rails across world.

At this moment the first high-speed rail with full autonomous train has been in service (refer to §16.3.6).

Furthermore, the air-based drone also has a leg up over these on land in terms of smoothness of automations.

Original from military deployments, and branding with Amazon's ambitious goods delivery; however, Google had a leg up on obtaining federal license for this services, all in testing phase as for now.

§ 4.5 THE FOUNDATION AND ORBIT OF THE CURRENT AI ON ASE: BRUTAL FORCE OR SHREWD PROTOCOL

Currently indications and efforts (http://www.mit.edu/~mitter/publications/121_Testing_Manifold.pdf) have shown the initiatives to grip the core issues among others in related technology; and emerging AI business entities strongly prove that the current data flow, networking, and utilizing of information have reached the developmental thresholds. Major expansions are yet to make. Data shows most of the current AI entities are working on one particular direction: autonomous vehicles, put in a broad sense, Autonomous Sentient Entity: ASE. Ase has a broad implication, including these powered space/air-based objects (spaceship, drones), water-based objects, land-based objects, data (information) based objects (IoT), and many more.

As we have elucidated in the preceded sections, the

soul for all the high-tech ASE (Including drones, partial of F-35, and small portion of Boeing 737 Max) is artificial intelligence (AI). In the above reference from MIT publication, a postulate is high dimensional data (speech, images, genomes, and other sources) is believed to lie near a low dimensional manifold is now called "manifold learning". We refer to the underlying hypothesis as the "manifold hypothesis." Manifold learning, in particular, fitting low dimensional non-linear manifolds to sampled data points in high dimensional spaces, has been an area of intense activity over the past two decades. In short, through machine learning, it is possible to tackle the issues existing in the AI research and development.

Facebook has been training its machine-learning systems to identify and label objects in videos—from the mundane, such as vases or people—to the dangerous, such as guns or knives. These neural networks are trained on a combination of pre-labeled videos from its human reviewers, reports from users, and from videos taken by London's Metropolitan Police, etc. The neural nets are able to use this information to guess what the entire scene might be showing, and whether it contains any behavior or images that should be flagged. If the system decides that a video file contains problematic images or behavior, it can remove it automatically or send it to a human content reviewer.

Facebook is still struggling to automate its understanding of the meaning, nuance, and context of language. That's why the company relies on people to report the overwhelming majority of bullying and harassment posts that break its rules: just 16% of these posts are identified by its automated systems.

All the AI projects are very promising, on paper. Once the real issues arise, the ability to tackle the problem sufficiently is always short half inch. Those are wide connected systematic symptoms and have to be addressed in more than one places.

CHAPTER 5:
THE COGNITIVE HUMAN INTELLIGENCE WORKS AT A "BANDWIDTH" IN MBPS

§ 5.1 PROTOCOL MATTERS THE MOST ON INFORMATION PROCESSING AND DATA FLOWING

Focusing on data and information processing, it is not only the speed that matters, what matters otherwise is the protocol that specific entity employs. Take a look at the serial bus USB bandwidth expansion history: now a two wire USB port can reach close to 1 GB/s. Comparing with earliest ~ 200kB/s, and classic 9-pin COM port maximum 115 kbits/s and 25-pin "parallel" port maximum 2.5MB/s, this makes the striking different. Of course, the USB protocol runs on top of the latest clock speed as well.

On the other hand, there are other deeper territories these must be explored to tackle the root causes. i.e. The current information process had been totally based on the human point of view, so far, the best description of the nature is language, albeit there must be different capacities from different languages. The truth of the matter is that the differences among these human languages are much smaller than differences among the communicating approaches utilized by different species. Here is a simplified imitation for that: almost all humans in the current world know the transparent of glass, so we are not running into it (of course, except the Apple Inc. whose employees sometimes do not know it, they collide into it even now), however, a bird, best for navigation in 3D space, with high intelligence, could not detect the difference, so the bird will run into it till crash and still does not get a clue. Butterflies always fly into the fire at night, on a similar scenario but worse consequence. What is this telling us: if one part cannot utilize the right protocol and chime in with the tailored tokens to hook on, the part will be an alien for the host system. There is no integrity and consequently, the alien is doomed to be ousted (in the nature selection process).

It is proper and natural that we start by exploring human territory with the unique matured languages. In some way, may be the tokens into which the information has been converted. Any king of language formulation on the nature objects has largely simplified the objects and tokenized them in a specific glossary.

§ 5.2 RISING OF HUMAN INTELLIGENCE: EVIDENCE OF CONJOINED TWINS CAN SEE THROUGH EACH OTHER'S EYES

We often compare computer to human brain , the closest and easiest example is the Datacenter. Inside the datacenters, the servers are acting more on switching than on the computing. As most of the datacenters, such like cloud storages, texting services, and audio/music/video services etc. are shouldering the tasks of data distributing or redirecting. Considering the gaming services, they are exponentially demending on the band-width, less emphasis on the smart calculating. The solutions for given tasks are processed within and delivered from, mostly, cluster, which is always less than or at the maximum equal (a datacenter holds one or more clusters) a datacenter. This makes the "brainstorm" not exceed the physical boundaries of a datacenter complex. The task in computing has not been executed parallelly across clusters at this moment. The word brainstorm, here represents a synchronized brain activity, can be deeply understood with the following human examples:

In the early development stage, Tatiana was smaller and less robust than Krista. Tatiana's heart was working harder than Krista's and that she had high blood pressure because of it—Tatiana's heart was supplying part of her blood to Krista's brain. They both can sense each other pretty well in terms of touch and others, once comes to full view scope (visionary), less fluent. Krista and Tatiana Hogan share the senses of touch and taste and even control one another's limbs. Tatiana can see out of both of Krista's eyes, while Krista can only see out of one of Tatiana's. Tatiana controls three arms and a leg, while Krista controls three legs and an arm. They can also "switch" to self-control of their limbs. Surely remarkable.

The structure of the twins' brains makes them unique in the world. Their brains are connected by a thalamic bridge, connecting the thalamus of one with that of the other. The thalamus acts like a switchboard relaying sensory and motor signals and regulating consciousness. Just a note for this, the real iSpace Datacenters have so called express patch panel (acting just like the thalamic bridge), collected switches, with aggregated bandwidth to 6.4 Pbit/s (yes that is 6,400 Tbit/s = 6,400,000 Gbit/s = 6,400,000,000 Mbit/s), and that is one kind of work I am engaged at. So "brain-wiring" them across the globe with cognitive AI algorithms, which is currently residing in my own domain (enSpace == brain), not in a business implementation level yet.

Let's still use a physicist way to scale the twins: Given each eye around 1.2 Million optic fibers, the visual cortex is mainly on alpha waves (8-12 Hz), albeit some claimed they are in lower region (we use higher end to get the upper bandwidth boundary). We do not have double data rate here like DDR computer memory access. So, a first degree estimate of our visual bandwidth per eye is: 1.2 x [(8+12)/2] million bits(?) per second, further divided by 8, we have 1.5 MB/s, if using 8 bit per byte is not proper, we go back to the 12 Million bits per second. Times 2 for two eyes, we have 3 MB/s or 24 Mbits/s. This bandwidth corresponds to a 32-bit true-color uncompressed (true!) movie stream with a pixel matrix of 1000x750 which is above the DVD quality but runs at really low refresh 10 Hz/s ((8+12)/2). If runs at 29.97 fps, we will have 686x512, a typical CRT TV broadcasting quality.

Given the fact the girls of Hogan can sense but not able to see (perfectly) through each other's eyes in certain way, that give us an estimation, that these two brains, they can pretty well under control in all kinds of situations, the maximum bandwidth between their brains is less than 24 million bits per second.

Before this makes you jump, let examine another first-degree modeling on human brain: the corpus callosum, which is the nerve fibers that connect the left part and the right part of our brain, consists of 200-300 million of axion fibers. Since nobody complains his/her brain does not catch the time, we consider the corpus callosum is effective and sufficient. In the first-degree estimation, if still use the 10 Hz (brain wave is not for axions, it is for neuron soma cluster), we have an estimation on our brain internal communication bandwidth 2-3 Gbits/s, or ~ 200 MB/s.

§ 5.3 TATIANA HOGAN AND KRISTA HOGAN, CRANIOPAGUS TWINS, HAVE BEEN COMMUNICATING WELL VIA A THALAMIC-BRIDGE WITH BANDWIDTH BELOW 3 MB/S

And we also know, our conscious awareness can be rooted even lower.

Of course, we are trying to use modern English digital glossary to describe a nature phenomenon, the validation can be disputed from the very beginning. Be that as it may, we are trying to use the same game rules to regular our research entities. The way as it goes always.

Using the same terms in network and computers, based on English manifold, we have demonstrated that even in the range much more than GB/s range, the data center entities have far from reaching primitive consciousness similar as the brain. The human brains, on the other side, albeit run at much lower speed, are conscious and with perfect integrity.

While the datacenters around the world practice with whooping bandwidths in the PB/s, no cognitive sensibility has achieved; On the other hand, craniopagus twins, have been communicating well via a thalamic-bridge with bandwidth below 3 MB/s. The fact exposes the key challenge in artificial intelligence study and development is the protocols, not the bandwidth or computing power.

CHAPTER 6 AI: NOT SO FAST, HOW HAD THE THINGS GOTTEN HERE

§ 6.1 THE ORIGIN OF THE DATA AUTOMATION ON THE INFORMATION PROCESS

Decennial Census: The Decennial U.S. Census counts every resident in the United States. It is mandated by Article I, Section 2 of the Constitution and takes place every 10 years. The data collected by the decennial census determines the number of seats each state has in the U.S. House of Representatives and is also used to distribute billions of federal funds to local communities.

Since the US Constitution has been considered never (better not making enemy out of it) wrong comparing to our individual moral judgement, so, better get this done, not quick and dirt but quick and neat. The Constitution came into force in 1789, it might be a preschool reasoning that the first US Census happened in 1790. The population of the United States as of Census Day, August 2, 1790, is 3,929,214, and, guess what, the most popular city, New York, has a population of 33,131. (The 2010 census gave population of

308,745,538, New York City 8,175,133. With a cost of $13 billion for the census, the Census costed approximately $42 per capita the process).

U.S. marshals (known for witness protection and hunting fugitives) were required by an act of Congress to count the inhabitants in their respective districts (hiring roughly 650 assistants for the first census in 1790 and sent them door-to-door). Assistant marshals continued in this role for nearly a century. In 1879, regarding the inefficiencies at last census prompted Congress to replace them with specially trained enumerators. Congress further created the U.S. Census Bureau in 1902. Now we get here, the processing of the 1880 census data took so long (eight years) that the Census Bureau contracted Herman Hollerith to design and build a tabulating machine to be used for the next census. Herman Hollerith was not awarded the project, he earned it.

Following the 1880 census, the Census Bureau was collecting more data than it could tabulate. As a result, the agency held a competition in 1888 to find a more efficient method to process and tabulate data. Contestants were asked to process 1880 census data from four areas in St Louis, MO. Whoever captured and processed the data fastest would win a contract for the 1890 census.

Three contestants accepted the Census Bureau's challenge. The first two contestants captured the data in 144.5 hours and 100.5 hours. The third contestant, a former Census Bureau employee named Herman Hollerith, completed the data capture process in 72.5 hours.

My Dashboard   Log out

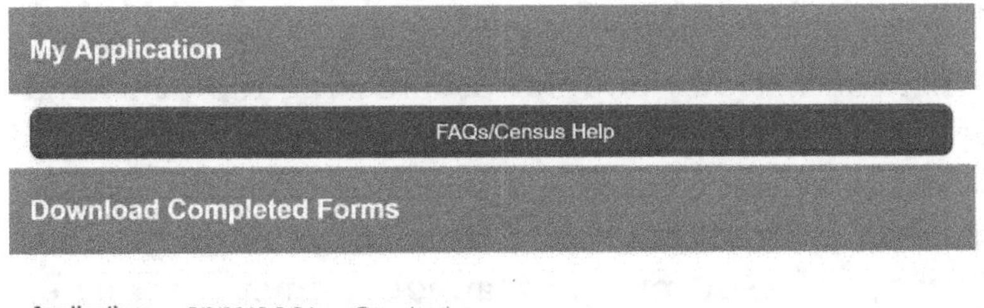

Welcome to the Census Applicant Portal

Thank you for your interest in working with us!

Available - Your application can be considered for employment.

My Application

FAQs/Census Help

Download Completed Forms

Application: 5/8/2019 2:34 pm Download

19.1218.1458

For the 2020 US Census, I am willing to be part of the solution.

Next, the contestants had to prove that their designs could prepare data for tabulation (i.e., by age category, race, gender, etc.). Two contestants required 44.5 hours and 55.5 hours. Hollerith astounded Census Bureau officials by completing the task in just 5.5 hours!

Herman Hollerith's impressive results earned him the contract to process and tabulate 1890 census data. Hollerith was working on the 1880 US census, which was laborious and error-prone, so he took on the mechanization. Using punched cards (round holes, 12 rows x24 columns, 3 1/4 x 6 5/8, in inch) to record information, Hollerith designed a tabulator and sorter for the work. These machines reduced years job to a few months, saved the 1890 taxpayers five million dollars, and earned him an 1890 Columbia PhD. This was the first wholly successful information processing system to replace pen and paper.

Now, we know the emerging of tabulating machine was from the Constitutional need, and thus the emerging information carrying media, punched cards and information automation.

However, these were mainly mechanization, using mechanical mechanism to do the manual work. No storage and no internal capacity.

With the nation's population growing rapidly, hand-counting the results was proving impractical—the 1880 census took a full 7 years to tabulate. Policy-makers worried that the 1890 census wouldn't even be counted by 1900, making reapportionment of congressional seats—as required by the Constitution—impossible.

§ 6.2 HERMAN HOLLERITH'S TABULATING MACHINE

Herman Hollerith's tabulating machine came with a sorter, which could select a particular group of cards based on multiple criteria. Differentiating different subsets of the general population was the critical step for the census. For example, in El Paso, Texas, United States:

Very small subset of Census attributes set

Percentage Attributes

83.00% Hispanic or Latino
92.00% White alone
3.90% Black or African American alone
1.00% American Indian and Alaska Native alone
1.30% Asian alone
0.20% Native Hawaiian and Other Pacific Islander alone
1.50% Two or More Races
11.60% White alone, not Hispanic or Latino

In the past, this final information would need to go

through many layers manual work: individual data first was written down to a card, then manual sorted in to different "baskets" then count, aggregating upwards in each layer, all manually and many portions are repeatedly. Now with the new tabulating machines: sorters and counters, they can be arranged properly in different decks of cards then counted and recorded in new cards for upper level for further statistics computing.

The counting unit of the tabulating machine was a major component. "On the tabulating machine, there was a contact point where there were little cups of mercury—as many cups as there could be holes in the card," It kept a running count of the number of cards with a hole punched in a particular position. It had 40 counters and hence could simultaneously count the number of cards with holes punched in up to 40 positions. Conducting "Probe" through the hole touching the Hg (liquid mercury, part of the circuit) thus close the electrical circuit to initialize a "counting" action via forces generated from solenoid further move the face dial was the main mechanism on the counting.

§ 6.3 INFORMATION SORTING, ROUTING, AND COUNTING WITH MECHANIZATION ANALOG VS DIGITAL

The key is information sorting, routing, and counting. As we see from here, the tabulating machines' major automation contributions were retaining some portions of the tasks in "memory/media (here card)" as-it form, then later on, this information could be used as-is for input for further processing.

Understanding the basics on these tabulating sorters and counters are very helpful for us to advance to the computer mechanism from their cradle. The mechanical calculating machine in the early stage more or less shared the similar principals in their design. Most of the early calculating machines were analogy. i.e. Sir William Thomson (who later became Lord Kelvin, and declared the "perfection of 18 century physics" as we will use that as an example in our late context) designed and built the tiding machine was a special-purpose mechanical analog computer, the main mechanism is the machine sums a number of harmonic variations, transmitted vertically to pulleys, round which passes a wire or chain which is fixed at one end and carries a recording pen at the free end. As seen in this picture:

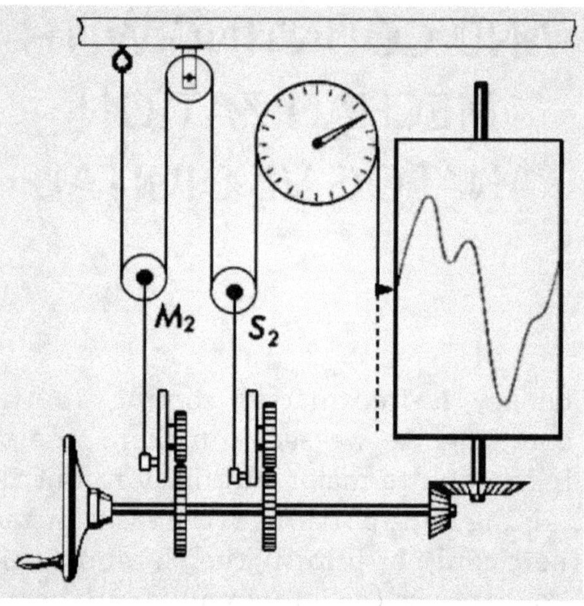

Schematic of the tide machine. Source: http://test.tidespy.com/images/TideMachine.png. A typical analog device.

§ 6.4 IBM AS MECHANIZING MACHINERY COMPANY

In 1911 Hollerith's company merged with several others to form the Computing-Tabulating-Recording Company (CTR), the later IBM.

While so many current events in the society are targeting for automation, the consequence of the automation itself has not been automated. Quite often, users were in long queue to wait for feeding the machine, to get their information imputed, and get their results. The original IBM computer announced in 1959 was a tremendous business success. The 1401 is considered to be the Model-T Ford of the computer industry, because it was mass-produced and because of its sales volume. Over 12,000 units were produced and many were leased or resold after they were replaced with newer technology. Here is a brief background on it. It has to be started from the tabulating machines.

With these explain, we can fast-forward to the computers these are closing to us. We start from the "IBM Card", as then, the IBM Cards were the major type of information carrying media. The information on the card could also be read with human, most of the time, the data was dual, both in machine read holes and printed text. IBM Card, the first generation of information media carrier: information unification and automation come at the cost of "material" efficiency

§ 6.4.1 IBM's 80-column punched card format and character set

"IBM card." Measuring just 7⅜ by 3¼ inches (187.325 mm × 82.55 mm).

Thomas Watson Sr., head of IBM at the time, asked two of his best inventors, Clair D. Lake and J. Royden Peirce, to each develop a new card. Both had a long history of inventing punched card technologies and had more patents between them than most American inventors of the twentieth century. He asked them each to develop a solution independently of one another. Each formed a team and went to work. Peirce wanted to use the existing card with round holes, but make it possible for each hole to represent more than one number or symbol—thereby doubling the storage of data but with half of it devoted to alphanumeric characters.

Lake's team proposed smaller holes, rectangular in shape, which would be easier to read by the metal tabulators but also require new machines, specifically punches and readers. In the middle of this contest sat James W. Bryce, IBM's most prolific inventor of the century with more than 500 patents. He knew both colleagues and understood their proposed innovations. Watson asked him to choose the best solution. Bryce voted for Lake's approach because it could be implemented quickly and required the least adjustment in how tabulating machines worked. Bryce also knew there was little demand for alphabetic information, and wanted to move away from round-holed machines which were more common. Nobody had rectangular holes.

Watson accepted Lake's proposal for both technical and business reasons. It was distinctive, it could be protected with patents, and it would work. He wanted to promote it as the "IBM card." Introduced in 1928, this card had 80 columns (nearly twice the number as the old card), 10 rows for coding numbers, 12 in a modified version of the card introduced in 1930. It was unique, well accepted by customers, and served as a model for other special purpose cards and hardware products introduced from the 1930s through the 1950s. By the late 1960s, most of IBM's punched-card machines were no longer in production, although the punched cards themselves lived on as the dominant input/output medium for electronic computers.

Remington Rand was IBM's main competitor in the punched card space. In 1927, Rand purchased the Powers Accounting Machine Company and, in doing so, kicked off a fierce innovation battle with IBM. The race of one-upmanship resulted in a slew of accounting developments focused on speed and automatic operations.

Beyond accounting purposes, the card had other uses in IBM. Until the early 1990s—long after IBM had ceased selling the punched cards for data processing—it was common practice for IBMers to use them for speaker notes for presentations, as they fit comfortably in the inside pocket of a suit jacket. Secretaries, too, used these cards for transcribing phone messages and typing driving directions. Even IBM executives routinely carried them around with their calendar for the day typed on them.

The IBM card will forever be tied to the modern age of information, serving as the most commonly used method of data storage for nearly a half century. The punched card was an essential part of IBM's development, and undoubtedly helped shape the company as we know it today. When the card was designed, the main purpose of its applications was numerical not alphabet. The interconnection of numbers is more obvious than text, which is the major "language" media on today's networks. The intelligent context from the alphabet piles are more challenging to find out than from the number games, that is one source of the fundamental problem to be resolved for out topic here: the artificial intelligence. Even though, at the bottom of everything, there is a binary representation for everything in the computer machine. In today's accepted practice, the digit "0" is express as 30H -> 45 -> 00110000, AND "A" is 41H -> 65 -> 01000001 and so on.

§ 6.4.2 How Information Becomes Data: Blank (Formatted) and "Printed-out" IBM Cards

Above is the "blank" IBM Card, I wonder the the 80-column (x12 row) IBM Punch card essentially is the decimal layout of the alphanumerical, same mechanism with today binary layout, only different is the "bases." I digitized it as following,

```
|......................................................................................|
|......................................................................................|
|0000000000000000000000000000000000000000000000000000000000000000000000000000000000000|
|1111111111111111111111111111111111111111111111111111111111111111111111111111111111111|
|2222222222222222222222222222222222222222222222222222222222222222222222222222222222222|
|3333333333333333333333333333333333333333333333333333333333333333333333333333333333333|
|4444444444444444444444444444444444444444444444444444444444444444444444444444444444444|
|5555555555555555555555555555555555555555555555555555555555555555555555555555555555555|
|6666666666666666666666666666666666666666666666666666666666666666666666666666666666666|
|7777777777777777777777777777777777777777777777777777777777777777777777777777777777777|
|8888888888888888888888888888888888888888888888888888888888888888888888888888888888888|
|9999999999999999999999999999999999999999999999999999999999999999999999999999999999999|
```

And this is a sequence representation of the numbers and alphabet together with special characters: The Space character has no punch, "&" is 12 only (means a hole in the row #12, the topmost row), "-" is 11 only, "/" is 0 + 1, and so on.

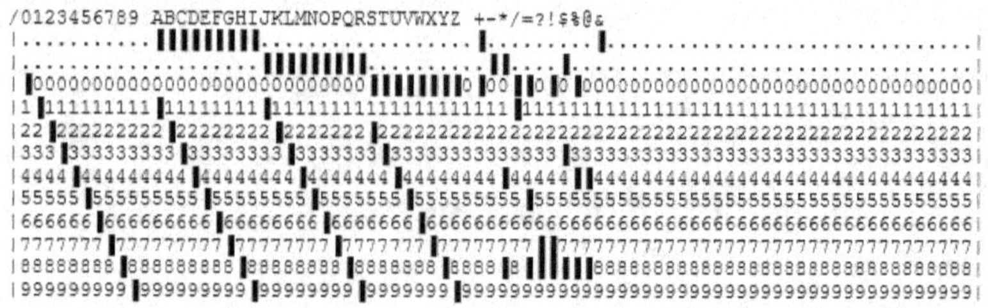

*§ 6.4.3 HELLO GOOGLE! LARRY WORKS 40 HOURS&EARNS $1/52. (*Larry Page Annual $1, "was")*

As the example for the "'O' is express as 30H -> 45 -> 00110000, AND 'A' is 41H -> 65 -> 01000001", in IBM card, it can be translated as: "O" is express as "..□123456789," (read vertically from top to bottom) and "A" "□.0□23456789." If you could not get an idea of how it works, you can use the following example (stating Alphabet CEO earns $1 salary per year, albeit Larry is preferring a "duty-free" civilian over the $1 CEO now: Larry and Surgey had both announced their stepping down from their company executive positions) with total 47 capitalized characters:

THE RISING AI MIND FROM GLOBALLY CORRELATED BIG DATA C...

HELLO GOOGLE! LARRY WORKS 40 HOURS&EARNS $1/52.

```
/HELLO GOOGLE! LARRY WORKS 40 HOURS&EARNS $1/52.
|  ||....|..|..|......|........||....|...|.||.............................|
|..||||..||.|..|.||...|||......|.|....||..|.............................|
|000000000000 |00000 |0 |000 |00 |000 |0 |00000 |000 |0000000000000000000000000000000000000000000|
|111111111111111 |111111111111111111111 |11111 ||1111111111111111111111111111111111111111|
|2222222222222222222222222 ||22222222 |22222 |22222 |2222222222222222222222222222222222222|
|33 ||333333 |333 |3333333333333333333333333333 |3333 |33333333333333333333333333333333333|
|4444444444444444444444444444 |4444 |44444444444444444444444444444444444444444444444444|
|5 |555555555 |5555555555555555555555555 |55 |55555 |5555555555555555555555555555555555555|
|6666 |66 ||6666666666666 ||66666666 |666666666666666666666666666666666666666666666666666|
|777777 |77 |77 |7777777777777777777777777777777777777777777777777777777777777777777777|
| |88888888888 |88888 |8888888888 |88888888888 |8888 |88888888888888888888888888888888888888|
|9999999999999999 ||9999 |999999999 |9999 |99999999999999999999999999999999999999999999999|
```

§ 6.4.4 Fact Check: Had IBM Cards Held Nearly All the World Information?

Although I was with IBM for the 100 anniversaries with the copy of that book "Make the World Work Better." The book had been missed for the moment it was handed to me. I read the context today from (https://www.ibm.com/ibm/history/ibm100/us/en/) and cannot be so sure about the statement, "taken collectively, the IBM card held nearly all of the worrld's known information for just under half a century—an impressive feat even by today's measures". Considering the card is thicker than paper and highly inefficient usage on the surface space (less than 1/12 used on the 12x column matrix card), plus the fact of the general purpose of original card had been designed for numerical over alphabet, which is the main system of recording symbols in printed matter for information. I just could not imagine that IBM cards had held all the world's know information (picture this: the works of Shakespeare on the IBM Card. never heard of that). Even though, at the minimum, these cards had formatted and routed some very important information, originally scattered, into forms of machine-readable symbols, physically, portably, and most importantly, logically interconnected.

§ 6.5 TURING MACHINE INFORMATION DISTILLING AND REPRESENTING

From lord Kelvin's tiding analog calculating machine, to numerous large and small calculators/computers; those were "isolate" items, because they were not built for scale and for large amount of information processing. Not until Herman Hollerith's tabulating machine, which was born with mission of gobbling down mountains of "formatted" information carrying card, these are the real modern information processing prototype "AMU" that we are talking about.

The new breed of languages, Turing-Machines, and ridicule inefficiency in the iSpace: one of the root causes accounting for the incompetence of the classic computers. Their greedy

In the tabulating machines, the data was specifically "distilled" and "transformed". The meanings and interpretations on these symbols on the card are totally different from the existing human languages. In fact, they must create a new "dictionary", "glossary", "grammar", and so on. These items, attributes, and interacting mechanisms are the principal requirements for a typical language. This development, not uttered from the animal vocal cords, but executing via so-called Turing-Machines (a hypothetical machine first described by mathematician Alan Turing in 1936, is a mathematical model of computation that defines an abstract machine, which manipulates symbols on a strip of cards, tapes, etc. according to a table of rules).

§ 6.5.1 Automation Comes at the Cost of "Material" Efficiency, Now and Then

Digitalization had brought us enormous extraordinary things. Ever since the beginning, the efficiency of the utilization on the resources was at a low grade. Think a fully utilized 12x80 card, if fully loaded, contains 80 alphabets. Still (1-80/(12x80)) ~ 92% waste. Now, the media carriers are cheap, they are more symbolic than materials, i.e. a thumb size USB flash driver's capacity

range from MBs to nearly TBs (10^9). The SD card in your camera or phone, for example, only feasible in a format called FAT (File Allocation Table). They are highly inefficient. For a normal 64 GB SD card that is typical now, the cluster size is 128 KB (exFAT). What does that mean to you, which means that the minimum storage unit in that card is 128 KB (Kilo bytes). If you have one letter, i.e. "i" storage in that card, it occupies 128 (1024 x 128 =) 132072 bytes. (Actually, the efficient is lower than this because there is other overhead, file Name space, FAT space, hidden sectors, and unpartitioned space on card). That will give you an efficiency lower than 8 ppm (<0.0075%). Of course, it will increase the efficiency when the file size is increasing. But that is just roughly the idea of how inefficient on the storage. Although not a lot of people really care about it, since the capacity of the storage media is very big currently.

The IBM Card, was one of the media carriers of these languages in "written" in volumes. These "books" were then read, comprehended, and executed by the earlier IBM computers, the real prototype of modern computers. These IBM cards were more physical than technology, so the design on the card and adoption on the automation has always been an efficiency lift in certain filed with the cost in the others.

In a large sense, the human being privatizing the individual space (houses, yards, even vehicles, and so on) was also a resource digitalizing. The individual space goes to a stage that not more resource can be allocated (New York, London, Toyko, etc.), then they start going higher, or squeezing inner ward, resulting in the crowded urban areas.

§ 6.5.2 An Important Leap Forward: Computer Languages as the Second Step of Information Tokenization

The languages executed by automatic machinery have developed in such a way that these were totally strangers in the view of the English speakers, in spite the languages have been created in tokens extracted from English. So to speak, the languages of automation machinery had been built on the English speaking language, with extra meaning tokens assigned. The languages have been developed not one, two, three, there are hundreds out there today. Bill Gates and Paul Allen wrote the ROM BASIC with ASM (Assembly) language. Larry and Sergey were mainly using languages like Java and Python to start their search engine. All these languages bear the same general purpose to be understood or understood after compiled, by machines, the computers, and to perform a designated functions or actions.

These specialized computer languages have become so dominated and prevailed that many specialize courses have been created to train the people(mostly college students) to understand the logic and grammar of a special sub set of these instructions.

Furthermore, as mentioned in the previous content, every career, every business, even the street gang, and so on, has created their specific sub set of, meaningful only in a subtle way, language, either slang or professional jargon, these specially alerted or modified English "apps", are the key to achieve various of goals. For example, If you are in IBM, you will be familiar with (Lotus) notes, which is the IBM email system; if you are in Google, you will be surely know "MK", which is not that "Michael Kors", loved by Ladies; MKs love by everyone in Google. MK stands for Micro Kitchen and is one kinda infamous Google subsidy system. Featuring fresh fruits, dried fruits, healthy unhealthy drinks, many kinds of snacks, and so on. Normally MKs sit between sessions or by stairwells, so people can come across each other in different departments and make connections. Here is the "MK" in Microsoft, which labels the complex as "Hub", the following pictures were taken in my latest visit to one of their campus, for purpose of this writing:

A picture of Microsoft "Hub": snacks and cold/hot beverages. What I had there were Zico Coconut Water, 11.2 fl. oz carton (in the lower "Microsoft" fridge) and mini-cookies (not visible in picture: under the "Microsoft" nut jars). Last but not the "least", did I mention that I had just one of a kind! I am believing I deserve this Silk nut-milk while I am writing this part of the story, as it is happening—this is the selfie of this book page and the beverage that the author is working on and with, in an early Saturday morning, the life I am enjoying so much (The top left inset). I also found here, everything is Microsoft, the story, the "hub", the snacks and beverages, the girls and the Microsoft Office word.

§ 6.6 KNOWLEDGE OF "LANGUAGES" AS ASSETS OF EXPERTISE

Moving into specific system, the language subset of each programming entity has evolved so "narrow" and "jargon" that requires their employees' long time learning, so far so deep that to change their temperaments.

In these internal brewing living business entities, view angles, mindset, as well as the solution approaches are away from your day to day common sense. In one place, they are golden keys, a piece of garbage in another organization. Here is a technique tiny sample, "XOR", is a logical operation that outputs true only when inputs differ, so called eXclusive "OR" or exclusive disjunction. This "operation" has been heavily used in your password's cryptography.

In a "bit" operation:

XOR logic:

0 xor 0 = 0
1 xor 1 = 0
1 xor 0 = 1

0 xor 1 = 0

Encrypt:

The original text:

01010101 01010011 01000001 (USA)
To xor with the key/password:
01110101 01110011 01100001 (usa)

We have The ciphertext:

00100000 00100000 00100000 (3 "space" characters)

Can you figure out the decrypt text using the cipher-text and the key.

Started from encrypted text:

00100000 00100000 00100000
Let it, " ", xor with key/password: usa
01110101 01110011 01100001

What we get here is the original text: USA

01010101 01010011 01000001

So, the "XOR" is a very important operations in computer languages, especially in terms of encryptions and decryption (recovered into original text) because twice xor the same key will simply go back to the original content.

I was acquainting with this from a very interesting event. The setting was long time ago, when GUI (Graphic User Interface) OS was not the base interface for PC. In a large big-data-base type document book-keeping, one of a big university's entire file was locked down because of the mistakes of the secretary (CPS) missing password. I was working in a key accelerator laboratory on my "energized particles (electrons, protons, alpha particles, and so on) interaction with matter" study. We got a call from the university president's office and they asked us for help. The task fell into my hand, not because I was an expert on data ciphering but only because they thought I might be able to get it done, and quickly, albeit there were many senior PhD candidates in the same lab with the same supervisor.

It would be super easy now, since we are so familiar with passwords these days, plus there are so many tools out there for password cracking. But I was not that luck at the moment. First of all, I knew nothing on the ciphering and I knew nothing on that specific word processing GUI (under command line OS) software, my project was, as mentioned, study the expected and exotic phenomena of the elemental particles' interactions with matters. I knew the importance of the task (in my humble student view). And there was no internet at the moment (Berners-Lee was just barely starting working on it in his limited lab scale, properly on COM ports, again, in my humble understanding then), plus there was no place to look for. I ended up cycling to a closed city bookstore (hours on bike) to get an idea of what the hell on a wrongly password encrypted document in an alien language. One of senior PhD student under the same professor helped me to source a journal on computer encoding. Started from that limited information, I was able to reverse engineer the critical arithmetic operation for the cyphering was "XOR" bit-wise operations. With help from some hex editor software, I guessed the most of the data could be recovered. The real encrypting is always much complicated than the simple "xor", for that cyphering, you can never find the original key. I actually forgot the details but "XOR" was one of the first few things I knew from when the computer was only equipped in prestigious research laboratories.

From IBM Lotus to Microsoft "Hub", from Facebook Oops@ to the lost password of University, these are just tips of numerous icebergs. Today, the password cracking/hacking is mostly related to greed, dollars, payments and do not carry social norm or ethics; quite often, it is on the opposite side: money makes the mare go.

§ 6.7 THE SPECIALIZED SUBSET TOKEN LANGUAGES CAN BE GOLD IN ONE PLACE BUT MIND-BOGGLING WEIRD BITS AND PIECES OTHERWISE

The skills and knowledge can serve you as ornament but it is rare, most of the time, they may be otherwise. If you missed news on the story of a south Korean couple who had let their baby die while they played (addicted) a video game. I had an infamous tenant who went out for her indulging "adult life" and left an unattended baby die (in her previous residence) here in US. However, they distorted this story as SID (sudden infant death) and made themselves famous and profited from it, that is the "typical" mindset in this land. The US edition of "Office" starring Stephen Corral et al, had this narrative in its pilot episode, in the "screen face time" from Jim, "If I left, what would I do with all this useless information in my head? You know? Tonnage price of manila folders? Er, Pam's favorite flavor of yogurt, which is mixed berry." But Jim's useless "information" was still "materials" and rosy. If you have beef with Facebook, do you seek help with one of your friends who is a Facebook employee, and to file an online form, "Oops@" (email "hotline") to just get your issue resolved faster than normal? As Facebook internal voice, "There is not a truly functional infrastructure" for "growing so fast and have never emphasized organization, polish, or stability."

In the industry revolution era, jobs were more physical and material. What you see is what your work on. Now, all the things are behind the "menus" and "tabs", these you are rather familiar and in the same time non-native. Giving everyone headache might be the business reimbursement process (taken from my friend's complain in his employer CBRE Group, Inc.), let's not mention the publication process for certain research results, which is even more time consuming and review intense. Normally, when you are request a business travel, you will need tightly follow the designated business protocol: your option of travel agencies, your per diem allowance, your estimated total cost, your place of fund source (normally called cost center), and many more. All these are subject to approval step-by-step wise in order and gating. Remember, your tiers of approvers are not working for your 24/7, the process takes its course. Some companies have company business credit card, which solves some of the issues. Otherwise, after travel, you will have a lot of forms to fill to get your cost (paid in the name of yourself on a business travel) back. None of these is clearly displayed in front of you, and you definitely have no one to ask for all the information at one stop. Most of these need to find the correct online portal and fill the form.

Even with considerable good design, there are still road blocks here and there preventing you from going through smoothly. Most of the time, you are so desperate to grasp the scope of this process, which is often worth nothing than a "clue" digital information junk in your head (suck like, check this or that box first; or from the nth tab of the left/right/top/bottom, fill your yada yada … then …); simply because you may not use it for the rest of your tenure. Most of these automation business processes cost a lot of high skill employee's valuable time than the real saving. These processes were handled by secretary in the old time. Now everyone needs to chime in to the digital portal, learn the designer's characterizing think pattern, and force you through other people's thoughts with glitches here and there.

Yes, there are a lot of business automations in place of the old human resources handling, however, they are more often costing more resources (especially in the employee hours) for the process to be able to take its course of automation. Furthermore, the increasing detailing and subdivided functions make the course work more specialized in their glossary, or in their process languages. In reality, any activity in the modern company needs certain special glossary. The benefits of automation become infinite dividing and documenting. The preparation for the automation process costs more that the share worth of the contribution that this automation bringing in.

The supposedly automated cost-saving on-line paper work processes, always played out otherwise, resulting with fusses and headaches, the on-line tutorials

are usually not sufficient and fail to function: people's "knowing-how's" is not sufficient aligned with the digital portals even in the high-tech companies. The work to train them to work with these on-line portals costs more work than simply get the original work done offline, especially when these activities are not very frequent.

CHAPTER 7: GIVE YOUR MIND A FLOSS: GOOGLE'S PANCAKE FLIPPING DOODLE ON THE 218TH BIRTHDAY OF JOSEPH ANTOINE FERDINAND PLATEAU

The Doodle designing team in Google has decided to use a flipping pancake GIF (Graphics Interchange Format. The acronym GIF most commonly refers to a short, animated picture without sound). For some time, Google was trying to create animation from math equations instead of frames of images (I was trying to get this information from the grave yard of their hundreds failed projects, and counting, this item is not there. Years ago, when one was trying to save these Doodles, one would find what s/he was dealing was a mathematic expression in the page sources … I was trying to make them local but was not successful, and I do not know that that project was called, so I cannot search in "Moma"), obviously not successful. However, the GIF animation provides better and easy ways to illustrate the plot in our context here. There are two major deviations from movie to GIF: 1) No audio; 2) GIF does lossless compress, limited in 256-color. Digital movies, no matter in what kind of digital formats, are normally in a none-reversible lossy compression. Today, Google's pancake animation is to celebrate Joseph Antoine Ferdinand Plateau's 218th birthday (The animated meme: https://www.google.com/doodles/joseph-plateaus-218th-birthday.)

§ 7.1 PLATEAU PHD IN 1829 "FILM PRODUCTION"

Born in Brussels on this day in 1801, Plateau was the son of an accomplished artist who specialized in painting flowers. In 1822 he entered the university as a student in law. However, he became interested in science; and in 1824, after he received a diploma in law, he enrolled as a candidate for an advanced degree in the physical sciences and mathematics. Plateau had been orphaned at the age of fourteen, he had to support himself during his studies by teaching elementary mathematics at the same time. He received his PhD in sciences in 1829. May be because of his busy schedule, Plateau had a relatively short volume PhD dissertation: 34 pages and around 13K words count (statistic calculations by me). Body of content started from Page 5 and ended at Page 31 (only 8 lines in P31). With 7 figures, which can be drawn from compass and rule, fitted in one single page. Totaling his dissertation at 34 pages. The dissertation had neither abstract in front of it nor summary at the end, starting as:

"Everyone knows that if you move a coal flame quickly

in the darkness, you will see a continue luminous curve ... quickly in a darkness with a coal flame on. This fact supports the fact that the sensations produced in us by the light have a certain drift, and that they still remain sometime after the disappearance of objects. Moreover, to convince oneself directly of this truth by looking at a piece of white paper exposed to the sun, and suddenly closing the eyes, we then see the white image of the paper still remaining for a noticeable long time..." (the truth of the "seeing" may be subject to argument, the effect was from some harmful effects, Plateau eventually blinded himself by this trick he enjoyed, a typical craziness of scientific enthusiasts).

Fascinated by the persistence of luminous impressions on the retina, he performed an experiment in which he gazed directly into the sun for 25 seconds. Later in life, Plateau lost his eyesight, which he blamed on an experiment during which he stared at the sun for 25 seconds. Plateau's long (he continued to do research even after his retirement) and productive career is especially remarkable because he was totally blinded in 1843.

Plateau's doctoral dissertation detailed how images form on the retina, noting their exact duration, color, and intensity. Based on these conclusions, he was able to create, in December of 1832, a device called Fantascope. The name came later, as Phenakistoscope, coined in the French newspaper Le Figaro in June 1833 and, it implies visual trickery, which is one way to think about movies. The newspaper explained that Phenakistoscope (phénakistiscope) is from the Greek word phenakisticos, or "to deceive," and óps, meaning "eye" or "face." In other words, an optical illusion. The invention is seen as a precursor to cinematography.

Picture on this scene near 200 year ago, Plateau was in the center of a gathered crowd, these had never experienced a man-made motion picture before. Plateau claimed that he bore magic charm, and he could make, the snakes, for example, to move, as illustrated in these GIF (Phenakistoscope) animations.

§ 7.2 DISSECTION OF PHENAKISTOSCOPE

Plateau got his PhD by animation movie. The original image, which is https://upload.wikimedia.org/wikipedia/commons/c/c2/Phenakistiscope_Snakes_16_sections_-_animated.gif and has the following information:

File Size	2.9 MB
Gif Version	89a
Image Width	1000
Image Height	1000
Color Resolution Depth	8
Bits Per Pixel	8
Background Color	0
Animation Iterations	65535
Frame Count	16
Duration	1.12s

According to the metadata info, we immediately get that the frame duration is 0.07s. Considering human eyes have "persistence of vision", which is in the range of 0.067~0.1s. The above image is pretty smooth for most of the people. To make a point on this, I have thus changed the duration in different time pieces:

	Frame duration	frame rate
(1)	1 s	~ 1 frame/s
(2)	250 ms	4 fps
(3)	50 ms	20 fps
(4)	100 ms	10 fps with reversal

(16 total frame "round-trip" ~ 32 frames)

The results can be viewed via (since the MS Word does not support in-line animating, I thus host these images elsewhere) in blogger sites:

Phenakistoscope with 50 ms interval ~ 20 fps

https://1.bp.blogspot.com/-25z7M0jIzRY/Xg19k8sycxI/AAAAAA-AAACE/DcDRvXsZX74LDm9ce9bWYJW8jH1fV73RwCEwYBhgL/s1600/PhenakistoscopeAt050ms.gif

Phenakistoscope with 250 ms interval ~ 4 fps

https://1.bp.blogspot.com/-5PiatY4SrMU/Xg19lCzsfiI/AAAAAA-AAACE/O2SavkSTWYoXHqWS1WJpznA1zz1ts8NVACEwYBhgL/s1600/PhenakistiscopeAt250ms.gif

Phenakistoscope with 1 s interval ~ 1 fps

https://1.bp.blogspot.com/-rR_ABAPsi94/Xg19nLmQC_I/AAAAA-AAAACI/hFtwFZoZS_Mg6V7RJvr0roBHlY3GyTQ8QCEwYBhgL/s1600/PhenakistoscopeAt1S.gif

If most people cannot detect the flick like discontinuation in the original Phenakistoscope GIF animation; the 1 full second frame rate will suffice. It is also obvious to detect this in the 4 fps one, while the 20 fps (0.050 ms) is much faster and smoother. However, since our still images are only 16 frames for the whole process, a sharp vision can still detect something: this is still an animation.

For the persistence of vision issue, to the Phenakistoscope GIF animation, we speculate that the ancient Belgians would be shocked if Joseph Plateau played it as a wicked show. That is a typical human internal perception on the outside world; they may be pretty much distorted and not exactly one to one matching in every manifold dimension, in this case - the temporal dimension. The human eyes are seeing the world around through biochemical reacting process, which takes much longer than physical absorbing of a photon by elemental particles. That reaction duration limits human vision's temporal resolution at 0.067-0.1 s. The innate idiopathic proneness of human being in the vision does not pose a danger in the nature environment. However, in a temporal scale of elemental interaction, there are rich things we just cannot perceive. The truth of gaps of blankness in our perception lets all kinds of cognitive interpretations happen: the magicians can always play with these native deficiencies and make us believe that something is believable while what we believe is not the loyally reality: i.e. the "silk through the phone tricks", which has many versions and even tutorials (by simply Googling the quoted "silk through the phone tricks"). That trick explores and utilizes the one kind of vision deficiencies.

§ 7.3 THE BRIEF HISTORY OF GOOGLE AS "DOODLE" AND GBIKE ETHICS

Before we steam our engine away from here, a note for the Google Doodle origin. It was said in August 30, 1998, 5 days before Google incorporated as a company (after failed to sell "PageRank" algorithm to any of the big internet business players, for $1 Million); What in the hell that Larry and Sergey could find time to attend the "Burning Man" ("Burning Man is the place to find out "who you are", then take it a step further." per their front page), the event takes its name from its culmination, the symbolic ritual burning of a large wooden effigy ("The Man") that traditionally occurs on the Saturday evening of the event. Which was August 29, 1998. That was why you have the stick Burning Man "Doodle" as the August 30, 1998 Google header logo. The impact of Burning Man event, in its 21st anniversary, was a Google internal announcement, as follows,

"Sep 4, 2019 Sprocket's Spin: Ep 6: GBikes + Burning

Man

"Hello GBike nation! Community is much more than belonging to something; it's about doing something together that makes belonging matter. As you may know, Burning Man, an event celebrating art and community, just took place. Unfortunately, a few individuals acted out of community spirit and took GBikes to the event (yes, they're tracked!). This has been a trend the past few years and one that we'd like to avoid to keep our beloved bikes safe and stocked up for the Google community to get around campus.

"Let's be GBike superheroes and only park GBikes at Google buildings so they don't disappear and end up at Burning Man or other places they shouldn't be. Thanks for listening and don't forget to wear your helmet and safety check those brakes!"

Don't you feel that these contexts akin to the teacher's gentle words in the kindergartens while little Joe breaks little Jane's crayon. Yes, there are. As you can get the context from the section of "Absolute freedom in Google," it was these kinda spoiled never wrong mindsets—to add one more clause, for that dissection.

The fissures in human's moral abyss luminate here and there in the GBike ethics, one of my colleagues told me there were selling GBike online somewhere around bay. GBike unethical activities have gone to a degree that the bay area law enforcement has been heeded. I witnessed an event when I was returning from NASA Ames Exploration Center, a police officer was politely nodding a GBike rider to check if he was a Google employee. That was greatly appreciated and I did say "Thank you for the checking, officer!" before his explain.

CHAPTER 8: TAKING THE STOCK OF "FLIPPING-PANCAKE" ANIMATION TO MOTION PICTURES: FILMS, MOVIES, AND THEN THE MEDIA DIGITAL REVOLUTION

Since the beginning of motion pictures, there are many technologies have been developed on the subject. Movies (including 3D MAX), TVs, Internet Videos, the 3D realities, and more. Not only they have not been distrusted by our authentication, but also they have been serving for the humans' entertainment, education, documentation, commercial, and many more. After a century development on the cinematography, most of the movies had been stored in movie films (for theater) or VHS tapes (for home entertainment etc.). Since 1990s, many new media formats have emerged, the most common one is MPEG digital media standard (more on this later).

There were several major developmental stages on the cinematography. For the professional 35 mm (1.378") film gauge: which has four perforations for each still image size portion. The theatre movie plays at a speed of 24 fps, resulting 35 x 24 => 0.84 mps (meter per second ~33 inch-per-second). In 1970s, VHS tape gained popularity with the process unit VCR (Videocassette recorder) entering into household. The information stored in the VHS tape is converted into magnetic signal and stored in the thin layer of magnetic media, which is not the same as in the film, in which, the original pictures are stored. In the standard play mode, the VHS tape runs at a speed of 3.335 cm/s (1.313 inch-per-second), gives a resolution of 250 lines. The broadcast TV analog signal was about 500 lines. Till then, those formation and information storage are all in analog.

The first general public digital media format is VCD, then DVD, with the current HD format, blue-ray, 3D and so on. VCD stands for Video CD, a digital audio/video format. With a resolution at 352x240. Corresponding the VHS resolution, of course, it is not, see discussions later on. VCD had never gain public enthusiasm in countries with VHS domination, for many reasons; the major one always the existing VHS industry business profits protection. But not until DVD and later.

§ 8.1 THE GENERAL DEVELOPMENTAL PATTERN IN THE FOR-PROFIT SOCIETY WITH GREEDY BUSINESS-PROTECTING PRACTICES: THE TENDER EMERGING ENTITIES CANNOT STAND UP TO THE OLD FOES FROM THE BEGINNING BUT TIPTOED COMPLIANCES

There are developmental patterns in the history of all emerging technologies. Most striking is the migrations of the infrastructures, the new emerging systems have always tried to accommodate their resource demanding within the existing infrastructures.

The advantages of this are many and disadvantages are more.

The design based on existing hardware saves a lot of effort. The foremost advantage is implementing a new thing without alerting the inertia of the people's mind. General population does not accept radical changes; and corporate businesses never welcome their existing profits shrinkage by embracing brand-new technologies that will phase their current hardware out: as for the household air conditions, refrigerators, and son on, for decades, there were so many smart units out there around the world: quiet, gentle, efficient. For all that, most of the US houses and apartments are equipped with the system half century ago and there is no sign of any change soon.

While this is all good for the stereotype mindset and conservative business profits in certain circles, the approach causes more issues with the further development on the emerging technologies.

When internet was starting entering household, they had already developed well in the academic/corporate environments. With LAN as the major form of connections using ethernet cables. However, this kind of hardware deployment was not practical to implement into household setting (the protocols of the LAN are not for long distance) at once. So came the AOL business on top of the century old phone lines. When A.G. Bell first successfully laid the coast-to-coast long-distance telephone line in 1915, and grew into big business, he never thought his nearly century infrastructure building would lay last golden egg to AOL, who advertised then "information highway" with their heavy-duty toll booth sitting at every "information highway" entrance. They drained the golden egg from Bell's duck and let the duck die in exhausting without a shape. Then the dialup faded away, then DSL, cable modem system. Now the optical fibers have already gone into household. The developmental pattern was very obvious. Some big internet players, such like Amazon, Microsoft, and Google, are now working to make much faster network with their own infrastructure as backbone to boost the whole world both wired and wirelessly.

§ 8.2 VCD, DVD, BLUE-RAY, AND NETWORK DELIVERY OF THE MOVIES, MUSIC, AND BIG DATA

§ 8.2.1 MPEG-1 VCD

The VCD was using then compact disc as physical carrying media, hold around 80 minutes of compressed video/audio streams in an original 80 minutes uncompressed Audio CD (for 700MB data disc). With either 352x240 (NTSC at 29.97 fps) or 352x288 (PAL at 25fps) video screen pixel matrix.

VCD stores single program stream (including Video/Audio/Data) media in MPEG-1 standard for system, video (1150 kbps), and audio (224 kbps) with total bandwidth up to 1.5 Mbit/s (here is a little calculation: these video/audio streams are stored in "raw" format, without CRC, cyclic redundancy check — a 703 MB data disc thus stores 846 MB raw data. Using maximum data rate at 1.5 Mbit/s, which is ~ 225 KB/s, gets about 75 minutes of MPEG-1 movie content. Since the data rate is not all way through with 1.5 Mbit/s, so fitting 80 minutes movie into a CD-Rom is not an issue). The systems layer provides the information about the audio and video layers, with stream identification and synchronization information essential to the decoding and subsequent rendering for each of them. The audio and video are bounded while the systems layer is viewed as an unbounded element and can, therefore, be a very complex environment. The systems layer is required to carry not only the multiplexed audio and video information but all of the other non-audio/video information, and in many cases private, data needed for a successful and pleasing user experience. The MPEG stands for Moving Picture Experts Group, a working group of ISO/IEC (officially ISO/IEC JTC 1/SC 29/WG 11) with the mission to develop standards for coded representation of digital audio, video, 3D Graphics and other data. Since its establishment in 1988, the group has produced standards that help industry offer end users an ever more enjoyable digital media experience.

For the video layer, MPEG-1 ISO/IEC 11172-2 specifies a video codec which was originally designed for the application domain of video for CD storage. The intended picture resolution is CIF or SIF.

A number of requirements apply in the context of storage and replay of stored data, which mainly are related to random access:

The video sequence must be re-playable forward and backward;

Fast forward/reverse modes have to be supported;

Editing (e.g. extracting or replacement of frames) must be possible.

MPEG-1 part 3 defines the audio system, MPEG-1 Audio (MPEG-1 Part 3), which includes MPEG-1 Audio Layer I, II, III, and published in 1993 as ISO/IEC 11172-3, part of MPEG-1 standard ISO/IEC 11172 (https://mpeg.chiariglione.org/standards/mpeg-1). ISO/IEC 11172-3 has three types of Audio encoding protocols, called layers I (MP1) II (MP2) III (MP3).

§ 8.2.2 MPEG-1 Part 3
Layer III is MP3

Do not mix the ISO/IEC 11172-3 "3" with the MP3 "3". I found there is no place explaining this. the "3" in ISO/IEC 11172-3 called part number, it happens to be same number "3" in MP3, which is a subset of ISO/IEC 11172-3 (most successful one of the MP1, MP2, and MP3). A MPEG-1 program (total entity) can chose from any of these three layers, I (MP1), II (MP2), or III (MP3), resulting in different quality of audio and audio stream bandwidth in the same video stream. Hope this clear some of the never explained confusion. MPEG-1 Layer I or II Audio is a generic sub band coder operating at bit rates in the range of 32 to 448 kb/s and supporting sampling frequencies of 32, 44.1 and 48 kHz. Typical bit rates for Layer II are in the range of 128-256 Kbit/s, and 384 kb/s for professional applications. MPEG-1 Layer 3 Audio (or MP3) is a 1- or 2-channel perceptual audio coder that provides excellent compression of music signals. Compared to Layer 1 and Layer 2, Layer-3 (MP3) provides a higher compression efficiency. An uncompressed Audio-CD hold 80 minutes full spectrum audio data (.wav/wave file), while MP1 and MP2 can achieve compress ratio of 4:1-6:1; MP3 reaches 12:1.

§ 8.2.3 MPEG-2 DVD vs Portable MP4

DVD uses MPEG-2 standard, which supports much higher quality with a data rate (also called bit rate) of from 1.2 to 15 Mbps. MPEG-2 is the format most favored for video on demand—DVD, and is the format for transmitting digital television.

MPEG4 was developed much later, as an encoding method for devices with limited resources. MPEG4 is the preferred format for portable devices, as it yields a 1:5 file size in media storage; MPEG4 also made it practical to buy and download videos online, as MPEG2 videos are quite large, and take a long time to download. However, MPEG2 provides a far superior image quality. The difference in quality is minor when viewing the files through a tiny screen, like those installed in mobile phones and even netbooks, but when it comes to large displays, like most current HDTV displays, you can clearly notice the difference in the final picture. We can attribute this to the amount of data lost, since both MPEG2 and MPEG4 are lossy compressed methods. MPEG4 simply discards more information, which results in poorer picture.

Then we have MP4, MP4 is an abbreviated term for MPEG-4 part 14. Again, like MP3, this brings some confusions. MPEG-4 is a method of defining compression of audio and visual digital data (Audio/Visual Objects). With the development of MPEG-4, it is divided into a number of parts (each part covers a certain aspect of the whole specification) including MPEG-4 part 2 (e.g. XviD video codec), MPEG-4 part 3 (e.g. AAC audio codec), MPEG-4 part 10 (H.264 video codec), MPEG-4 part 14 (MP4 media container) and others. MPEG-4 Part 14 or MP4 is a digital multimedia container format most commonly used to store video and audio, but it can also be used to store other data such as subtitles and still images. Like most modern container formats, it allows streaming over the Internet. The only official filename extension for MPEG-4 Part 14 files is .mp4. MPEG-4 Part 14 (formally ISO/IEC 14496-14:2003) is a standard specified as a part of MPEG-4.

§ 8.3 MPEG-1, MPEG-2, MPEG-4, MP3, MP4: DISSECTING THE DIGITAL VS ANALOG STORAGE FORMATS

§ 8.3.1 PCM Audo as Function of Values vs Time

We had deeply analized the video formats both in Chapter 7 and the previous sections of Chapter 8. The original sound stored in CD is in a formation called: PCM (pulse code modulation) - which transcodes an analog signal into discrete unit and then maps into certain representation for play back. This process is independently from computer system.

You can see this the following way:

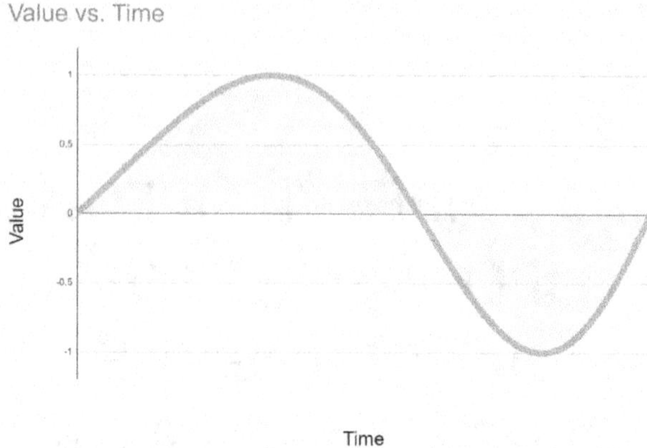

Let's reproduce the sound from microphone to a speaker. In the recording, the horizonal axis is representing Time and vertical axis representing a Value (i.e. amplitude, current, voltage, mechanical offset, and so on), the record can be illustrated as the above figure (certain time period). For the analog system, the output module will convey the "V vs T" and apply them to the speaker. For this kind analog setup, the two parameters here are time and value, whose fidelity is tied with the microphone-system-speaker performance, once the hardware built, no parameters is tunable anymore.

§ 8.3.2 Pros and Cons for Analog vs Digital

If, for a good reason, the sound has to be stored for later play out, then there is a recording process. For the classic analog record, it was normally recorded on tapes, which have thin layer of magnetic materials coated onto plastic base strip. For recording, the magnetic writing header was modulated by the input signal, for simplification, it is proper to use current in place of the "value", higher sound volume produces higher current (it is the truth), then the higher current will make the writing header coil generate stronger magnetic field, which again exerts on the recording tapes, the stronger magnetic field results larger angular rotations in the magnetic materials on the tapes. In the later play back, a reading header picks up the signals from the magnetic domains and amplified to the output.

The analog recorded information does not have rigorous correlations to have the fidelity locked in. During storage and transferring, the degree of "deformation" can make the recording audio/sound deviate away from the original signal, the play back system has no way to detect and the degradation can be gradual and slow, but can continue forever.

The audio in an Audio-CD, as PCM, has already digitalized. However, the process is more into the detail and refine. The Audio-CD uses LPCM (Linear PCM): with sampling rate at 44.1 KHz (44,100 is the product of the squares of the first four prime numbers $2^2 \times 3^2 \times 5^2 \times 7^2$ and hence has many useful integer factors.) and a Bit-depth of 16bit. Linear means during the whole audio event, the sampling rate and bit-depth keep constant.

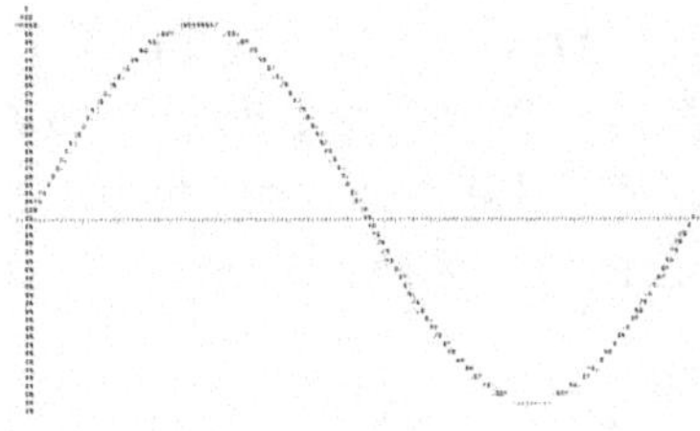

Take the above illustration, the LPCM data is pretty much keep the loyal representation of the original sound wave by sufficient slicing the above wave record: if the above horizontal scale is 1 second, the LPCM in CD will slice the 1 second in 44.1 K time pieces; while slicing the vertical recording signal value (i.e. amplitude, voltage, current, etc.) into 2^{16} = 65536 pieces. With 2-channel (studio), then the size of a 1 second LPCM data chunk size will be (16-bit = 2 "bytes"), in [channels x bytes/sample x sampling rate]: 2 x 2 x (44.1 x 1000) = 176,400 "bytes". In one minute, it will be: 10,584,000 = 10.0937 "MB"/m. An important conception has to be declared here: the "byte" and "MB" here are borrowed conceptions. Data stored in CD is not the same data stored in the computer disk. The data on the disk is digitalized laser signal degree of modulation (dye variations or surface pits' reflections), these variations in the laser reflection strength have been picked up and transcode directly into output sound system. The disk, cluster, sector, byte, bit, file, etc. conceptions do not involve. All the CD-player see is a stream of passing audio units: since the CD rotate at a fixed speed, the player only deals with (audio) scale (i.e. amplitude) information.

To let computer use and process the signals on an Audio-CD, IBM and Microsoft worked together in early 1990s. Through one to one mapping, the computer transcodes the audio unit information into computer file. As people normally are aware of, the sound comes directly off a CD called .wav file, which is the Windows/DOS based operation system one to one mapped LPCM data, so without compression, the CD ripped Wave file size is the same 10.0937 MB/m. The process doesn't lose necessary data to reproduce the same signal in quality.

§ 8.3.3 Digital Audio as Radical Processed Soul Food

Enough background on the Video/Audio digitalization (the motion pictures, movies, using 24-30 still images per second to represent the real continue moving objects was a digitalizing process) for the modern media stream information. The major hints that we are trying to dissect here are the human visual clue and perception on the natural world. After Joseph Plateau's discovery on the persistence of vision and invention of Phenakistoscope. Motion pictures have explored the mechanism and were able to deliver the serial images appear as moving objects thus videos and movies were born. The persistence of vision at 0.0667 to 0.1 second level results a classic film playing speed at 24 fps. That is well known so far. However, the major development on the MP3 encoding had enabled the fast transfer speed of audio/music on the internet, what that had imposed into the audio stream and impact to our auditory system has much less stressed.

The mp3 audio has cut many chunks away from the original digitized L-PCM audio stream. There are usually some frequencies that most people can't hear, so this data removed first. Secondly, some sounds are naturally loud, and they usually mask some quieter sounds. This always makes MP3 get rid of some 'hidden' sounds. Lastly, sound compression exploits that human ear hears particular frequencies better than others. It is pretty clear that MP3 is a lossy data-compression.

While the LPCM CD-Audio is sufficient to map the ana-

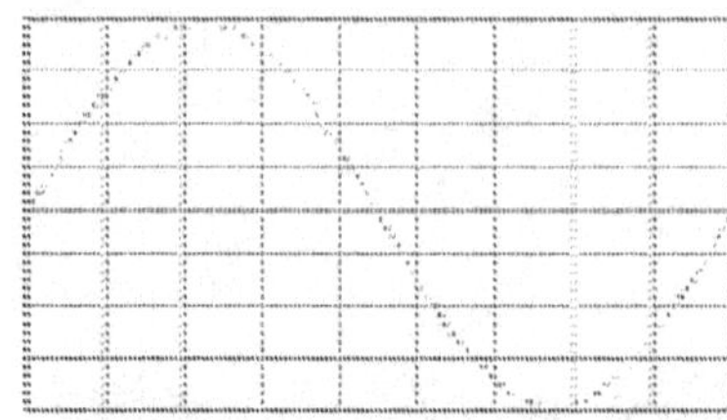

log sound with fidelity by 44.1 KHz and 16-bit depth and accounting to a 10 MB/m stream. The Audio sub stream in the MPEG data stream is a processed data. The most popular MP3 format (MPEG-1/2 Part-3 Layer 3), supports 32 KHz, 44.1 KHz, and 48 KHz sampling rates, and varieties of stream sizes in KB/s.

First, take a look at these charts, in which, the audio signal is to be represented a rougher digitalized data. As the data values of the mathematical method

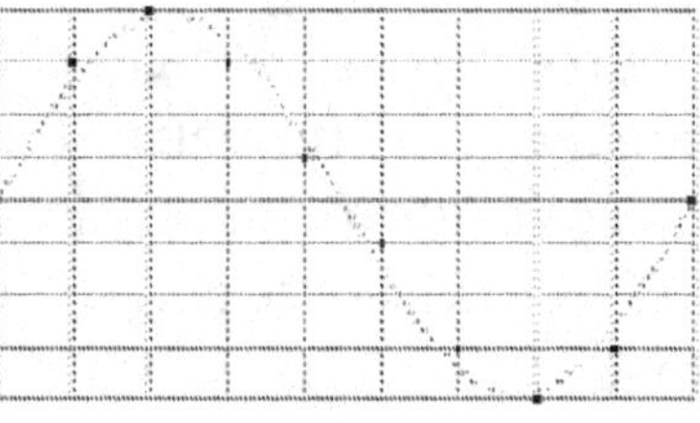

only takes the intersecting points, the smooth sound signal values will be replaced by these black spots, which, obviously, are not a fidelity representation.

The data of MP3 is not uniform as seen from the above illustration.

MP3 format uses characteristics of the human ear to design the compression algorithm:

Omitting certain sounds that the human ear cannot "hear": Adult hearing loss & psychoacoustics effects, mostly noticeable, the auditory masking, which occurs when the perception of one sound is affected by the presence of another sound, including simultaneous masking or frequency masking (frequency domain); temporal masking (time domain).

The first and easiest savings are to go ahead and cut out a certain frequency range if the music allows for it. At best, tests have usually shown that we can hear frequencies in a range between 20 to 20,000Hz. Our ears are also most sensitive between 2KHz and 5KHz, and they can detect changes between frequencies in increments of 2Hz—that's the effective "resolution" of hearing. As the average person gets older or the delicate cells of the ear are damaged by loud noise, high-frequency perception is reduced. most adults have their hearing reduced to above 16KHz. Without getting to the bottom of any hard algorithm, the volume has been reduced by 20% [(20-16)/20]. But there are much more than that following.

Simultaneous masking occurs when a sound is made inaudible by a noise or unwanted sound of the same duration as the original sound.

Temporal masking occurs when a sudden stimulus sound makes inaudible from other sounds which are present immediately preceding or following the stimulus.

Haas effect, which states that two identical sounds arriving within 30-40ms of each other from different directions will be perceived as a single sound coming from the direction of the first. It's often used in public address systems to reinforce the sound "from the stage," even if the loudspeakers are located farther to the side.

There are certain sounds that the human ear hears much better than others.

If there are two sounds playing simultaneously, we hear the louder one but cannot hear the softer one. Regardless the definitions and categorizing, the resultant audio from CD to MP3 ripping has been stripped away a lot of context based on frequencies, coherence, etc., plus many algorithm-based reductions.

§ 8.3.4 Human sensibilities vs the digital representations: Does internet music MP3 audio hurt your cognitive intuitiveness? The answer is not a simple "No!"

The full Audio-CD spectrum is being represented by limit representative resources: in frequency, rhythm, and cadence.

As the end users of the MP3 listeners, you will hear less frequencies, less events (audio peaks, variations, coherences, etc.) Questions are, what the impact of these reductions to your auditory and long-term cognitive capabilities?

Even something is not consciously aware, this does not warrant an omission is cognitive impact-free. In one aspect, explore the full audio spectrum, experience the elegancy of ample and richness on the full spectrum sound manifesto, then the experts can retreat and create something like the beautiful tree with the forest as background. The higher trees may shadow the distant or lower trees behind, however, without these trees all together, a forest cannot be formed.

On another hand, all the superiorities of human being over the other creatures are based on the elegant advances or differences during the course of evolutions. The industrial/technological frontiers are not here serving to smear flat the positive freedom variations and annihilate these subtle potential evolving buds. The unfortunate consequences are large-scale "manufacturing" the "human cognitive perception (auditory)" abilities, chopping off all these deviations, which are often the new emerging trends (thinking about Einstein as an not-so-normal-kid, and Newton, a not-so-normal-adult), and producing army of "aliens of identical personality treat".

§ 8.4 THE GOOD, THE BAD, AND THE UGLY: DIGITIZING SOCIETY, HIGH PROFILE ORCHES-TRATED-MARATHON, IDENTIFIES THEFT, EMAIL PENETRATIONS, PASSWORD CRACKING, GENE EDITING, ELECTRON MEDDLING, AND MANY MORE

§ 8.4.1 Take every respect and measure to pave a great future for all the creatures in this planet and beyond.

Now, it may be the moment in the history for the homo sapiens, to reflect and to correct. To deeply explore the impacts on the species in an historical responsibility from interventions exerted upon the nature to the general welfare and natural courses; before the unwelcomed outcomes become realities; these could not be undone; and before the human beings really know what they are doing. Take every respect and measure to pave a great future for all the creatures in this planet and beyond.

From the beginning of the digital era, mostly, people, from all kinds of motivations, feel the urges to alert the digitalized natural recordings and force their unwelcomed presence and cut into the nature self-sustaining events; i.e. the gene editing (after gene mapping, a digitizing process), in the big scheme; password cracking, in a curiosity based small tricks (or money based greedy); election meddling, in political and strategic interests nationally or internationally, and so on. Digitalizing the nature things or events helps human being deeply understand nature and for the best, find ways to better comply; it also provides the opportunities to perform reverse engineering on certain subjects. However, too much artifacts on these subjects may pose unprepared consequences.

§ 8.4.2 Eliud Kipchoge Ran 1:59:40 an Over-Engineered Marathon

There is also a tendency of over-driven on the engineering to the organisms, a bliss or a misfortune, time will give us the answer. One of the recent events, the marathon, was an example of this: What materialized was perhaps the most finely tuned, carefully orchestrated marathon-length run in history. How the two-hour Marathon limit was broken. In the October Saturday morning in Vienna, Austria, Eliud Kipchoge, the world's finest marathoner, became the first person in history to run 26.2 miles in under two hours. His time of 1:59:40 required him to maintain an average pace of just under 4:35 per mile

On a course specially chosen for favoring a faster speed, in Vienna, Austria; in an athletic spectacle of historic proportions, Eliud Kipchoge of Kenya, an eight-time major marathon winner and three-time Olympic medalist with a prime age, 34 years old, of marathon*, ran 26.2 miles in a once-inconceivable time of 1 hour 59 minutes 40 seconds. Matching a laser guided constant speed of 4'35"/mile or 13.1365 mile/hr (17 second per 100 meters) most of his running course. People hailed the extraordinary historical event, and most unique of this was the deeply tinted human digitally-engineering driven with heavy business interests. The run, organized by the petrochemical company INEOS, featured a cycle of hype and commercial buildup more reminiscent of a heavyweight prizefight than a road race. The weather was not too warm, not too cold with an altitude 500s feet above sea level, the geolocation time zone is close to Kipchoge's Kenya home time. The starting time was hour to hour finely selected that it was not finalized till less than 16 hours before the event. On Oct 12, 2019, Kipchoge got up 4:50 a.m. then followed oatmeal breakfast. After three-hour, at 8:15 a.m., Kipchoge set out from the Reichsbrücke bridge, spanning across the river of Danube, and charged across a stretch of downhill road followed by ~10 kilometers flat circuit, a straight line, and portions of the road were painted with lines to highlight the fastest possible path ... may be the experience of last unsuccessful attempt Kipchoge in 2017 had make Kipchoge more determined. When a similar event had organized by Nike, he ran a 2:00:25 marathon on 1.5-mile loop of a Formula One track in Monza, Italy. It was by far the fastest marathon ever run, but it was not officially recognized as a world record because it was not run under normal race conditions and had not broken the 2-hour mark, a temporal barrier that many would have deemed untouchable only a few years ago.

*Reason to say this is Eliud Kipchoge prime are based on in-depth studies: (1) "What's the Ideal Age for Marathoning", while the marathon performance peaks around 30 for the statics, the historical marathon champions' spans pretty wide. (2) According to current digital running app Strava, middle-aged runners consistently average faster marathon times than their younger rivals. As a result, Eliud Kipchoge is not far away from his prime age.

§ 8.4.2.1 Form Factors of Tech-Luxury with Physicist's Aerodynamic Analysis

Kipchoge was running with selected 35 pacers (in 5 groups: 7 pacers each, forming 7+1 "X" shape with Kipchoge in the crossing point of "X"; six more pacers were on reserve. These pacers, selected all over the world, including former world and Olympic gold medalists plus other "qualifiers") surrounding to minimize wind resistance for the whole journey except the last hundred seconds. The pack is guided by an electric timing car driving 4:34 per mile (in case of glitch, a second car on standby). Equipped with advanced Garmin Edge 520 GPS bike computer, built for competition and armed with a barometric pressure-based altimeter, the lead-timing car projected green laser beams in front of the running pack showed the pace Kipchoge needed to maintain and the immediate next step size. At predetermined times, the seven pacemakers would make way for another group of seven to slide in and take over. A team member on a bicycle periodically pedaled into the pack to deliver Kipchoge a carbohydrate-heavy cocktail of gels and fluids.

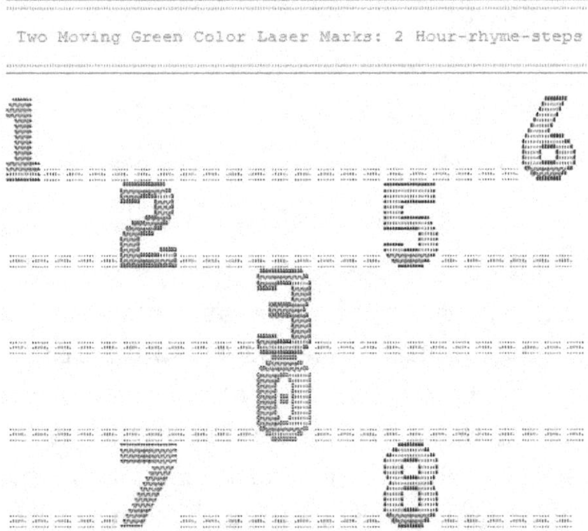

From a physicist's aerodynamic analysis as the author of this book, the 5-1-2 forming "V-1-^" matrix was not only shielding the wind disturbance, it also serving as a pushing effect, in which, the faster the whole matrix move, the more forward force pushing on Kipchoge back. Analyzing the above moving structure, you will find the zone "0" is occupied, at the tip of "3" has negative air pressure, as the pack moving forward, the "0" experiences suction: a forwarding pushing. That subtle aerodynamic design gave another positive impact on the result.

Kipchoge showed the subtlest signs of strain on his face in the first half of the run and fell a couple seconds behind his desired pace in a few portions. He ran the final stretches of the marathon with his lips curled into a gentle smile (his smiles were interpreted as two folds: the first one was he was suffering, and the second one was he was happy, per Kipchoge's own records). Afterward, he walked with a barely perceptible limp.

§ 8.4.2.2 "Like the First Man on the Moon" in Kipchoge Own Words

"Berlin was about running a world record," Kipchoge said that past week. "Vienna is about running and breaking history, like the first man on the moon." This was about breaking barriers and showing, as the marathon logo stated, that no human is limited. If that is true, presumably the glass ceiling for those famous 26.2 miles has yet to be reached. Technological advancements are not unique to athletics. Kipchoge was not at all troubled by the fact the IAAF would not recognize that feat as a record, a scenario perhaps impacted by the detail that he had been holding the world's best official marathon time anyway (See the latest world record in the list in next section).

Heavily engineering manipulations on relevant or irrelevant things with large business in the background, besides the attentions gripping and the commercial driving, the real benefits and accelerations on the "things" are subject to a deep discussion.

As it pointed out in the above content, the IAAF (International Association of Athletics Federations) did not recognize Kipchoge's 1:59:40 record because of the artificial designing and engineering. However, both Kipchoge and the INEOS (a chemicals company headquartered in London) had achieved their goals: the headlines and social attentions. Comparing with Nike,

INEOS had been nobody, then was somebody known across the world. Kipchoge, through so many years world champions' glory, had a bigger ambition abyss to fill: he compared the 2-hour margin break as magnificent as the human moon landing (which will be in our deep dissection on the AI implementation in Chapter 13).

§ 8.4.2.3 Is 1:59:40 a Intangible?

Selection of historic world best marathon times

2:55:18.4 Johnny Hayes (US) 1908, London

2:36:06.6 Alexis Ahlgren (Swe) 1913, Polytechnic Marathon

2:17:39.4 Jim Peters (UK) 1952, Polytechnic Marathon

2:09:36.4 Derek Clayton (Aus) 1967, Fukuoka

2:05:42 Khalid Khannouchi (Mor) 1999, Chicago

2:03:59 Haile Gebrselassie (Eth) 2008, Berlin

2:01:39 Eliud Kipchoge (Ken) 2018, Berlin

1:59:40.2 Eliud Kipchoge (Ken) 2019, Vienna

If we take the world Marathon records progression (to be fair, only after year 2000) from 2002 and till the last world record by Eliud Kipchoge 2018, the profile is the following figure vs E.K. (linear) this single event.

In 2019 the Berlin marathon best result was by Kenenisa Bekele (men) with 2:01:41 (2 seconds slower than the world record) and Ashete Bekere (Women) at 2:20:14, they were both from Ethiopia (They are not related, with a "l vs r" difference in their last names). It is fair to say that 2:01:30s is kind of the current record attainable. Take the data after 2000 and plot a line via Eliud Kipchoge engineered 1:59:40; it will be the straight ling in the above illustration. The trend is not off the natural developmental data too much; it is very hard to believe that the Marathon will stall. In other words, result of the hyper events is not that supreme; the result is attainable in a few years. As a reminder, the cutting-off before the 2000 makes the gap more obvious, plot in a "zoom-out" scale the difference will be very small.

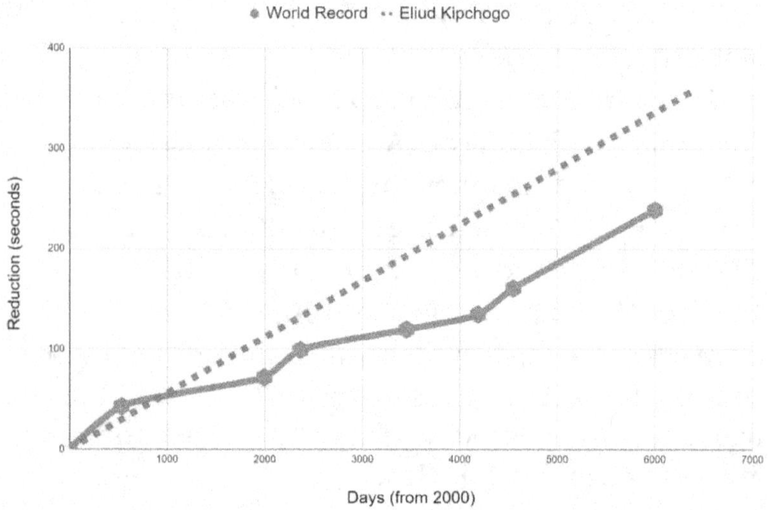

In this sense, the commercial impact and entertainment aspect of this event are more overwhelming than what is really achieved.

§ 8.5 WHEN THING APPROACHES NATURAL COMPLEXITY, THE EXISTING TOOLS AND ALGORITHMS ARE OFTEN FOUND INEPT

Now we have seen the awkward situation in the interface between human engineering and mother nature's elegancy. Through millions of years evolution, the self-assembling nature things have found their way through all kind of survival the fittest processes, which had happened naturally and in the ambient environment, which neither need go through a high temperature wielding nor complex lithography manufacturing. Human beings have tried all the efforts and approaches, to achieve superior situations, at the end of the process, only found their impact is still trivial, compare to the nature evolution.

When the project approaches nature complexity, the existing tools and algorithms are often found incapable to well define and tune into the simple nature things. An often very simple event in the nature takes great efforts in the current methodology.

The supreme issue of the whole western civilization: sophisticated technologies with enormous regulations. On the other side, the subtle nature always manifests her elegancy and intangible integrity here and there, in the brain's wonderful thoughts of consciousness, in infinity verities of proper existences, or in quantum weirdness, to just name a few.

CHAPTER 9: EINSTEIN'S SPOOKY ACTION AT A DISTANCE: TAKES 10,000 TIMES LONGER EVEN TRAVELING AT LIGHT SPEED

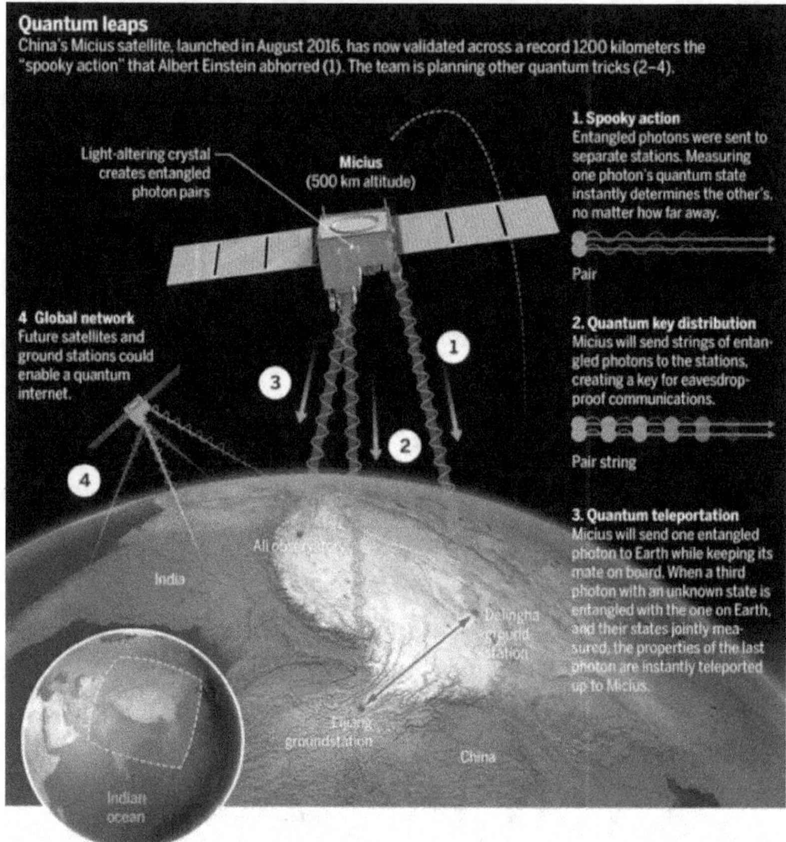

Image source Science Magazine: https://www.sciencemag.org/news/2017/06/china-s-quantum-satellite-achieves-spooky-action-record-distance

Einstein was troubled by the uncertain intangible quantum arrogance: "Subtle is the Lord, but malicious He is not." In middle of 2017, Scientist demonstrated the quantum entanglement from eerily intertwined quantum particles at a distance over 1200 kilometers, Albert went on: "spooky action at a distance." (foreseen nearly a century ago lol).

Of course, in the current US weird news seeking media market, the weirdest part of quantum weirdness is that all the popular media essays embrace quantum phenomena without really understanding them fully so far by standards from most of the physicists. They talked it like a pro and the movements of the jargons around their tongue like the fire season of California.

Firstly, how they did that: the team sent a laser beam into a light-altering crystal on the satellite. After hitting the crystal, the photons in the laser beam transduced into pairs of photons (a single photon transduced into two coherent photons, not necessary the same wave length) entangled so that their polarization states would be opposite when one was measured. The pairs were sent to separate receiving stations in different ground stations 1200 kilometers apart. Both stations were in the highland of Tibet, for the purpose to reduce the amount of air the fragile photons had to traverse. The team reports simultaneously measuring more than 1000 photon pairs. They found the photons had opposite polarizations far more often than would be expected by chance, thus confirming spooky action over a record distance.

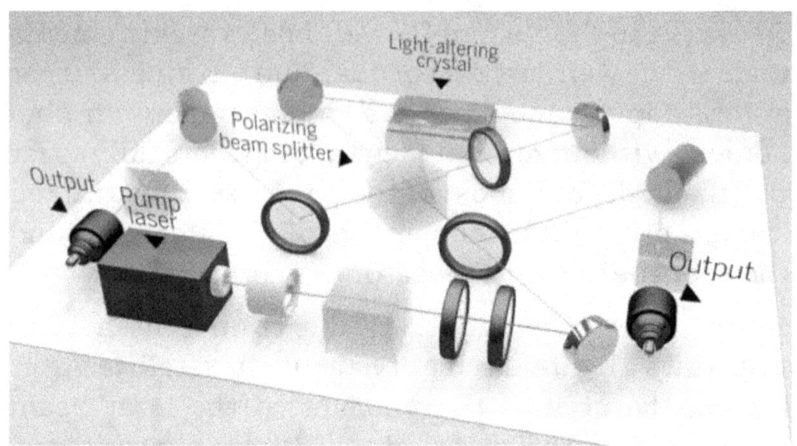

In Lab Optical Setup (Image extracted from Video, ibid.)

In the history of humanity civilization, a lot of mysterious puzzles gradually become clear truths and facts under new lights once the science develops to the degree.

Spooky and unpredictability, all of these uncertainties in certain civilizing stages become something predictable and by the course in later stages.

Einstein's "spooky action at a distance", which is now a fact. For the purpose of respecting another fact heralded by Richard Feynman, "When you follow any of our physics too far, you find that it always gets into some kind of trouble." I am gladly stop here before any trouble arises, albeit already looming close, may be.

With this experiment and others previously, through so-called "loophole-free" Bell tests have been performed in which the locations were separated such that communications at the speed of light would have taken longer—in one case 10,000 times longer—than the interval between the measurements. According to some interpretations of quantum mechanics, the effect of one measurement occurs instantly. However, all interpretations agree that entanglement produces correlation between the measurements and that the mutual information between the entangled particles can be exploited, but that any transmission of information at faster-than-light speeds is impossible.

CHAPTER 10: QUANTUM ENTANGLEMENT, QUANTUM COMPUTING, QUANTUM SUPREMACY, AND Q—

§ 10.1 FULLY UNDERSTANDING RICHARD FEYNMAN'S TROUBLES PLEASE TAKE COURSES OF "IBM CARD" AND "SPOOKY ACTIONS AT DISTANCE"

In 1980s, Richard Feynman (a figure every college physics student knows around the world, if one had college physics course and not knew him, simply because the physics textbook was not profound enough) proposed that a quantum computer would be an effective tool with which to solve problems in physics and chemistry, given that it is exponentially costly to simulate large quantum systems with classical computers. Feynman knew the redundancy of the classic computing (the day-to-day devices ever person is using).

As we have explored the IBM punched card efficiency, with less than 10 percent of utilizations. And the popular SD card, can be below 8 ppm (0.0075%). Those are just a media carrier layer, aka, external storages. Insider the computer, a 64-bit system (almost all the devices, including the phone and pads) always processes the operation in 64-bit. Picture this: the data flows inside a modern computer (CPU, GPU, registers, RAM, Cache, VRAM, and so on) like a thin stick figure with extreme long ghost shadow, such as the below inflable tube man

Although the inflable tube man occupied a huge space, the little valuable "mass" only occupies tiny space. However, these "flat" space (RAM, Operations, etc) re-sources are always allo-cated in a linear way inside a computer. As the result, considering the intermedi-ate parameters, even the input and output data sets are all small, they can swallow enormous system re-sources.

All the original design flaws loom bigger and bigger, fixing here and mending there, with the majority of the driving factors are business, profits, national, or even military priorities, the architectures for all the tech-nological machineries and/or theories, together with their mathematic tools, are required back compatible and carrying big burden on their back to test and valid-ate while their full power should have been on the edges of advancing.

The human beings are one kind of these creatures thriving in planet earth: born the way with a "gravity" cursed on their body. As a consequence, these creatures, which are the only kind so far, are capable of high intelligent cognitive thoughts and nothing short of communicating tokens: languages, have gone great effort to engineer a way of escape the curse: they concepted an idea of escape velocity, at 11186 meters per second, or 6.951 miles per second, pop goes the human. Even though, they are not capable thinking of none gravitational environment natively, even with these observations in the international space station. With all kinds of limitations like this, the fully comprehend of the nature is a big challenge. Out of dilemmas, the quantum physics had created out of stopping questing further type: shut-up and accept.

Should a theory exist without these rude bulling: surely, if you pick the right expression manifestos, tokens, and models. Unfortunately, these have not been properly established and that is one of the purposes of this book serial.

Now the era is coming, in the fiercely competing front, with the national priority as backbone, the quantum entanglement phenomenon shows the potential.

Again, may be because of the curse, the creature could not full understand and employ this phenomenon so far in their traditional theorems, if one little creature need travel a while to reach the water hole following Mom creature, how these entangled two things can interacting each other instantly: i.e. the 1200 km apart experiment conducted in 2017 via the help of an object escaped from planet earth, a satellite.

But they want make this phenomenon immediately to

be used by national or business priorities instead of staying back and enjoying a little bit, to let the nature run its course.

§ 10.2 GOOGLE'S QUANTUM SUPREMACY?

Without further ado, Google thus decides to claim the advance of edging out competitors by declearing that they had achieved quantum supremacy (Quantum supremacy using a programmable superconducting processor, Nature 574, 505-510, 2019. https://www.nature.com/articles/s41586-019-1666-5).

Before you "escape" away, just a simple fact:

(1) Google Quantum supremacy deals with a random number of binary 53 bit.

2^{53} = 9,007,199,254,740,992 ~ 9×10^{15} which is 9 PB (PB: 10^{15}, TB: 10^{12}, GB: 10^9/your phone has hundreds GB, MB: 10^6, KB: 10^3, B: 0|1)

(2) As we have pointed out in the last section, your phone/PC are all 64-Bit width, such like the picture of inflable tube man, working with binary 64-bit all the time, regardless you notice it or not, 64-bit CPUs have been used in supercomputers since the 1970s (Cray-1, 1975). AMD's introduction of first 64-bit x86-64 processor in 2003 made it into households. So, your phone's CPU registers:

2^64=18,446,744,073,709,551,616   =>
2^(64-53)*GoogleQuantumComputer =2^9 GQC =512 GQC

(3) IBM Summit supercomputer can write down 250 PB data once. The data scale is ~ 20 times of Google quantum computer data scale.

§ 10.2.1 IBM Was Not Impressed While New York Times Seems in Fever Pitch

Google's Quantum Supremacy was a big bold claim. The result: The big old edge chaser IBM had a word or two, they argued a not so extraordinary laboratory event had been exaggerated: like, this is a day-to-day thing, suddenly, Google, after an overnight sleep, claimed they can announce this way.

While NY times lectures (again, they think they understand better, as we said the typical media weirdness of quantum weirdness) "Why Google's Quantum Supremacy Milestone Matters", used same phrase as we are using here "the weirdness of the quantum world", as in their original text: "This is 'quantum interference,' and is behind everything else you've ever heard about the weirdness of the quantum world." (They had not copied us—simply because we have not published this context so far, and I am assuring you I had put these paragraphs down way before that article, we are not using theirs).

NYT article claims: "The calculation doesn't need to be useful: much like the Wright Flyer in 1903, or Enrico Fermi's nuclear chain reaction in 1942, it only needs to prove a point." Well, this sound like the quantum cornerstones (and already knighted a stature): you just cannot to be picky on this, shut-up and accept! wow! Ask the authors who had tried to publish mass or mess of words in Nature magazine, which is famously for its picky weirdo (I searched in Google scholar citation, the Author has not been published anything on "Nature" albeit there were in the same magazine family branch in *nature physics*. If you are a scholar, you will know that, i.e. in this site, https://www.nature.com/siteindex, you have 53 branches started with "Nature" and hundred all together, they are not the "Nature" magazine itself at all. If an exhaustive search finds the content within this pair parentheses is true, I do not understand—well, please read on the following quoted text before I continue—)

"Over the last decade, together with students and colleagues, I helped develop much of the theoretical underpinning for quantum supremacy experiments like Google's. **I reviewed Google's paper before it was published.** So the least I can do is to try to explain what it means."

—The understanding that I do not have is, seems to me, if this was the case, this author was not qualifying for a peer-review for the very "Nature" magazine.

People know physicists are always picky and seeking perfection, which is why Einstein had so much feuds with Bohr. So, what is going on here.

Let's read on:

"(Google's Quantum Supremacy was using) a protocol that I came up with a couple years ago uses a sampling process, just like in Google's quantum supremacy experiment, to generate random bits. While by itself that's unimpressive, the key is that these bits can be demonstrated to be random even to a faraway skeptic, by using the telltale biases that come from quantum interference. Trusted random bits are needed for various cryptographic applications, such as proof-of-stake cryptocurrencies (environmentally friendlier alternatives to Bitcoin). Google is now working toward demonstrating my protocol; it bought the non-exclusive intellectual property rights last year."

§ 10.2.2 Yikes! The NYT Author Was Partnering With Google's Team

Yikes! Google had purchased the author's "non-exclusive intellectual property". First, the NYT author acted like bigotry. Second, the dude had actually financially benefited from this. For a pure business play, there are protocols and regulations in place; for these academic bigotries, they are more profit prioritized than pure for-profit business, in an arrogant way.

The author of the NYT article was actually on the same boat with Google's journey, Google was working to demonstrate the NYT article author's protocol...what a !!!... now you are pretty clear, they are mutual protected or appreciated each other.

I thought out other examples:

GOP vs NRA

or similar

Putin vs Trump

Do I need to elaborate further? No, you will say.

The mutual protection and mutual exploitation are obvious, this is the same bureaucracy in scientific institutions as that in the capitol hill.

Now where we resort Ivy schools.

§ 10.2.3 Mikhail Lukin, Director of Harvard Quantum Initiative, on the Google's Quantum Supremacy

Riding the quantum computing 'wave': Harvard Quantum Initiative Co-Director Lukin on 'quantum supremacy' and Google's announcement of its achievement.

Now, I am just quote as is: "Google points to one specific calculation and says, 'We crossed the threshold.' I think, in practice, it's not quite like that."

"50 or so qubit systems already have been used in other labs, including ours, for the past two or so years. There have been a number of experiments done with systems of that scale which classical computers have a hard time catching up to. In this sense, I would describe what's going on now as not a singular event but more like a wave that is coming."

"at Harvard. I believe that we've already crossed into the domain where we have useful quantum advantage for scientific applications. Using our 51-qubit system, we have made one of the largest quantum superposition states, and we have already discovered new phenomena that have not been known previously, and that you would not be able to uncover using brute force classical simulations. In fact, here at Harvard, in different labs, we have at least two systems which have either entered or are entering this domain [of quantum supremacy] for scientific applications."

Well, this is quite different tunes, not only similar events happened normally, the ivy university has made it practically useful for scientific applications.

With authors like the dude of the NYT article as peers to review, may be cartel-review in this case, the picky Nature magazine does not bother to do the second check.

Harvard dialogue continued: "The specific problem that Google is trying to solve is akin to generating random numbers in a quantum way. The algorithm they're using is not designed to be practically useful. So, in this practical sense, quantum supremacy by itself, to me, does not mean very much."

There, random result as quantum supremacy has been claimed a "milestone" and "matters", so far, the only useful direction is based on Shor's algorithm. The quantum algorithms before the Shor's algorithm are usually considered as toy experiments. It attracts investments beyond academic after Shor's calculating algorithm, which is a useless math toy on integer factorization. From which quantum computer can crack another human made trouble: RSA public-key cryptography schemes to demo quantum supremacy.

§ 10.3 QUANTUM SUPREMACY WHAT IS IT? DO NOT COME WITH DIRAC NOTATION OR FOURIER TRANSFORM

What all these about? Please do this with neither Dirac notation nor Fourier transform, the must-have enclosers for any level publications touching quantum computing today

Now the ivy scholar claimed "quantum supremacy by itself, to me, does not mean very much", well that is the whole point Nature magazine has tried to make in the shield of that NYT article.

- First, let not be confused with this pollical campaign like movements. Let go back to the strictly "numbers."
- Second, Google's research has not touched anything on Shor's number game yet.
- Third, we even do not need go to the number games (Shor's algorithm, the efficiency of Shor's algorithm is due to the efficiency of

the quantum Fourier transform, in short, Shor demonstrated an exponentiation operation of factoring a number can transcode into a polynomial operation with the successful Quantum computing.)

- The last, the key of Google work is "RANDOM".

Random is not always really meaningful and useful. Another word is chaos, which is normally considered no positive aspect. That random is akin to chaos.

In a time, the statistics kicks in and the profit driven businesses are seeking and exploiting the benefit from random and statistics: the lotteries, the casinos, the gambling. All these are based on randomness and statistics.

From here, the ordinary people can grasp the key for Google's achievement, which no-part so far has explained clearly in the public eyes what was it. So exactly, what was it?

What is Quantum Supremacy? Let's make it simple without mimicking your kitchenware (hardware) or underwear (soft-wear) these you are toying and feeling all day long, we do not make metaphors on anything, because it's essential a simple random, and we talk straightly on that with neither Dirac Notation nor Fourier transform.

Nobody (although Harvard claimed they are close to practical applications, but not reported so far) has found a way to utilize the quantum computer in a meaningful way to this date.

§ 10.3.1 What is Quantum Mechanics? Awesome Crash Course

Let's talk about quantum mechanics (QM), for dummy. QM is the basic conception or "science" of quantum physics, our day to day quantum phenomena. We do not go to the weirdness too much, just touch base. When we are talking about QM, I am not going to Dirac's notation, and here specifically, when we are talking about Quantum supremacy today, I am not introducing Shor's algorithm directly from Fourier transformation. We are going to use "conceptions" in lieu of complex math equations, which you see in every place if it touches the quantum computing.

I am not sure if I really know QM, to be frank, not in the Einstein's way, though.

When I graduated for the Physics major in college and my score for the graduate school examination on Quantum Physics was 100%. I was pretty happy with my understanding on the QM. Then after study in graduate school, I was totally throwed out of the window of QM, on which I did not have a clue any more. Reason was simple, I was not taught any conception on QM in graduate school "Advanced QM" course but I had to use all my time during classes to take note with a scale of ten-letter-size-page per session. The exams were the same, to be frank, I really did not know how to fill the blanks. For the exam of advance QM, our scores were so poor, as the teacher would use a math formula to boost our score by:

S = 10 x Sqrt (R)

R: Real score

S: Score (after boost)

Sqrt: Square root

in a 60% pass scale, your 36 real score will pass:

100 x Sqrt (36) = 10 x Sqrt (6 x 6) = 10 x 6 = 60.

My score was 80s, but my brain was empty. And the poor original feel-good on QM were totally flooded away by these notations.

Our professor was a "WFS" university alumnus.

The WFS stands Worker (Blue collar), Farmer, Solider.

They were not studying industrial technologies, neither agriculture technologies nor modern warfare advancements; instead, these college students were really doing the shift works inside the mills/factories; doing "I am a farmer, I grown it" (a song mocking "I am sexy and I know it") things, and disaster relive things like hurricanes or fires. As a result, their knowledge on text book or, this "WFS" university graduated alumnus as a professor, especially on QM, was limited.

Now, after quantum physics in my undergraduate education, armed with advance QM education I came out blank, as blank as US president Trump's knowledge on climate change.

At the same level, I am trying to make the course on this session an obvious conception to Trump, or except Trump, that simple.

§ 10.3.2 Let's Talk About "Random," Well, Not Really, the randomness was from the specific hardware based

Something seems random may turn out a revelation of profound subconscious cognitive threads. Like Trump's Twitter's content, you may think there are random—in this part, we had a very lucrative conclusion: that these Dreamed on US president Trump akin to these themes from the Out-of-body experience. These were narrated in my new book (*Cognitive Big Data Analysis on the Mind*, ISBN-13: 978-1085867863/ ISBN-10: 1085867862 available in print or eBook around the world, bookstore or online).

So, we are talking about real random.

Wait a second, Google claimed their result were not really random, because of the hardware limitations (quantum interference, in their words), their random was a specific hardware character. That is fatal blow to anybody in the community: you cannot repeat their actual result in your machine.

As the progress of my nth time proof-reading on this manuscript, I spot a paper yesterday, so I put it here as quotations:

"Random Hardware Errors Make a Quantum Computing Future Unlikely

https://scitechdaily.com/random-hardware-errors-make-a-quantum-computing-future-unlikely/

"As someone who has worked on quantum computing for many years, I believe that due to the inevitability of random errors in the hardware, useful quantum computers are unlikely to ever be built. (Michel Dyakonov, a theoretical physicist at the University of Montpellier in France. In an article in IEEE Spectrum, the flagship journal of electrical and computer engineering.)"

§ 10.3.3 Google's Quantum Supremacy is Moderate Size a Random Number, Albeit a Fake Random Number: Some Experts Said, "Random Hardware Errors Make a Quantum Computing Future Unlikely"

Now, we go to the random directly.

What's on earth was the random Google was talking about?

Actually, it is extremely simple:

a random number with 53-bit (0|1) length

Or in the day-today conception (decimal)

Any integer number between "0" and "9,007,199,254,740,992"

Why the hell they want to do these random numbers?

TL;DR: Why Quantum Supremacy was actually a ran-

dom number: They do not know what else to do!

 (TL: Too long; Didn't Read, for these impatient readers like, again, Trump)

The whole effort Google was playing with this number games can be elaborated as:

(1) They imagine certain property of a physical entity representing anything "random" mixers of probabilities weighted combinations. If they grab any of the item, which may look "black" or "white".

(2) They assign "black" as "0", white as "1" or vice versa.

(3) They queued 53 these entities hand-in-hand, for whatever interactions out of their control, they got a random 53-bit number every time they measure. (max decimal digits: 15 digit, 10^15)

(3a) The interactions between these qubits cause their measurement result: a random number, on which the statistics show they were not really true random. Because the physical building process for the circuits and qubits (from SIS: Nb-Al_2O_3-Nb stack, there is some "delta" variation in the "2" and "3" in the aluminum oxide) had not been tunable and controllable, precisely.

(4) They were trying figure out, by measuring many times, to see does this fake random number follow a pattern.

(5) They claimed the processing of the estimating the fake-random number was **quantum computing**, and beyond classic computer's reach.

(6) IBM does not respect their claim.

(6a) Nor does Harvard University's scholar.

(7) The Google's quantum computer was from a company in Canada, D-wave. Made from Superconducting Qubits.

(7a) These Superconducting Qubits are made from circuits with Josephson Junctions. These circuits I-V curves show step like (like the stairs of the building), they assign "0" to ground step, "1" as first step. The process only involves ground step and first step. If your measure result showing the qubit is at ground level, that is "0"; at first step "1". these 53 bit "(0|1)" form aforementioned 53 bit or 15 digital numbers in decimal.

Basically, that was the whole story about. so, you do not even bother to know the Shor's algorithm yet.

§ 10.4 HAND-ON CODING IN QUANTUM COMPUTER, HELLO WORLD! RUNNING IN LONDON-BASED QUANTUM COMPUTER

N ow, by using the Quantum computer in London, I am leading you through the simple program process for a real Quantum computing code and run though, step by step, then you will really know from inside out.

Here is the simple code for the Quantum computer in London with 5-Qubits:

---Code of "Hello World!" on a Quantum Computer---

```
1 OPENQASM 2.0;

2 include "qelib1.inc";

3

4 qreg q[5];
```

```
5 creg c[5];
6
7 h q[0];
8 cx q[0],q[1];
9 measure q[0] -> c[0];
10 measure q[1] -> c[1];
```

---End---

In the above code, I am explaining it line by line:

1 OPENQASM 2.0;

This is saying to use Quantum ASM (Assembly) language Version 2.0

2 include "qelib1.inc";

Call a library, in this case, a header

4 qreg q[5];

5 creg c[5];

This a declaration, both Q and C registers are 5 quantum bits long

7 h q[0];

Apply "h" operation to Quantum bit Q (0)

8 cx q[0],q[1];

Apply "cx" operation between quantum bits Q(0) and Q(1)

9 measure q[0] -> c[0];

10 measure q[1] -> c[1];

measurement the value of the content in these two

bits.

This code took the quantum computer in London 45.8 seconds to complete the operation. And the result:

For these four possibilities: 00 01 10 11

Expressed in 5-bit long bits: 00000 00001 00010 00011

The measurement of 00 (00000) at 46.704%

The measurement of 01 (00001) at 4.004%

The measurement of 10 (00010) at 3.943%

The measurement of 11 (00011) at 45.349%

What Google's work is to find after large number of measurements, to see if these percentage holds (in the above calculation, I let the computer run 8194 times, and this is why we got a statistic percentages of the outputs).

Before we close out this session, we are trying to warn people, there is so far no straightforward way to walk through the whole mess without using Matrix/Dirac notations and Fourier transformation. The book here is the first of this kind.

§ 10.5 IF GOOGLE'S QUANTUM SUPREMACY HAS NOT EVEN TOUCHED THE GOLD STANDARD OF SHOR'S ALGORITHM, WHY THAT ALGORITHM SO GOLDEN?

When you writing something all in weird equations without a way to articulating your mind, we have a real problem:

Either our tools (I mean mathematically or conceptionally) of basic manifesto are not there or the scholars on this do not have a way to really illustrate the physical phenomenon into a conception.

I am not going to do any of them, but I am trying to articulate the whole mess so far on the quantum computing, only after we have sorted out Google's result, which is not even on the track yet.

The social network-oriented gadgets and their software are doing all the dirty and inefficient tasks. It is

not the hardware design that matters, it the task that they had been designed for matters.

Once again, because the original design flaw (like the IBM cards, only 10% usage), the digital computing was nevertheless redundant and always greedy, in most of the cases, they are useless digital worms just eroding the system resource.

§ 10.5.1 The Gadgets in Your Hand Are "Supercomputers" But What Have You Used Them For?

If you have a i.e. iPhone 10 series, not mention the 11 or newers. Here is a comparation between iPhone XS with a supercomputer:

Peak Performance

Cray-2   vs   iPhone XS(2018)

1.9 GFLOP   ~1 GFLOP

GFLOP: 10^9 floating point operations

Price (USD)

Cray-2   vs   iPhone XS(2018)

> $30 millions   ~$900

Memory for operations (RAM)

Cray-2	vs	iPhone XS(2018)
256 MW		4 Gigabytes

MW: Mega Word

Storage

Cray-2	vs	iPhone XS(2018)
~32 GB		512 GB

What clay-2 was used for: The Cray-2 was predominantly developed for the United States Departments of Defense and Energy. Uses tended to be for nuclear weapons research or oceanographic (sonar) development. However, the first Cray-2 (serial number 1) was used at the National Magnetic Fusion Energy Computer Center at Lawrence Livermore National Laboratory for unclassified energy research. It also found its way into civil agencies (such as NASA Ames Research Center), universities, and corporations worldwide. For example, Ford and General Motors both used the Cray-2 for processing complex Finite Element Analysis models of car bodyshells, and for performing virtual crash testing of bodyshell components prior to production.

What is the public iPhone XS are used for: texting, phone call, listening music, watching video Tweeting ...

What is the core issue here? PROTOCOL & CODE: Clay-2 was for computing while iPhone for (lol) ornament.
Most of time, you iPhone is running AD-based thing in

background. Idling process, yes, to idle the machine (in this case a phone) you need run something.

§ 10.5.2 Super Inefficient, Redundant, And Resources Greedy, The Original Sins of Digital Computers

Because of the redundant and greedy, even a simple result involving large intermediate operations.

Do you need really that big matrix for a computing,

may not be. Einstein came out a formula $E=MC^2$. These large computings seldom results in good faith concise conceptions.

Now, Python, an interpretation language is the #1 language used in the technology industries. Google was started with Python and Java code. Python is sloppy and resource greedy (all the interpreting languages are less efficient). Java a little better. Decades ago, I was comparing same process between Java and C. The result showed C was more than 5 times faster. Instagram are mostly on Python.

The path to the problem solving is the correct modeling, not a sloppy way of blindly piling up of awkward big equations with "bandages" here and "patches" there.

§ 10.5.3 The Key to Shor's Algorithm Is Based on Fourier Transform, which we do not need.

Shor's mathematical tool has been based on Fourier Transform, which we had promised not to be used. We will have our way, and here is how to think our way out:

Periodic is everywhere in numbers, why? The truth is simple but need a genius to figure it out: I am telling you all of them at once. Shor's algorithm is a good example of this application with Fourier transformation.

A few words on the Fourier transformation, now that they need Dirac's Notation to narrate the Quantum computing, Fourier transformation's utilization will be not a surprise. We have our words on the Dirac's Notation already; what about the core of the Fourier transformation; there is a lot of simulations online now to show that any trace of data can be expressed by certain of round movements combination. If the specific trajectory bears certain periodic pattern, then Fourier transformation will able to find them out.

So, the only thing to remember here is Fourier transformation will be able to figure out a periodic entity (movement, development, or any other abstract entity, such as sound, planet rotation, organism life cycle …), if no periodic at all, the Fourier transformation fitting will approach infinity expressions thus not very helpful.

Now you have seen the fact is so simple, I do not

understand why shall all resort to complex equations for Fourier transformation. As our simple way through the book: go back to numbers, any number will have periodic. You do not need to know profound number theory.

Why?

If I tell one clue, you will immediately out of dark:

All the number rule has periodic pattern.

Why All the number rule has periodic pattern?

Simply because that is the principal of the civilization creation on numbers:

The creation of numbers in the human civilization is because of simplification (Chapter 12):

To use limit symbols to (only a "handful" signs) to represent the infinite nature. Thus, the number system is a periodic system, as simple as this in English.

In number system, we have number bases:

Then you have the binary number: 0,1, the most bottom set that the digital computer had utilized. Then the periodic length is 2.

Again, we have Octal (8) system, decimal (10) system, duodecimal (12-a dozen) system, sexagesimal (60-clock) system, and so on.

The base system is actually a periodic system and for the repeating. So, as a result, **any number problem has a periodic mechanism built intrinsically, smart guys able to find them, if work hard enough.**

That is the whole foundation of Shor's algorithm, which is the light of the dawn gives scientists a hope to clinch the possibility of make quantum entanglement useful.

So, do we need go to the detail of Shor's algorithm, certainly not.

But you should know, **Shor was a smart guy, this was why he taught at MIT.**

Till now, we have successfully elucidated the conception of Google's Quantum Supremacy and beyond their own comprehension.

We were not touching complexities of the Dirac's Notation and Fourier transformation.

§ 10.6 THE QUANTUM ENTANGLEMENTS ARE COMMON AND UNIVERSAL OUT THERE. IT TAKES A STROKE OF GENIUS TO FIND OUT

Everybody in this planet lives in a micro-environment of specialty with certain degree of connections to the whole world. In a realistic tone, we view the world and beyond. There is no need for the fiction to kick in in this scenario. The primitive organisms only have rudiment sense of environment ... ameba, paramecium, able to interact the environment with contacts; in Euglena, there is an eyespot apparatus, which helps the single cell organism move toward to the light. This is actually a decision-making process, even without an eyespot. Tiny, brainless blobs might be able to make decisions: A single-celled organism can "change its mind" to avoid going near an irritating substance, according to new findings. (A Complex Hierarchy of Avoidance Behaviors in a Single-Cell Eukaryote, Current Biology, Vol 29, No. 24, P4323-4329.E2, Dec 16, 2019)

These eyespots do not differentiate the brightness or color spectra, just "0" (darkness) or "1" (brightness). So, the interpretation of a phenomenon (as for the human beings' observations) is far more comprehensive than simply detection (eyespot).

Amazingly, there is a highest-level similarity comparison with this in the human's vision.

It had long proved that a toad's eye is capable to see a single photon prior to the experimental study conducted with human objects. But an isolated toad's eye cannot tell, it was not guaranteed that the live toad could "see" it. This is not an issue once these experiments performed on a human object, and story could be told from the person.

After more than half hour in darkness conditioning, human subject can detect single photon with optimizing conditions: one of them is the eye was exposing to an off-axis dimmed red light to make the vision sharp. If a green light photon enters that "sharp" eye with the arrangement off-axis red light background, this person reports light detection more than the chance of guessing.

We throw away the probabilities, "0|1", and all the apparatus, conceptions, terminologies, we only see one single fact, boiling down:

The human eye can detect single photon (I notice, even the single photon conception is from Quantum Physics, I will let it go).

That is crystal clear in our head now.

Be that as it may, that event was not at anything close to clear at all to the person who was there to perfume the experiment.

You would say s/he saw a green shooing star roar through the sunset sky ...

No, not that.

All the observer got is a "deja vu", a remote sense of something totally out of blue (in this case dimmed red).

So, the person at the peak of sharpness of vision, detecting a single photon with a sense of something. The original study elucidated by the author as "a feeling".

Yep, that is the closest correlating to euglena's eyespot vision. An either "0" or "1" in its faintest realization with highest probability of uncertainty.

As the director of quantum computing sector in Harvard University said, the high fragile and uncertainty of the quantum computing results are among other hurdles to address first.

§ 10.7 QUBITS OF SILICON BASED SPINTRONICS

Researchers at Princeton University have made an important step forward in the quest to build a quantum computer using silicon components, which are prized for their low cost and versatility compared to the hardware in today's quantum computers. The team showed that a silicon-spin quantum bit can communicate with another quantum bit located a significant distance (4mm) away on a computer chip. The feat could enable connections between multiple quantum bits to perform complex calculations. (Resonant microwave-mediated interactions between distant electron spins by F. Borjans et al, Dec 25, 2019, Nature. We had briefed this previously).

§ 10.8 Q—CRAZINESS: QUBIT [0,1], QUTRIT [0,2], AND QUDIT [0,9]

Quantum entanglement is not happening only in Google purchased D-Wave Quantum Computers, which were based on superconducting Josephson Junctions (called weak links). There are other types of Quantum entanglement expressions (one of the example is prenented in § 10.7): the photons in laser; quantum well trapped entities; Nuclear magnetic resonance (NMR, your NMR medical examining); spins of particles... to just name a few. The most common one is the aforementioned coherent photons, from which 1200 km apart two photos expressing instantly heralding (meaning that once a part is defined, the coupled part immediately defined without delay, at least many orders faster than light speed from the experiment data).

More interestingly, there are not only qubits (which is mess of 0|1 and in-between, there are qutrit as well (in qutrit, the state can be in 0|1|2 and anything mess among them, for that case, a 53-trit "Google" counterpart will have:

3^53 = 19,383,245,667,680,019,896,796,723

a 27 decimal digit number instead of Google 15 decimal digits and will be more than 2 billion folds of Google supremacy's number); not only qutrit; there are qudit, in which 10 different quantum states in one entity.

Not only from the quantum entanglements of qubit, qutrit, or qudit; either from these experiments on earth or in space to verify the faster than light speed of heralding (the same time of event happing), but also from a deep mind view of physicist, the quantum entanglements are common and universal out there, in confined experiment or in nature environment. That, strikes the core of the current whole infrastructure of the science and civilization.

CHAPTER 11: THE ORIGIN OF SPECIES

§ 11.1 LANGUAGES AND THE CAPACITIES OF LANGUAGES IN ARTICULATION AND ILLUMINATIONS

L anguage and associated connectivity are apparatuses serving the functions of organizing and articulating the enSpace cognitive apprehensions.

Strikingly differentiated from other creatures on the planet earth, human being has evolved from rudimentary responding to the environment to systematically tokenizing their views of the nature into expressive languages, not one, not two, but hundred and thousands of languages with dialects. The enSpace(cognitive activities) abstract symbols of the tSpace (external world) have empowered the recording, sharing, editing, modifying, observing, improving, planning, and innovating, drafting, plus creating in their lives and beyond.

As common ground, language enables different human

beings gradually converge into one kind of standard on certain thing. We like to use gallon to measure volume, mostly, on liquid. Most of the countries around the world are using liter. Since they all serve for a volume purpose, so we figured out that 3.78 liters can fill a gallon, so 1 Gallon = 3.78 liters. For colors, we have red, green, blue, as the very basic. We examine the English vs Latin on these words.

Red   :English
red   :Latin

green   :English
viridi   :Latin, blooming, youthful, fresh, green

blue   :English
caeruleum :Latin, blue, cerulean, dark, greenish-blue, azure, of river/sea deities, of sky/sea

Except red is the same since the root in English was simply from Latin; the other basic colors were originally describing something properties of plants (and other things). Gradually, the two languages speaking people figured out that they were talking about the one of the "looking" under the sun light.

Helen Keller, the first deaf-blind person to earn a Bachelor of Arts degree, had wrote her account of colors: "Now, heat varies greatly in the sun, in the fire, in hands, and in the fur of animals; indeed, there is such a thing for me as a cold sun. So I think of the varieties of light that touch the eye, cold and warm, vivid and dim, soft and glaring, but always light, and I imagine their passage through the air to an extensive sense, instead of to a narrow one like touch. From the experience I have had with voices I guess how the eye distinguishes shades in the midst of light. When I feel my cheeks hot, I know that I am red. I have talked so much and read so much about colors that through no will of my own I attach meanings to them, just as all people attach certain meanings to abstract terms like hope, idealism, monotheism, intellect, which cannot be represented truly by visible objects, but which are understood from analogies between immaterial concepts and the ideas they awaken of external things. The force of association drives me to say that white is exalted and pure, green is exuberant, red suggests love or shame or strength. Without the color or its equivalent, life to me would be dark, barren, a vast blackness."

And further into Ms. Keller's articulation, in her account of consciousness: the consciousness was arising from nothingness of void darkness:

"Since I had no power of thought, I did not compare one mental state with another. So I was not conscious of any change or process going on in my brain when my teacher began to instruct me. I merely felt keen delight in obtaining more easily what I wanted by means of the finger motions she taught me. I thought only of objects, and only objects I wanted. It was the turning of the freezer on a larger scale. When I learned the meaning of 'I' and 'me' and found that I was something, I began to think. Then consciousness first existed for me. Thus, it was not the sense of touch that brought me knowledge. It was the awakening of my soul that first rendered my senses their value, their cognizance of objects, names, qualities, and properties. Thought made me conscious of love, joy, and all the emotions. I was eager to know, then to understand, afterward to reflect on what I knew and understood, and the blind impetus, which had before driven me hither and thither at the dictates of my sensations, vanished forever."

This is interesting, and above all, Ms. Keller told a story the runaway path from her "anguish", a state that Hellen describe with only basic instincts in primitive survival temperaments, always threw her into uneasy, angry, and anguish. Amazingly, one often overlooked important conception here: the ability to thought. Ms. Keller's statement was simply and flat, but the revelation needs to be broadened beyond her own account.

§ 11.2 IT TAKES INTEGRITY OF LANGUAGES AND THEIR CORRELATIONS TO ACHIEVE COGNITION

lthough patient H.M. (Henry Molaison, 1926 – 2008) was the most famous case in the history of neuroscience, Clive Wearing (1938 –) is a stupefying case alive. Henry could not form new memory rooting from his bilateral low temporal lobe complexes removal while the long-term memory retained. In the case of Clive Wearing, he can hold only a few seconds span of thinking cognitive activities before they disappear and reappear anew. While tumbling from a renowned artist in music conducting, Mr. Wearing must have been able to sort out large mass of information threads and find the cadence in his composing and conducting career. The top-ranking human beings these can express thoughts and subtle cognizance in their best, once the thread of continuous brain cognitive activities has been broken into pieces, Mr. Wearing complained his account of anguish simply because of incapable of thoughts. Clive Wearing is the living manifesto of the truth that connectivity and integrity are of paramount importance for the homo sapiens' elevated intelligence and shrewd creativity.

When Hellen Keller was not capable of language, she was not able to form thoughts simply because there is nothingness in there and there is nothing to form. On Clive Wearing side, he has ample of elements and building resources, however, the digitization and disassociation expeditiously rob the thoughts and meaningfulness of the life. It is not hard to say that the language elements and their associated connectivity are among the essential resources for the enSpace intelligent activities to function and sustain.

People grown up with visionary and auditory sensory awareness, most of us make senses out of something around the world from these two senses as the initial stages. Letters, words, and other language units enter to our awareness via all these the rudimentary senses in multiple "manifolds" domain. So, when the "Mom" comes into an infant's awareness, s/he has pleasant smell (olfactory), a smile and comfortable face (visionary), a sweet voice (auditory), a gentle touching (tactile), warm chest (temperature), plus feeding, soothing, caring all sorts of "dimensional" parameters accompanying with that. These feral children, once discovered, they generally cannot differentiate these sensations, the first and most obvious one is temperature. Among the most important smell, touch, vision, and hearing, Hellen missed two, the visionary and auditory senses.

Before Ms. Keller was "civilized" by Ms. Sevillian, Ms.

Keller was uneasy, anguish, temperaments of instinct needs, uncontrolled angry; according to her description, she was filled formless and empty, darkness was over the surface of the deep nothingness. It was a remarkable revelation that Hellen's teacher Anne Sullivan, through touching, the primary channel of information injection (words of English language), elevated Hellen Keller to an educated professional lady, with great personality and achievements, even by the standard of a healthy person. The language, in its fundamental role as building blocks, cataloging and refining Hellen's original primitive reflections to "the world I live in."

Using the generations of language deposition and condensation, through patience, Ms. Sevillian had successfully illuminated and enlightened Hellen's world of temperaments and anguishes. The greatness of that had been recognized, howbeit, the trajectory of education had already been paved before that miracle:

The raw data was there (color -> red, green, blue; fruits -> apple, orange, banana...)

The tools were there (again, these things expressed in English, in alphabet, words, sentence, grammar...)

The mechanism was there (methodology of vividly teaching, spelling vs expressing, and so on)

The examples were there (the ultimate goal was to train Hellen like everybody else around)

Full loaded all kinds of "cookbooks".

§ 11.3 THE ORIGIN OF ARTIFICIAL INTELLIGENCE: IAAD VS DAAI

Languages as tools to articulate the enSpace reflections of the tSpace phenomena have evolved and matured in the homo sapiens. Languages serve as beacons in the "darkness" over "emptiness" and have illuminated enSpace (human mind cognitive activities "space") world with the rising of intelligence. The things in the evolving physical universe (tSpace) have been mapped into human mind (enSpace) through languages.

Now imagine there is something in the world but not to be sensed by the human yet, or never be. The challenge will be in a different dimension. In this scenario, let everybody be in Hellen's situation:

For a very simple start, the mammal bat, which can fly at total darkness without trouble and with extremely poor vision. How does the bat do it?

If one does not have sufficient knowledge, s/he does not

understand the whole mechanism and s/he probability resorts magic and fairytale narrative. Because according s/he living environment and sense of interactions with it, s/he does not have a clue how the bat does that.

The bat can send an ultrasonic signal out, which is not a big deal, since the bat is small. Small animal makes sharp sound, human can make all kinds of sound; moreover, the bat can detect the echoes of its sound: thus, it is able to get the information about the direction, distance, and find the clear path for itself. That is remarkable and hard for human to experience and relate. So, without some basic background, one probably does not easily to figure how that bat flies at night without trouble.

Along comes the quantum entanglement.

Under the same token, human beings have not very successfully comprehended the mechanism governing it, or a better domain of manifolds for a good illustration.

The dilemma demonstrates "There are known knowns; there are known unknowns; there are also unknown unknowns" — accepting our limitation with dispassionate mind for all that due diligence.

In a large sense, there are two classes of evolutions.

At one side, IA: information artificiality (A/D: analogy information to digital), these entities with large amount of existing data and infrastructures, are crying for a neat, quick, and general systematic protocols of aggregating and distilling, to make sense out of them. We are going to denote this process IAAD (Information-Artificiality : Analog-Digital, detail discussion later).

At other side, AI: artificiality intelligence (D/A: applied digitalized data to analogical world) human beings are still short of senses on certain domains expressed in certain manifolds out of human beings' sense of awareness, i.e. the mechanism of quantum entanglements at the profound end; the protocols and methodologies of executions on autonomous vehicles; plus many more. We are going to represent this process DAAI (Digital-Analog: Artificiality-Intelligence)

We are going to look into the details of each side.

----The alpha and omega of artificial intelligence

— The Alpha Mission: IAAD accomplished but might not have been loyal to their original subjects.

— The Omega Mission:the DAAI is trying on the re-creation of things in the tSpace from enSpace plots via iSpace tools; ableit either the sources or the approaches might not have been built on a solid ground.

CHAPTER 12: INFORMATION-ARTIFICIALITY : ANALOG-DIGITAL

§ 12.1 THE START OF IAAD JOURNEY

Before the artificial intelligence to be made possible, the opposite course of AI, IAAD has to be in place.

The evolution of homo sapiens has empowered the species to reproduce "yesterday once more". Through storytelling, writing, audio and video records, plus other kinds of marks on the surface of the planet in the tSpace domain, and beyond, as well as "learning by heart" within enSpace. There are a lot of views on the universe. In virus "eyes" view, the world might be full of "meals" in omni-directions, it can easily penetrate the porous thin net holding the meals in form ("cells" or even organelles) and inject its whole-body inside. In the observation of fish's eyes, the world is wet and that is the only life-sustaining environment. In bird's-eye view, while the thin air is as the water for fish, more than that, the uninhabitable solid crust embeds infinite mystery beyond its little head's comprehension: some are delicious meals, some are deadly, equipped with sharp vision, still get hit by little projectiles with an infinite speed (at least more than 8 times the diving speed of "our" Peregrine falcon, clocked at 200 miles per hour, who "runs" fast like "deer". Even this is in a human's think in lieu of a bird). Orion, the constellation, may only see a distorted space (general relativity) as the possible existing "manifold" domain for him/her to live in, other than that, not so much: the black hole is unimaginable.

In different scopes, the same "universe" has been "articulated" in dramatically different narratives. Although there will never be arguments between different species, still, the insulation of communication has neither established peace nor pulled-off win-wins. Species that more closely represents the nature can dig deeper and exercise more leverages in the course of "survival the fittest" and resource exploitation. The unfortunate species may experience extinctions. If the powerful dinosaurs had extinguished by "observing" meteor shower too close; The whales, as species, are gigantic and too big to fail into an ordinary species mouth, be that as it may, the fish lover Asian-Pacific island homo sapiens, albeit considered smaller in size of its own species, have hunted the big "foe" around the globe thousands miles away and alomost eliminated the whales, as a species.

§ 12.2 FROM PRECURSOR TO INTELLIGENCE AND KNOWLEDGE: INFORMATION HARNESSING AND LANGUAGE DEVELOPING

Homo Sapiens (humans) have been so far the most "sapiens" (wise); through tens of thousands of years' evolution, humans have largely dominated the planet earth, in a comparative manner. However, in the absolute scale, the brightest species still have no clue about their precise position in the domain of universe.

In the course of history, the homo sapiens, species of wise, had in many occasions proclaimed "declaration of independence" and celebrated the comprehensive maturity of adulthood. Only found later, they were still inferior. With a self-delightful doctrine, universal Bible, the Catholic church had embraced their perfect theory on the universe: the core was that the earth was the center of the universe. When the experimental observers disputed the principals, they would annihilate these unorthodox with whatever effort they could put together, in an attempt to restore their sanity and keep the followers away from "infections." Their resistance had led to many culminating trials, based on their own believes, including Galileo affair, ending life-time arrest in—house; Execution by burning of Giordano Bruno, and the charges made against Bruno by the Roman Inquisition were:

- holding opinions contrary to the Catholic faith and speaking against it and its ministers;
- holding opinions contrary to the Catholic faith about the Trinity, divinity of Christ, and Incarnation;
- holding opinions contrary to the Catholic faith pertaining to Jesus as Christ;
- holding opinions contrary to the Catholic faith regarding the virginity of Mary, mother of Jesus;
- holding opinions contrary to the Catholic faith about both Transubstantiation and Mass;
- claiming the existence of a plurality of worlds and their eternity;
- believing in metempsychosis and in the transmigration of the human soul into brutes;
- dealing in magics and divination.

From history to now days, the church has been mending their theory again and again to accommodate all the new developments. The issue was simply originated from their primitive declaration of perfection (frozen of development) of the interactive tSpace.

Then In the field of strictly science research, there is Lord Kelvin's declaration of perfect theory in physics: albeit a little troubling two clouds; howbeit they turned out to be two revolutionary scientific leaps: One gave the birth of the theory of Relativity and another of Quantum Physics. In a lecture delivered at the Royal Institution of Great Britain, on Friday, April 27, 1900, physicist - William Thomson (Lord Kelvin, Queen had knighted him the Lord Kelvin), had the following open remarks,

"THE beauty and clearness of the dynamical theory, which asserts heat and light to be modes of motion, is at present obscured by two clouds. I. The first came into existence with the undulatory theory of light, and was dealt with by Fresnel and Dr. Thomas Young; it involved the question, how could the earth move through an elastic solid, such as essentially is the luminiferous ether? II. The second is the Maxwell-Boltzmann doctrine regarding the partition of energy." (sic)

As one of the world's most eminent physicist, Kelvin declared that the physics (classic) theory was "almost" perfect ("beauty and cleanness") albeit with only two remain trivial issues — I. & II.

In a classic thinking pattern, things seem smooth out. When all was said and done, small bumps normally did not pose great challenges while dealing the classic equations. Notwithstanding these two cases.

(I) On the first cloud, when Lord Kelvin was delivering his lecture, a 22-years old young man name Albert Einstein was in his freshman second semester on his PhD course. Einstein was bewildering at what he was trying to do. After switching his advisor (in his freshman summer 1901), Einstein's mind was still an indecision. One year later, Einstein was conceiving (no! No! NO! I know what you are thinking, not that) — to withdraw the tiresome damn PhD course, he said, "the whole comedy has become tiresome for me." Nonetheless, Albert finally got a degree, with title: A New Determination of the Molecular Dimensions (Original: Eine neue Bestimmung der Moleküldimensionen), in 1905. The two professors reviewed as, "the arguments and calculations to be carried out are among the most difficult in hydrodynamics." And "the mode of treatment demonstrates fundamental mastery of the relevant mathematical methods." May be as the requirements to qualify the PhD degree, be that as it may, Einstein published a few papers in that year 1905, one of them was, "On the Electrodynamics of Moving Bodies", and Einstein could not stop doing "That Thing You Do!" until he was finally stuck on a so called unified theory. Before Einstein successfully drove himself into that corner, he had already demonstrated that the first cloud in Lord Kelvin's lecture, was not a small one, a cloud related to the theory of relativity, from which real cloud (mushroom-like) loomed humongous.

(II) The second cloud, partitioning the energy, of course, led to the quantum physics, a change on our view on the universe from the marrow of the spine.

Lord kelvin's lecture published in a magazine called *Philosophical Magazine*. Exactly one hundred years later, the author for this book also published a paper with the same magazine (*Philosophical Magazine Letter*, Vol. 81, No. 10, pp. 683-690. October 2001) on superconductivity mechanism (well, do we remember the

Google's quantum supremacy was based on superconducting qubits ?!). After patiently waiting for quadruple 5-year (as comparing the 1901 paper to 1905 Einstein's paper on the theory of relativity), there has been no new theory evolved from the mispredictions in the paper. I am about feeling the confidence that my paper might have been right all way through: c'mon dude! U R declaring a perfectionism again. Oops!

Not only in the business of science, but also in NBA, a basketball game profession, people are declaring the perfection too. Kevin Durant said this (about his play style after joining Golden State Warrior) to the Wall Street Journal while he was taking his new headspace: "So me? Shit, how you going to rehabilitate me? What you going to teach me? How can you alter anything in my basketball life? I got an MVP already. I got scoring titles" (https://www.wsj.com/articles/kevin-durants-new-headspace-11568119028).

Roman Catholic Church did it, Lord Kelvin did it, I did it (not really), Kevin Durant did it, … Y'all had done it, T'all, and W'all had done it, that was easy.

Even in the modest and sincere scientific territories, the knowledge-soaked scholars can "tread water" and stop advancing in the due diligence. The root course is simply because the homo sapiens, wise creatures in the planet earth, do have gotten upper hand in the race of exploring the universe that they are living in and living on.

All in all, with the condensations of thousands of years history, from views of all sources of languages' facets, they had achieved the crucial infrastructure construction of the enSpace universe with building blocks of knowledge, which in both a correct attitude and a modest developing perspective, may or may not 100% represent the universe, neither on the comprehensive scales of completeness nor on the microscopic levels of accuracy.

§ 12.3 LANGUAGE AT IT'S WIT'S END

The enSpace spectacles rarely see the sunlight; language is gold howbeit as a manifest tool it has innate limitations; the digitizing programing language had been ridiculously truncated; and after twice information revolutions, the enSpace human large knowledge has been transcoded into the iSpace digital big data.

The information has never been a trouble in any ancestor's view, the wholesome humans had always greedily absorbed as much as they can, then integrated into the individual enSpace, the conscious mind. While the curiosity killed the cat, it is always the right mindset for a school pupil. Every piece of information, made the homo sapiens wiser and equipped more skills to cope with the external universe. This type of generation to generation passthrough had its limitations. The enSpace is unlimited, the human life span has a limit. The nurtured enSpace spectacles seldom entirely manifest their fullness, albeit limited aspects of them had been put into language records. As a familiar example, there are so many NBA players right now on the conference games. Some puts on a show of high scores (quite a few games had one play scored 60s points already, weeks into the regular season). Let's push back LBJ and KD a little. For the full greatness of NBA Michael Jordan, his instinct, his skill, his mindset of competition, plus many more attributes, had converged and integrated into one head, four limbs, attached on a torso. The wholesome player had performed epic shows on the planet. First, Jordan himself had not written the book; the Biography was written by Sam Smith. Second, Jordan himself had not, may never be, put all he had into a "to-go package" and delivered by Amazon to your door yet. If so, you or at least you can bring up somebody with a "bible", again, even "the Bible" had trouble, for the Galileo affair and Giordano Bruno case.

So, the writing out was not a fullness representation of our enSpace. With the distortion of the first abstracting: the external tSpace universe creeps into human enSpace with specialized language as tokens; although a lot of declarations of perfection, the process had been completed with great reduction and remodeling. With the same token, an enSpace fullness of integrated entity, experiences mourning losses to fish out and expressed into language tokens again.

§ 12.4 THE POWER OF LANGUAGES

Even with the limited written down of the human enSpace attributes, humans, the homo sapiens, had achieved more than any peer so far in the universe.

The obvious differences between human's ability of inherent and other creatures enable the species to pass through the expertise over external channels on top of the biological genetic limit. That, by far, is the driving force for all the great human achievements. Some other creatures, for example, octopuses, which are capable of learning through simple observation, among others, is at excel on the problem solving and issue resolving. However, it may be a bit challenge for octopuses to write down words in water: not only the paper always gets wet, but also the fact that the sea water simply bleaches the ink away, not mentioning the regulations requiring these octopuses have to submit a copy of their book to the congress library.

§ 12.5 "CHIEF'S" PEE-PEE "DOCUMENTATION" IN THE DIRTY LIMIT

If let speculations creep in for a moment, although there is no hardware proof in human's observable environment, that there are some sorts of "literature" recording from other creatures, existing out of homo sapiens' perceptions. To the "dirt" limit, human cannot see anything or smell anything to enter the territory boundaries of the circle of the lion pride, albeit that circle had been marked with the pride's chief's pee-pee, which has been always well received and respected by the creatures.

As a little note to the inability of "written" records on the other life forms on the planet earth, some life forms are totally different from our comfortable life survival environment. These extremophiles, some thermophiles live around deep sea floor hydrothermal vents with temperatures reaching more than 120 Celsius (248 F); some in ice environment (Synechococcus lividus -20 Celsius, 3 F); some in salty, acidic, alkaline, ionizing radiation or UV, as well as high pressure environment. The thermophile archaea, are using sulfur for growth or respiration. The sulfur, instead of oxygen, is in place for an electron acceptor. Some acquire energy from oxidizing sulfur instead of oxidizing C or H. If they write out their alchemy, it will show some inconsistencies with the homo sapiens'. If they are looking for lives in the universe, they are surely heading to the different directions that the NASA does.

(https://www.jpl.nasa.gov/edu/news/2019/12/30/nasas-9-most-teachable-moments-this-decade-and-beyond/)

§ 12.6 LIMITING IAAD ON THE PAPER

It appears that is not a high-risk factor so far that we just discard the chief's code of conduct or "wet" marks, and we are concentrating only on the abstract languages' tokens of human marks "on the paper". We start to realize, with all the respects and due diligences, before the IAAD, the information-artificiality : Analog-Digit transition, the data is in fixed form and immobile. It does not make much different that you put in paper or in IBM punch cards, people do not have the ability to perform a quick access and they are not presented with an aggregated platform of lateral information array. Most importantly and relevantly, the resultant information on the paper, undergone the phenomenon-to-languages total transition, cannot be read, understood, and processed by computers. There was a giant gap between the computer computing and the materials readiness (picture this common scene: line of many people holding the "IBM Cardd" in their hands to wait for the IBM 1401 to process their data like the scene of Charle Choplin was waiting for a job in his silent movies). Strides have to be made to render these paper format information and data into tokens these can be understood and process by computer with quick access speed. Basically, this total converting process constitutes another "civilizing" and "liberating" processes to release the paper format total information encoded in languages' entity and tokenizing most of this information, if not all, into a "computer universe", the iSpace, as we have symbolized in the opening of the book. The process is akin to artificially creating another layer of languages, which is called programming languages, such as Python, Java, C, etc., that had been done and still carried on till today. With the help of second language revolution (computer languages) and information liberation (from paper languages), the transition had been made possible from permanent publications (or if relevant, from IBM punch cards) to random mass accessible media such like hard disk drives (HDD) , optical discs, solid-state drives (SDD), cloud-based storages (HDD & SSD based), or as IBM Watson computer running model for TV show Jeopardy: total RAM-based memory.

To give our own example, here is how we were working in the RAM while this book was edited.

This transition had really broken the ground and laid the foundation for the IAAD leap: digitizing and "materializing" elements in the iSpace universe.

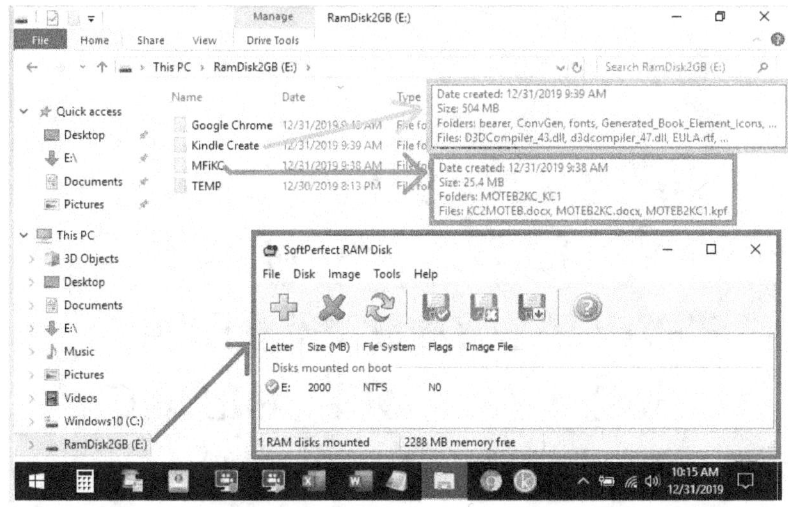

As the last proof-reading stage, this book is being edited in RAM, not only the traditional way: software is using and executing in memory. The Kindle Create (software in E:\Kindle Create) and book content (materials in the folder of E:\MFiKC\) are all residing in a 2GB RAM disk, created with "SoftPefect." In another view, if somebody (hackers) managed to shut down this computer, this book content would have been totally lost. Since you are reading, that had not happened. And the following screenshot is this very screen:

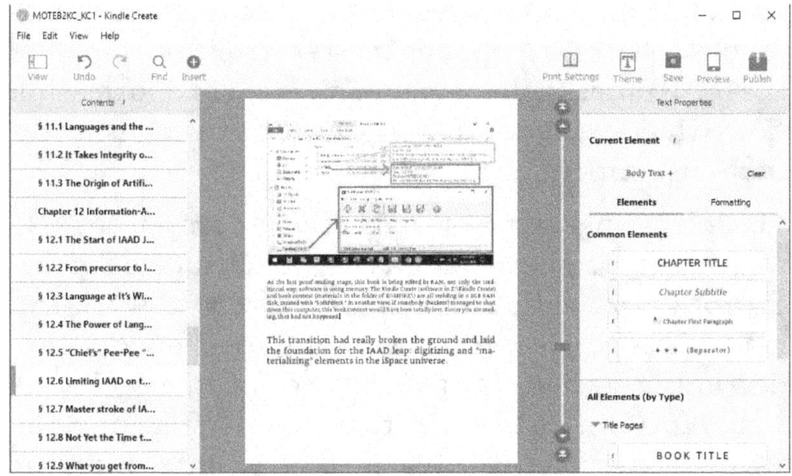

§ 12.7 MASTER STROKE OF IAAD EPOCH: THE "PAY-AS-YOU-GO" REAL-TIME DATA DEMANDING AND DELIVERY

However, even with the fullness of total information and data transition, the attainment of complete set of data for the computer to manipulate, there is a missing master stroke to complete the IAAD process: the degree of freedom of information flow, which expresses "physically" as the establishment of the network infrastructure.

The increasingly glued social networks are part of day-to-day life, people should have the attitude of appreciation for scientists and engineers whose work had made these connections possible. All the network connections have been started from so-called world-wide web. Tim Berners-Lee, a British scientist, invented the World Wide Web (WWW) in 1989, while working at CERN. WWW was originally conceived and developed to meet the demand for automated information-sharing between scientists in universities and institutes around the world. Although there are some users take it for granted, i.e. using Twitter a lot, but still curses all the scientific developments, like the President of the United States. These social network infrastructures had been built step-by-step with all the nuts and bolts by these students (candidates seeking academic degrees), engineers, and, scientists while all others were in Star Wars' fantasy or the shockwaves of rock and Roll music.

With all the efforts and due diligence, internet has been constructed from the laboratory research tool into a house-hold essential component. Picturing this 30 years ago, asking T.B. Lee, that the optical fiber was going to enter the ordinary home and doing daily video chatting during the grocery shopping, he would definitely express his doubt: at that stage, even the digital video had not been born. For a similar scenario, also as the national priority, the quantum computing is at the front of agenda for a lot of powerful business entities and government agencies. Although there was voice like, HP, in the dawn of the announcement of quantum supremacy from Google and voice from IBM, together with others, has made this kind headlines recently, "Beausoleil, a former quantum physicist from Stanford who is now a fellow at HPE, says he explained his rationale to senior management, and they understood and accepted it. He felt that quantum computing wasn't feasible for the kinds of data sets enterprise customers want to analyze. Beausoleil also says he couldn't come up with a use case in quantum computing that HPE was likely to have. He says the types of things HPE focuses on in its day-to-day work don't directly apply to building a quantum computer, so quantum computing no longer became a priority. It's really not a good fit. For the majority of our customers, it's not going to make a difference to them. Some of the challenges of building a quantum computer today include making sure temperatures remain close to absolute zero – otherwise, the particles required for these computations will become unstable. Instead, HPE decided to focus on building more computing architecture and software that its customers could use."

Quantum computing aside, the huge leap of world wide web during the past quarter of century orchestrated the master stroke of the IAAD epoch, which spans from the beginning of homo sapiens all the way to current generation civilization.

§ 12.8 NOT YET THE TIME TO CELEBRATE THE EPOCH OF IAAD

To ease the surge of blood pressure on this perception, please conceptualize this as an exponential function, with which the current world "classic computers" have some troubles and thus cry desperately for the quantum computers. On the data aggregations and manipulations, the homo sapiens expend their capacities of information throughput and data gobbling-down speed through their invented digitized iSpace elemental building blocks. Providing the grandness of the master stroke during the IAAD epoch, in which the information aggregates and data moves with exponential expansions, there are increasing congestions and crying demands on the computing power and instant proper data distributions, accompanying that very IAAD epoch. To address the problems arising the creation of the grandness of IAAD epoch, the homo sapiens have been on the quest for Citius, Altius, Fortius computers, the supercomputers, together with spirally increased network bandwidth. Taking only Google's hardware infrastructure, through its worldwide-allocated data centers, in terms of amount of per-capita-resource, Google now offers a whopping >200MB RAM, >700MB (SSD storage), >5 GB (Hard Disk), with a computing power akin to an Clay-2 super-computer, for each person of the 7 billion population on the planet earth. Aggregating with Microsoft, IBM, Facebook, Twitter, Instagram, Amazon, ... and many more, such like gaming data-center-services, navigating, weather forecasting, and many more, plus government and military agencies, the number will be astonishedly huge.

Up to today, with all these enormous digital apparatuses and data mountains, in the scale of universe domain, all but akin to snail's world to the earth. Humans are still facing similar obstacles when they are trying to solve all the knots in the universe. Speaking the elements and problems in the enSpace only, the iSpace machinery so far has only shined occasionally like the shooting stars. Stuffs in the real world, transduced in certain way inside enSpace, are mostly depicted as multi-body system. To the extreme end of certain type of limit, the electron itself cannot be considered as a "point particle": even considering all electron's electric charge is distributed on the surface of a sphere, with the static electric energy resulting a rest mass (reverse thinking of $E=MC^2$ => $E/C^2 = M$) that sphere's radii is much bigger than proton' and neutron's, simply meaning it is "too big to be true," on the other hand, may be so. Of course, all these conceptions are in a classic doctrine (interested, Feynman had calculated this in his lectures when he taught in Caltech, collected in his book "The Feynman Lectures on Physics", I believed it was in Volume 2, but do not nail down the volume number relied on my memory). Purely in terms of all human created events, the chess match (IBM supercomputer Deep Blue versus Garry Kasparov); the TV quiz show Jeopardy (IBM Watson Supercomputer vs Jeopardy winners Brad Rutter and Ken Jennings); and board game Go! match (Google AlphaGo vs Ke Jie, AlphaGo awarded the highest-ranking stature after the match), are the limited digital successes in computing.

Below is the Google AlphaGo Displayed at the entrance of one of their restaurants in Sunnyvale Campus--the inset are the original server racks.

There are numerous problems out there the current computer cannot solve and find out the exact solution. Just to satisfy any curiosity, i.e. In programming language theory, the POPLmark challenge (the challenge is about measurement of how well programs may be proven to match a specification of how they are intended to behave, and the many complex issues that this involves). In natural language processing, Is there any perfect stemming algorithm in the English language? There are tons of algorithm problems, the one we have mentioned, integer factorization be done in polynomial time? (classic computer); P versus NP problem; shortest path problems (graph), and many more.

§ 12.9 WHAT YOU GET FROM IAAD EPOCH: PILES OF BIG DATA; WHAT YOU MISS: THE COHERENCE OF THE DISCRETE DATA

With the great master stroke, plus thousands of years of cultural depositions, shock and awe technologies, the completion of the IAAD epoch, when the real problem arises, these resources are still short of a miracle. That is the awkwardness of the digitization and current computing. To add insult to injury, actually, to reveal a secret, all the analog problems are out of the comfortable zoom of the classic computing. I am giving a very practical example of a related "game", or can be called a "race": the game of drones (which absolutely has nothing to do with game of thrones). The drones are among the most popular toys in the general population both in their nature attractions and technology densities. Although it is excited for the live bird-view and taking image on the fly, with normal Wi-Fi based protocol, the digital video is a little bit delayed, which one does not care much, for now. In some situations, it is wanted for a trad-off to get an instantaneous responding from the console over the quality of image, but it is hardly possible, regardless the image quality (not that great!). In the tournament of drone race (actually there is a national event), the operators are zipping the drones through gates, arrays, and event tree branches. Have you been in any air show across the country, the drone show is just way more spectacular and crazier than that simply because there is no life on board. In such scenarios, fractions of a second make huge different, an enhanced instant ripple butterfly effect. Once again, this has no any algorithm involved, in the era of fast speed network and data gobbling, the communication between the drones and the headsets of the operators, has resorted to analog communication, which is faster (in speed), clearer (in quality), and more reliable in signal communication, from my own first-hand humble experience.

The innate transduction course of IAAD digitizing approach is the origin of the entire issue. The whole story of the IAAD epoch, out of no better option, is using discrete data to represent a continue "event." Thus, called IAAD: information/intelligence artificiality : Analog to Digital. At the end of the day, while everything is done, all you get are discrete data points. While these discrete points are to be transcoded back to describe the original event; the critical intelligent information that is needed is the coherences, the mechanism of evolving trend and the correlations between these data. Although you can plot out the discrete data and they are looking like something coherent. But the principal mechanisms, functionalities, and the flowing beauties of the original universal event do not come out as equations, theory models, or amalgamated entities. For a video or sound, the IAAD was remarkably successfully; for the data point-representations of series of hypotenuses square vs the squares of the other two sides, when these data aggregated, they are not giving the "Pythagorean theorem!" The process needs high degree cognitive creative thinking with deep relevant knowledge as the background. And this is normally happened in highly cultivated scholar's heads. Recalling the failed undisclosed Google Doodle project, which I couldn't find a trace even in Google's internal portal, was using the mathematic equations to create animated images (movies). Could be considered a well intented try, albeit failed, obviously, without a mention.

§ 12.10 THE FABRICATION LINE-UP: TSPACE > ENSPACE > ISPACE <> SCREENS | ENSPACE (VIEWERS) TELLS THAT THE INNATED DEFICIENCY CAN BE INFECTIOUS TO THE YOUNG GENERATION'S BRAIN AND LIFE*

*This title has been distorted from Kindle Create, the original here:

§ 12.10 The fabrication line-up:

tSpace ⏭ enSpace ⏭ iSpace ↻ screens ⮌ enSpace (viewers) tells that the innated deficiency can be infectious to the young generation's brain and life

The discrete data in the digital world has been "fabricated" through aforementioned steps:

- from real universe (tSpace) to human cognitive thinking domain (enSpace);
- from enSpace (mostly in the forms of languages recordings) to iSpace (the digitized enSpace resources) discrete big data; These information entities ended up on the screens of all sorts of digital gadgets.
- Then these highly reduced and human-made virtual universe is presented to the view of the people, with the biggest impact on the young generation. Here is the piece of advice that may help a lot of parents to think twice when issues come up towards their children's activities on a computers, phones, and society media:

In the mental health regard, from the wholesome cognitive wellbeing, screen time is not an accelerating factor; instead, heavy screen time decelerates the nature tendency of wiring expending inside brain and renders the brain as a receiver: In the first fold, it is the interaction, what you see is what straight forward it is, the viewer never think the next frame of video by imagination, except passively receiver, retreated from an active participator. In the second fold, it is the memory loss; the brain has great potential, but no people heard anyone become a genius without thinking and learning. On that part, actively memorizing is a very important contributing factor, with the prolonged interacting, without cognitive expending of coherent consolidations, which is another type of active thinking, the capacity of the memory drops (memory weakening) and the mental health status declines. Thirdly, the most observable and directly impact part is the negative effect to the vision. Even this lies in two folds of impacts, first, it is the degradation on the vision: the focus on the bright screen, with fixed pose and fixed distance for a long time. The eye adjusts the directions with six external ocular muscles and tunes focus with circular ciliary muscle, in which failing is the cause of vision declines. When the eye is seeing the distance objects, the circular ciliary muscle at fully relax position (bigger circle), thus the lens of the eye become "thin". For the close objects, the circular ciliary muscle needs contract (small circle), so the lens become rounder, to focus on the objects. The lens does not decline, however, the circular ciliary muscle can loss its full health range of functionality if circular ciliary muscle has to work too hard and too long without proper care. It is much worse for watching the phone or the monitor screens than watching TVs, which was an old school argument between the parents and the children. Now the parents shall pray that their children to watch TV instead of watching on the closer and smaller screens. Long screen time for the children exhausts and depletes the functionality and power of circular ciliary muscle, and causes the vision to decline. Second, the most comprehensive and invisible descendancy for the delicate cognitive intelligence, is that the screen time not only hampering the vision on the eyes, it also interrupting the wholesome cognitive thinking process in the brain. What is the reason to account for that?

Ironically, the screen input is a high bandwidth traffic for the eyes, then for the brain to process, the intense visual inputs without a proper health cycle for relaxation effectuate the brain most sources and inhibit the normal collective consolidating functionality. In a long term, this can cause the brain cognitive power lose steam and so for the person's intelligence.

The smoking gun, is essentially the discrete treatment during the digitization and that constitutes one of the current computing core features, it's intrinsic and everything is based on that, for the good or for the bad. In the similar situation, the long screen time creates too much discreated information for the brain to effectively digest and properly correlate, as a result, it turns the viewer to a receiver, depletes the resources for a proper cognitive function, and damps brain's normal development.

We have also argued the negtive congitive impact of ridiculed portable music spectrum for the healthy hearing in the previous chapter:

§ 8.3.4 Human sensibilities vs the digital representations: Does internet music MP3 audio hurt your cognitive intuitiveness? The answer is not a simple "No!"

In the IAAD Epoch, the toy mission Version BKM 0.1 accomplished while the real mission version 1.0 is seeing increasing challenges for taking off from ground.

CHAPTER 13: DIGITAL-ANALOG : ARTIFICIALITY- INTELLIGENCE

§ 13.1 THE INITIATIVE OF DAAI, MOVING DATA AROUND

We are going to review the status and challenges of the reverse process of IAAD, the DAAI, Digital to Analog : Artificial Intelligence. This part has been briefly revealed in Chapter 12, IAAD. The demanding on the stronger, higher, and faster in the digital society iSpace has been accelerated, which is the nature drive force for a greater and bigger piles of data and is still growing. The emphasizing on the speed and bandwidth is the focus from everywhere around the globe. Slow websites, Google is now planning to give them badge of shame in its Chrome web browser (https://www.androidauthority.com/google-chrome-speed-badging-1053039/).

The reason is obvious, all the "instances" are kept while the users are connecting with the original information sources, if a specific web site is slow, no matter how fast the Google's system can handle, the user will still experience a slow information exchange; on Google side, such as what they are practicing, recording the linking and visiting counts, time duration, information utilization, and many more, for the "PageRank", AD service targeting etc., and no wonder Google gets a leg in the door for the individual website' speed affair.

In Tim Berners-Lee era, the computer communicated using "COM" ports, telnet, and later dial-up, the bandwidths of the networks were at KBPS level. After a protocol improvement and standardization at 56 kbps (bits, if in bytes, 7KB/s), the landline phone-based dial-up internet ISPs had grown like weeds. The internet data delivery companies, such as AOL, among others, were big and giant business entities and they suddenly became the society's big brands, akin today's Amazon, the old time Steel industries, and the automobile big names and beyond. The most famously "show of power" of AOL was in 2001, at the height of its popularity, it purchased the media conglomerate Time Warner in the largest merger in U.S. history. AOL advised that Americans had gone from the strongly connected US highway system into an information highway system, ironically, AOL collected heavy duties for the usages of the "highways" with a toll both at every entrance, without even paying a penny to the "clerks," who was replaced by computer's gating and automatic fee collection.

§ 13.2 DIGITAL LOSSY COMPRESS ARISING FROM NETWORK BANDWIDTH CONSTRAIN

During the dial-up time, there were a lot of corresponding software designed for the quick transportation through internet. The most famous two suits are Macromedia Flash, a very compact animation movie maker producing ".swf" file and RealMedia, ".rm", ".ra", ".rmvb", for video/audio compression; for a while RealMedia's files format and streaming became the internet media delivery standard. They used a heavy lossy algorithm to compresses the media file to achieve the largest compress ratio for the media to become portable. Although they are lossy, the quality of the picture was amazingly good. A full DVD movie (4700 MB, 4.7 GB) can be converted into .rmvb media about 700 MB, on the then mostly computer screens, or home TVs via computer monitor VGA-port, the quality was hardly having detectable degradations. With more aggressive lossy algorithm, a DVD can be further compressed into roughly the size around 150 MB, the quality is still enjoyable on the screens. Do a small math project, at 4700 MB DVD capacity, a 2-hour movie on the DVD will need a bandwidth of roughly 700 KBPS (corresponding to ~ 6Mbps bandwidth), which is two grades higher than that of the 7 KBPS of the then full dial-up internet speed. Taken the deep compressed size of 150 MB, the corresponding bandwidth was about 21 KBPS, three times of the maximum speed. So, most of the media streamed over the internet was using reduced video pixel scale, i.e. reduced the DVD from 720 x 480 resolution to typically 320 x 240 or lower, with more than a quadruple reduction, the media was finally fitting for the then household internet. In reality, there is always some reduction on the designated dial-up speed, the practical speed for live stream delivery was about 20 MB per hour, at 3 – 6 KBPS. And a move of 175 MB size often took a whole day to download with practically download speed at ~2-3 KBPS.

For the dial-up internet connection, the customer side does not have any hardware except the computer built-in (most of the cases) modem, the computer connected with the internet with a phone line through the phone jack of the modem. Leaps to the DSL (Digital Subscriber Line) and cable are both requiring separate modem hardware in the end-user side; however, the speed has been greatly lifted. With mbps (bits) the entry level, the current home portal internet speed ranges from MBPS to tens of MBPS. The latest development is the optical fiber goes into household, for a while already, which, for example, the Verizon FIOS, reaches 940 mbps (bits) downloading speed and 880 mbps (bits) uploading speed.

§ 13.3 IT IS THE SLUGGISH PLATFORM THAT IS FATAL INSTEAD OF BANDWIDTH

For certain cases, once again, it is not the speed that matters, it is the software madness: sloppy software, p2p services, adware or malware, those are the bandwidth killers. For example, we were (with 3 college students) sharing a 3Mbit/s cable internet package till I left this year. The students were able to perform their course work online and watch shows online. On the other hand, one of the houses I shared subscribing a 200 Mbit/s packages without even a computer in use. There are from some part of the southeast Asian, karaoke most of the nights, with gate rings and huddling like the necessary elements in the old villages. The owner is on disability but he seems as strong as a horse. Quite often, vehicles jacked up by the street and he was working on it, normally from his hometown fellows. They party like hyenas, akin to food contest, a lot of food wasted at the end, a weird disaster scene happening here in the San Francisco bay area. No explanations to lead the observers out of confusions as how these sloth and gluttony type of populations boom like viruses.

The bandwidth, which I am testing during my writing now:

Download: 249 Mbps
Upload: 12 Mbps
https://business.comcast.com/learn/internet-speed-test, which is the isp provider.
This bandwidth is a at idle 24/7.

§ 13.3.1 The challenges of service delivery based on collective digital resources: Epic failure on Disney+ launching event

The network speed and service, in a corporate level, sometimes are a matter of a success and profits. There are military operations, scientific experiments, society and social campaigns, with all these settings that the real-time none delayed communications are the core of success. We just had an excellent example of the "Disney+" launch (https://www.afr.com/technology/the-disney-streaming-service-debut-just-had-a-nightmare-debut-20191113-p53a2d), an example on the wrong (failure) side, and it also correlated with our popular theme conception in this book, the bandwidth. As you might have experienced, if you are the first wave to subscribe the Disney Plus service (with very low price), "The glitchy debut of Disney Plus is the stuff of tech launch nightmares" was the title in Washington post. Yesterday, hours after the debut, the Disney Plus streaming service had crashed its servers. Users flocked to social media to update their followers on the anticipated event. Many could not begin the new Star Wars show "The Mandalorian." Instead, they were greeted with a frowning character from the movie "Wreck-It Ralph" paired with a network error message, or Mickey Mouse stranded in space. "The Mandalorian" is the flagship launch show for about 500 films and 7,500 episodes of programming from Pixar, Marvel, Star Wars, National Geographic and others. The problems for some users undercut a huge day for Disney, which has touted the streaming service as a major part of its portfolio. "The demand for Disney + has exceeded our highest expectations," the company said. "We are so pleased you're excited to watch all your favorites and are working quickly to resolve any current issues. We appreciate your patience."

Disney chief executive Bob Iger set huge expectations for Disney Plus in his 2017 announcement for the service. "We're going to launch big, and we're going to launch hot," he said. Disney Plus costs $6.99 a month, and a bundle of Disney Plus, Hulu and ESPN Plus will set you back $12.99 a month.

Hollywood reporter titled "Disney+ Hit by Technical Issues on Launch Day" with blue screen of Disney+ death. An error icon would appear each time, showing Mickey Mouse and his dog, Pluto, in space outfits. It would then force users to exit the service.

"We are having a problem

Please exit the app and try

again.

Error code: 1017 - SERVICES_STARTUP_FAILURE"

Once the service did load properly, some titles, such as under the Star Wars category, were unavailable; that error page was just a blank blue screen that said, "Sorry something went wrong. Please try again later."

For shows and films that did not trigger an error message, some load times exceeded 30 seconds. However, in some cases, once the film or TV episode was exited out of, the app would crash.

The rocky premiere of Disney Plus comes as the latest front in an escalating streaming war for your eyeballs. Apple TV Plus launched Nov. 1, taking on HBO, Hulu and Netflix.

When in the old days, this was often happening undercover and not on the "national TV stage", for Disney+, this is their global TV stage, big, red, hot. But on the wrong side of the fence.

Not only the wired internet connection gains higher speed. The original cell-phone orientated data service, have been developed into the fifth generation with a data transfer speed expected at 2gbps (2000 mbps, bits) and with the existing 4G and 3G practical internet speed at mbps (3G, bits) and 20s mbps (4G, bits). The cellular speed is catching up the wired speed and represents the new breed of internet connections, especially for the portable devices.

§ 13.3.2 US DOD JUEI:
Modern military ware is
gearing up on the big data

As we have elicited the speed rankings in the previous section of the book, with the internal bus speed at hundreds of gbps (bits), the external network speed is still far less than the speed on the mother board. Now the external data accumulated larger and larger, the throughput of data processing is getting higher and higher, considering a graph of a matrix with mass data storage blocks distributed around the globe, the sampling on the matrix needs exponential growth both in the speed and the bandwidth. Now, it is the growing balance or race among the data, network, and processing power, as well as others (computer memory, CPU speed, and so on).

Many technology big players, especially these are relying on the networking platforms, have been investing heavily on the infrastructure constructions. Microsoft, Amazon, Facebook, Twitter, of course, Google and many more. While Google is quite happy with the current market and profit situation, more inclining to technology, business and enterprise perspectives, Amazon, Microsoft, and many other entities are very actively seeking large growth opportunities in all the directions, including government, military, and civil organizations. The current Trump government shuts Amazon out because of Trump's personal favorite, and Microsoft suddenly finds their luck, after several postponements, delays, and challenges, the US Department of Defense has awarded Microsoft the $10 billion Joint Enterprise Defense Infrastructure (JEDI), exclusively (https://www.nytimes.com/2019/10/25/technology/dod-jedi-contract.html). As the story develops, Amazon, as the No. 1 player in cloud service business, is petitioning for a contest plea, entertainingly, eyes on Trump (https://www.federaltimes.com/it-networks/cloud/2019/11/25/here-are-the-trump-statements-amazon-cites-in-its-jedi-protest/).

According to Amazon's own statement, Amazon Web Services (AWS) is the world's most comprehensive and broadly adopted cloud platform, offering over 165 fully featured services from data centers globally. In 2018, AWS became the first cloud provider to offer 100 Gbps of network bandwidth with the C5n EC2 instance types. AWS offers the largest global footprint in the market. No other cloud provider offers as many regions with multiple Availability Zones, with 69 Availability Zones (AZs) within 22 geographic regions around the world, and announced plans for 13 more AZs and four more AWS Regions in Indonesia, Italy, South Africa, and Spain.

§ 13.4 STATE OF THE WORLDWIDE CLOUD INFRASTRUCTURE AS A SERVICE

Gartner had high level reviews on a variety of entities with broad criteria.

Gartner Research Report on the cloud infrastructure as a service, ranking list:

1. Amazon
2. Microsoft
3. Google
4. Alibaba Cloud
5. Oracle
6. IBM

Although these all had made to the list, but they had not been made equally, not from the ranking but in reality. The front runners were far beyond while the second groups were niche players; leaving the challengers and visionary categories empty. Simply meaning, even the front runners have not gotten a clue what and how.

Gartner Research Report:

Magic Quadrant for Worldwide Cloud Infrastructure as a Service

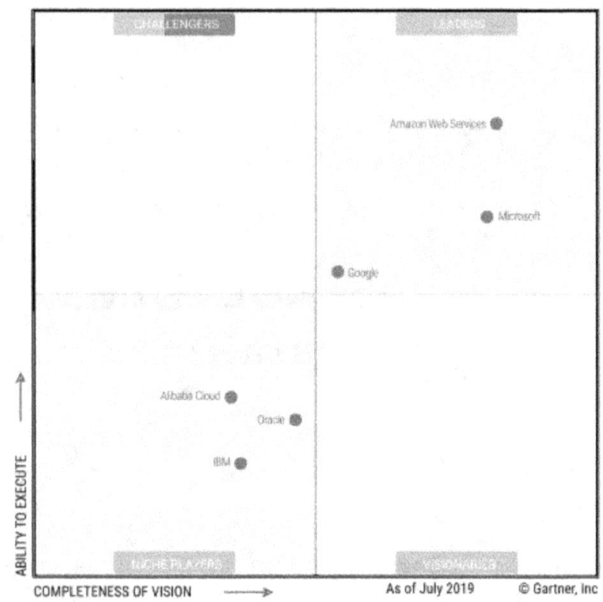

The Gartner Magic Quadrant constitutes with Leaders, Challengers, Visionaries, and Niche Players for each quadrant quarter. The latest Gartner Magic Quadrant for Cloud Infrastructure as a Service Worldwide (https://www.gartner.com/en/documents/3947472) reported that Amazon, Microsoft, and Google are in the leaders' quadrant, while Amazon and Microsoft are by far the front runners. Alibaba, Oracle, and IBM are in niche players quadrant while challengers and visionaries two quadrants are empty. Instead of sighs for Facebook, Twitter, Instagram, or games' domains.

Here are some details of the Gartner research, we select Amazon, Microsoft, Google, and IBM as examples.

§ 13.5 AMAZON

Amazon Web Services (AWS) is a cloud-focused service provider. It pioneered the cloud IaaS (Infrastructure as a service) market in 2006.

§ 13.5.1 Offerings

AWS is integrated IaaS+PaaS. Its Elastic Compute Cloud (EC2) offers metered-by-the-second multitenant and single-tenant VMs, as well as bare-metal servers. AWS's hypervisors are based on Xen and KVM. There is multitenant block and file storage, along with extensive additional IaaS and PaaS (platform as a service) capabilities. These include object storage with an integrated CDN (Amazon Simple Storage Service [S3] and CloudFront), Docker container services (Amazon EC2 Container Service [ECS], ECS for Kubernetes [EKS], and Fargate) and event-driven "serverless computing" (AWS Lambda). VMware offers a VMware Cloud Foundation service within AWS data centers (VMware Cloud on AWS). Enterprise-grade support is extra. It has a multi-fault-domain SLA (service-level agreement). Colocation needs are met via partner exchanges (AWS Direct Connect).

§ 13.5.2 Locations

AWS groups its data centers into Regions, each of which contains at least two availability zones (data centers). It has multiple Regions across the U.S., as well as in Canada, France, Germany, Ireland, the U.K., Australia, India, Japan, Singapore, South Korea, Sweden and Brazil. It also has one Region dedicated to the U.S. federal government. Two China Regions. It has a global sales presence. The portal and documentation are provided in English, Dutch, French, German, Italian, Japanese, Korean, Mandarin, Portuguese and Spanish. The primary languages for support are English, Japanese and Mandarin, but AWS will contractually commit to providing support in a large number of other languages.

§ 13.5.3 Adoption profile

AWS strongly appeals to buyers seeking agile operations, but is also frequently chosen for traditional styles of IT operations. AWS is the provider most commonly chosen for strategic, organization wide adoption. Transformation efforts are best undertaken in conjunction with an SI.

§ 13.5.4 Recommended uses

All use cases that run well in a virtualized environment. Applications that are potentially challenging to virtualize or run in a multitenant environment — including highly secure applications, strictly compliant or complex enterprise applications (such as SAP business applications)—require special attention to architecture.

§ 13.5.5 Strengths

Enterprises make larger annual financial commitments and deploy more mission-critical workloads on AWS than with any other hyperscale provider. This speaks to how enterprises perceive AWS as a strategic provider of cloud infrastructure and platform services relative to other providers in the market.

AWS has a broader range of customer profiles, ranging from startups and small and midsize businesses (SMBs) to large enterprises, than any other provider in this market. Enterprises using AWS benefit from the early adopters, which help to push new technologies into the mainstream, derisking such services and making them easier to consume and manage as a result.

AWS is the most mature, enterprise-ready provider, with the strongest track record of customer success and the most useful partner ecosystem. Thus, it is the provider chosen by not only customers that value innovation and that are implementing digital business projects, but also preferred by customers that are migrating traditional data centers to cloud IaaS.

§ 13.5.6 Cautions

AWS makes frequent proclamations about the number of price reductions it has made. Customers interpret these proclamations as being applicable to the company's services broadly, but this is not the case. For instance, the default and most frequently provisioned storage for AWS's compute service has not experienced a price reduction since 2014, despite falling prices in the market for the raw components.

AWS prioritizes being first to market with respect to delivering new services and capabilities. As a result, it is willing to launch feature-poor services or services without deep cross-platform integration, which it often defers to the future to address. The quest to be first to market sometimes results in services that need years of substantial engineering updates.

As the ambitions of Amazon's CEO expand into additional markets, the boards of directors for companies in potentially threatened verticals have directed their IT organizations to avoid the use of AWS where possible. This may ultimately limit AWS's success in some verticals, and may impact the associated ecosystem. IT leaders in these verticals should consider a contingency plan for board-level directives.

§ 13.6 MICROSOFT

Microsoft is a large and diversified technology vendor that is increasingly focused on delivering its software capabilities via cloud services. Microsoft entered the cloud IaaS market with the launch of Azure Virtual Machines in June 2012 (with general availability in April 2013).

§ 13.6.1 Offerings

Microsoft Azure is integrated IaaS+PaaS. It offers metered-by-the-second Hyper-V-virtualized multitenant compute (Azure Virtual Machines), as well as specialized large instances (such as for SAP HANA). There is multitenant block and file storage, along with many additional IaaS and PaaS capabilities. These include object storage (Azure Blob Storage), a CDN, a Docker-based container service (Azure Container Service), a batch computing service (Azure Batch) and event-driven "serverless computing" (Azure Functions). The Azure Marketplace offers third-party software and services. Colocation needs are met via partner exchanges (Azure ExpressRoute) such as those from Equinix and CoreSite.

§ 13.6.2 Locations

Microsoft calls Azure data center locations "regions." There are multiple Azure regions in the U.S., Canada, the U.K., Germany, France, Australia, India, Norway, UAE, Switzerland, Japan and Korea, as well as regions in Ireland, the Netherlands, Hong Kong, Singapore and Brazil. There are also six regions for the U.S. federal government; two are dedicated to the Department of Defense. (The two Azure China regions are part of a separate service operated by 21Vianet Group.) Microsoft has global sales. Documentation is available in English, French, German, Italian, Spanish, Portuguese (Brazil and Portugal), Japanese, Korean and Mandarin. Support and the service portal are available in those languages, plus Czech, Dutch, Hungarian, Polish, Russian, Swedish and Turkish.

§ 13.6.3 Adoption profile

Microsoft Azure appeals to both Mode 1 and Mode 2 customers, but for different reasons. Mode 1 customers tend to value the ability to use Azure to extend their infrastructure-oriented Microsoft relationship and investment in Microsoft technologies. Mode 2 customers tend to value Azure's ability to integrate with Microsoft's application development tools and technologies, or are interested in integrated specialized PaaS capabilities, such as the Azure Data Lake, Azure Machine Learning or the Azure IoT solution accelerators.

§ 13.6.4 Recommended uses

All use cases that run well in a virtualized environment, particularly for Microsoft-centric organizations.

§ 13.6.5 Strengths

Enterprises that are strategically committed to Microsoft technology generally choose Azure as their primary IaaS+PaaS provider. The integrated end-to-end experience for enterprises building .NET applications using Visual Studio and related services while deploying them to Azure is unsurpassed. Microsoft is leveraging its tremendous sales reach and ability to co-sell Azure with other Microsoft products and services in order to drive adoption.

Azure provides a well-integrated approach to edge computing and Internet of Things (IoT), with offerings that reach from its hyperscale data center out through edge solutions such as Azure Stack and Data Box Edge.

Microsoft Azure's capabilities have become increasingly innovative and open, where 50% of the workloads are Linux-based along with numerous open-source application stacks. Microsoft has a unique vision for the future that involves bringing in technology partners through native, first-party offerings such as those from VMware, NetApp, Red Hat, Cray and Databricks.

§ 13.6.6 Cautions

Microsoft Azure's reliability issues continue to be a challenge for customers, largely as a result of Azure's growing pains. Since September 2018, Azure has had multiple service-impacting incidents, including significant outages involving Azure Active Directory. The nature of many of these outages is such that customers had no controls in order to mitigate the downtime.

Gartner clients often experience challenges with on-time implementations within budget and that results from Microsoft setting unreasonably high expectations for customers. Much of this stems from modestly improving capabilities of Microsoft's field sales teams to appropriately position and sell Azure within its customer base.

Enterprises frequently lament the quality of Microsoft technical support (along with the increasing cost of support) and field solution architects. This negatively impacts customer satisfaction, and slows Azure adoption and therefore customer spending.

§ 13.7 GOOGLE

Google is an internet-centric provider of technology and services. Google has had an aPaaS offering since 2008, but did not enter the cloud IaaS market until Google Compute Engine was launched in June 2012 (with general availability in December 2013).

§ 13.7.1 Offerings

Google Cloud Platform (GCP) combines an IaaS offering (Compute Engine), an aPaaS offering (App Engine) and a range of complementary IaaS and PaaS capabilities, including object storage, a Docker container service (Google Kubernetes Engine [GKE]) and event-driven "serverless computing" (Google Cloud Functions). Google also offers GKE On-Prem (software for on-premises deployment), a container-based offering for enterprise deployments. It has a multi-fault-domain SLA. Colocation needs are met via partner exchanges (Google Cloud Interconnect).

§ 13.7.2 Locations

Google has multiple regions across the U.S., as well as a presence in Belgium, Japan, Singapore, Germany, the Netherlands, the U.K., India, Australia, Brazil, Canada, Hong Kong, Switzerland and Taiwan. Google has a global sales presence. Support is available in English and Japanese. The portal is available in English, Dutch, French, German, Italian, Polish, Spanish, Turkish, Russian, Portuguese, Korean, Japanese, Mandarin, Cantonese and Thai. Documentation is available in English, German, Japanese and Brazilian Portuguese. Google operates regions with availability zones, but these zones can be separate buildings or separate power, cooling, networking, and control planes.

§ 13.7.3 Adoption profile

GCP initially appealed to Mode 2 buyers with demonstrated strengths associated with big data and other analytics applications, machine learning projects, cloud-native applications, or other applications optimized for cloud-native operations. GCP is also beginning to attract enterprises with traditional Mode 1 workloads such as SAP.

§ 13.7.4 Recommended uses

Big data and other analytics applications, machine learning projects, cloud-native applications, or other applications optimized for cloud-native operations.

§ 13.7.5 Strengths

Google has leveraged its internal innovative technology capabilities (e.g., automation, containers, networking) by providing a scalable IaaS offering with PaaS capabilities, centered on open-source ecosystems. While catering initially to cloud-native startups, Google is in the process of expanding its reach to enterprise customers.

Google has differentiated technologies on the forward edge of IT, specifically in analytics and machine learning. This has driven some enterprises to select Google as a strategic cloud provider where they have deployed applications that are anchored by BigQuery.

Google has innovated programs to assist customers with the process of operations transformation via its Customer Reliability Engineering program. The program uses a shared-operations approach to teach customers to run operations the way that Google's site reliability engineers do. This has the potential to tether Google more closely to enterprise customers.

§ 13.7.6 Cautions

Google demonstrates an immaturity of process and procedures when dealing with enterprise accounts, which can make the company difficult to transact with at times. This can be attributed to its nascent focus on the enterprise market. The immaturity of process is most pronounced in areas such as contract negotiation, discounting, independent software vendor (ISV) licensing, integration with enterprise systems and support. Google is aggressively targeting these shortcomings.

Google has a much smaller pool of experienced MSP (Managed Service Provider or Management Service Provider, is a company that manages information technology services for other companies via the Web) and infrastructure-centric professional services partners than other vendors in this Magic Quadrant. Its own professional services are still gaining traction in driving customer implementations. Some prospective customers find that these ecosystem limitations heighten migration risk.

Google's overall enterprise coverage from a field sales and solutions perspective is behind its competitors. Further, enterprises often lament about Google's inability to craft appropriate solutions for enterprise requirements when engaging with solution architects.

§ 13.8 IBM

IBM is a large, diversified technology company with a range of cloud-related products and services. The IBM Cloud offering has been built on IBM's July 2013 acquisition of SoftLayer and its previous Bluemix offering.

§ 13.8.1 Offerings

IBM offers both multitenant and single-tenant virtualized compute resources along with bare-metal servers. It has S3-compatible Cloud Object Storage. CDN integration is offered via an Akamai partnership. IBM Cloud offers an Open Container Initiative (OCI)-based container service (IBM Cloud Kubernetes Service), event-driven serverless computing (IBM Cloud Functions), a Cloud Foundry-based aPaaS, and other PaaS capabilities. IBM also offers a Kubernetes- and container-based private cloud offering (IBM Cloud Private). Managed services are optional. Colocation needs are met via partner exchanges (IBM Cloud Direct Link).

§ 13.8.2 Locations

IBM has SoftLayer infrastructure in multiple data centers in the U.S., along with data centers in Canada, Mexico, Brazil, France, Germany, Italy, the U.K., the Netherlands, Norway, Australia, Hong Kong, India, Japan, Korea, Sweden and Singapore. IBM offers formerly Bluemix-branded services in the U.S., the U.K., Germany, Australia and Japan. IBM has a global sales presence. It offers support in the wide range of languages in which IBM does business. The portal and documentation are available in English, French, German, Italian, Portuguese, Spanish, Simplified Chinese, Traditional Chinese, Korean and Japanese.

§ 13.8.3 Adoption profile

IBM appeals to its existing customers who have a strong preference to purchase most of their technology from IBM. These customers primarily have Mode 1 use cases. However, IBM Cloud infrastructure capabilities may also be used to complement other IBM solutions, such as Watson.

§ 13.8.4 Recommended uses

IBM outsourcing deals that use bare-metal servers as the hosting platform, where the customer has a need for supplemental basic cloud IaaS. The infrastructure may also be used as a component of applications built using the IBM Cloud PaaS capabilities. It should also be considered in circumstances that require both API control over scalable infrastructure and bare-metal servers in order to meet requirements for performance, regulatory compliance or software licensing.

Disclaimer: IBM did not respond to requests for supplemental information or for a review of the draft contents of this research. Therefore, Gartner analysis is based on other credible sources, including public information.

§ 13.8.5 Strengths

IBM has a very large base of customers with critical applications that are beginning to adopt cloud services. IBM is well positioned to partner its service businesses to assist these customers through the cloud transformation journey.

IBM has a strong brand and existing customer relationships across the globe, and can offer support in local languages, local contracts and billing in local currency. IBM's base of strategic outsourcing customers may help to drive adoption of IBM Cloud infrastructure.

IBM has transitioned to messaging around hybrid and multicloud computing, which does not directly challenge many of the providers in this Magic Quadrant. Rather, it offers capabilities and tooling to enterprises, allowing them to choose the cloud environment that is best for their specific application requirements, positioning IBM Cloud as a niche or specialty offering during the selection process.

§ 13.8.6 Cautions

IBM's Next-Generation Infrastructure (NGI) project has produced incremental improvements to the infrastructure services formerly under the SoftLayer umbrella. However, it has not delivered on its fundamental goal — to produce a new set of cloud IaaS offerings based on the principles of hyperscale architecture. Given this, it is unlikely that IBM will become a competitive public cloud IaaS provider.

Despite having many worldwide data centers, the IBM Cloud experience remains disjointed, as many features are available only in specific locations. This and an unexceptional user experience cause IBM to have a higher level of user dissatisfaction than other vendors in this research.

IBM has a smaller ecosystem of partners that provide adjacent tooling (e.g., cost management, security, governance). Additionally, it has fewer partnerships (in comparison to other providers) with major software vendors (Microsoft, SAP, Oracle) that could culminate in deployments on the IBM Cloud.

§ 13.9 EXAMPLES OF HOW THE CLOUD SERVICE IMPLEMENTED IN REAL BUSINESS PRACTICES

With these serves from the cloud computing front runners in a nutshell, we can envision that many focuses of these services are capacity/hardware based (such as MSP) and mainly reply on computing power, storage capacity, and network bandwidth etc. These services, mostly like a linear aggregated pile of resources, opening to both business entities and individual requests. The bigger the data, the larger share of the resources, the infrastructure will grow and expend proportional to the demanding and they are linearly one-to-one mapping. The MSP, on-line markets, and many other listing and publishing services in Amazon are in this category (the VMware is under Amazon now). Microsoft, with the new awarded government project, adding their GitHub hosting service, and more, has already been the home for some business entities. Here is an example, NTT Data Corporation is a Japanese system integration company and a partially-owned subsidiary of Nippon Telegraph and Telephone (NTT). NTT Data is using Microsoft's Share-Point services, an MSP kind, to manage and host all their company services, including portals such like, human resources' benefits, company training programs, employee's time keeping, and many more. For NTT Data, they need neither a full IT department nor the whole hardware system, thus reduces the business running cost and infrastructure capital. Google also offers similar services, albeit going a little too far just for the purpose of avoiding Microsoft's various platforms - which actually has caused a lot of self-inflicted issues as listed by Gartner reported (additionally, as the business practice, the Google sheets, which is lacking a lot of functions and the full macro capability offered by MS Excel, to compensate, Google office suite, Google docs — Google Slides — Google Sheets, offers their own scripting language, which have never been welcomed by the existing excel users' communities and had never been embraced so far. Google is trying to make Google software suite as the only platform for many services, they have not made their production compatible with the existing office Suite. As the end-user, especially inside Google, the employees find it is extremely inconvenient to use an immature and insufficient office suite while the expertise in MS office have to be put on hold. To give a practical scenario, when to sort and review large amount of data array, the numbers of rows and columns are big, there is a function in MS excel to eliminate the identical rows. In Google sheets, if you ask for this function, they would suggest you to vote for this function to be added in in the future edition, exhibiting the latency and immaturity. Even though, Google sheets are the office sheets to use regardless.) Of course, they are ample success suites in Google products. The Gmail is one of them, one of the successful MSPs on Google's plate. Most traditional big companies have their own system for all the communications. Such as IBM, which has the Java based IBM (Lotus) Notes, including email service, IBM SameTime (Sametime Communicate, Sametime Conference, Sametime Complete, and Sametime Unified Telephony), and so on. Outside IBM, almost nobody uses them, although this gives IBM system a layer of protection; but in the same time, IBM became increasingly isolated. With the success of Gmail system, some companies, for the sake of avoiding the hefty cost of both software (MS office) and hardware (email servers, communication platforms), as well as human resource (large IT team), turn to "rent" these services from outside. GlobalFoundries (GF, it is not small, but relatively new) was a typical example. GF is an American semiconductor foundry headquartered in Santa Clara (this headquarter is now closed and the current headquarter is located in Malta, NY). GF was created by the divestiture of the manufacturing arm of Advanced Micro Devices (AMD). The Emirate of Abu Dhabi is the owner of the company through its subsidiary Advanced Technology Investment Company (ATIC). From 2015-2017, GF launched the transition campaign of "Going Google", after a period of preparation, GF fully switched to Google's Gmail for their company business email services and Google Slides, Google Docs, and Google Sheets as official business office suits. However, all the employees are still having MS Office installed. The real cost may be from the reduction of the IT head count, IT hardware maintenance, and the IT service hardware. For curiosity on how the Gmail for business is implemented, here it is. If you need use business email, you are on the same interface of the free Gmail portal; however, in the email user name filed, you will need to input the full email address for the specific company: your email address for the specific company is still the same. In this case, if Taylor Swift is with GF, what does she need to put in the email user name field is: taylor.swift@globalfoundries.com as the Gmail user name — her password is omitted here to protect her personal credential.

The cloud services, of course, always seek the biggest margin for the profits. Fundamentally, they have not changed the general course of the data flow and algorithms used to handle the interconnected information. The data piles up, the bandwidth adds up, the computing power enhances; with the exponentially "graph" connections, the growth of hardware and capacity are normally not able to match exponentially, best bet is polynomial. From this point of view, although some of these cloud front runners hold huge capitals, construct strong hardware foundation, but their core is mostly working on the moving the discrete data chunks, instead of DAAI scheme revolution. We have to examine other entities.

CHAPTER 14: LINEAR-PROPORTIONAL ENHANCED INFRA-STRUCTURE IS NOT A MATCH FOR THE EXPONENTIALLY BOOMED BIG DATA EXCHANGE (LINKS OF THE NODES ON A GRAPH)

§ 14.1
COMMUNICATIONS CAN BE FAST OR SLOW, THE JUSTIFICATION IS GET THE JOB DONE

People are now increasingly connected and dynamically interacting each other with full 24/7 spectrum. Sometimes at work, I got a ping form HR and was requested a video conference call, after everything sorted out for the meeting agenda, I realized the caller was actually 2000 miles away. It was not surprising if we had a scheduled video conference, however, when this kind of fully unprepared event happened and moved on, I was still a bit surprised by the format and the approach to address an issue in a matter of minutes (< 3 minutes) with the current existing infrastructure.

About two decades ago, when we were on a timely

scheduled distance-driving to Atlanta to catch a flight, my vehicle's fuel pump failed without warning (always the case for these "viscera" parts), the vehicle was in a total silent without any trace of noise or sound that could lead to a quick diagnosis (I did not know the issue by then). Stalled along the side of highway, then the relatively new gadget cell phone was really put into full display on the power of communication, sorted out all the issues quickly (calling for airline to postpone our flight, calling for AAA service to tow our vehicle. Really saved us from that difficult situations. As compare, half decade before that event, when we locked our car key inside the car, we had to go to a McDonalds' along the highway to borrow their landline phone to call a locksmith. That was the back trip from our first Disney visiting after first time obtaining the driving license.) In a larger theater of total operation, the dynamically developed and randomly generated events often warrant the attentions and immediate responses, the detecting, assessing, and addressing an issue are critical for smooth operations.

§ 14.2 DURABILITY IS NOW ON SOFTWARE: F-35 JOINT STRIKE FIGHTER VS BOEING 737 MAX PASSENGER PLANE WITHOUT MENTIONING STARLINER

The challenges of DAAI deployments expose the intrinsic shortcomings in the IAAD establishing process, as we had addressed in the previous sections. Since the IAAD process had not fully grasped the entire representation of the original entity, the re-creating process subsequently face challenges of recapturing the full feathered bird.

In a micro- scrutinized examining, one will see the bandwidth issue, hardware vs software resource balance, and ultimately to the final flashing software's error handling and bugs. I am tirelessly bringing this topic up again, the F-35 Joint Strike Fighter. Software was a great portion of the F-35 jet, which has been designed with synergy among sensors for many specific requirements. The aircraft's "senses" had been expected to provide a more cohesive picture of the battlespace around it and available for use in any possible way and combination with one another. **The sensor fusion software has been described as one of the most difficult parts of the program. The difficulty of integrity, which is the primary function of DAAI process.** Much of the F-35's software is written in C and C++ because of programmer availability; Ada 83 code (Ada was a result of blending and extending from Pascal and other languages) as a heritage from the F-22 program. The Integrity DO-178B real-time operating system (RTOS) from Green Hills Software runs on COTS Freescale (Freescale Semiconductor, Inc. was an American multinational corporation, On December 7, 2015, NXP Semiconductors completed its merger with Freescale) PowerPC processors. **The final Block 3 software was planned to have 8.6 million lines of code.** General Norton Schwartz has said that the software was the biggest factor that might delay the USAF's initial operational capability. Michael Gilmore, Director of Operational Test & Evaluation, wrote that, "the F-35 mission systems software development and test is tending towards familiar historical patterns of extended development, discovery in flight test, and deferrals to later increments". **US congress described this software suite as complicated as anything on earth on the wake of a serial of software bug related issues** (for a few times, the F-35 had been grounded for related flight incidents).

Now the Boeing 737 Max fleet is still grounded, the price has to be paid for the rushing into market because of business competing with Airbus. Boeing's reputation of reliability was pretty solid comparing with peers (outside the military contracts). Boeing had been apt to adopting new technologies fast and spearheadedly, this tendency had caused Boeing to have lost the lucrative government contract on the very F-35 program to Lockheed Martin. In that instance, Boeing was using carbon fiber for the jet frame structure while Lockheed Martin used more expensive and harder obtained full Titanium-alloy; and the later won the contract. Now, ironically, on the fate of software suite delivery to the planes, they have converged into same ill-fated software glitches. While Lockheed Martin can mend their mistakes largely hidden, which is always the benefits of government and military contracts, Boeing is treading water now for the responsibilities on the software glitches, which had not only deployed prematurely, knowingly manipulated the public understanding on the matter, especially airline customers' awareness, not only in a strategic and systematic level, but also in multiple disastrous accidents with great numbers of fatalities.

More items in the basket of nonfulfillment were numerous reports on the autonomous vehicles or ASE (Autonomous Sentient Entity), most publicized were Tesla electronic cars and Uber's Ride hailing services. Although there are many parts for the developers to check out, these incidents have a common ground: rushing into the markets without extensive test cycles, either eyes on competing market share, or creating social splash, and so on. Whatever the reasons for their accelerated deployments, the challenges and difficulties are rooted deeply inside the DAAI execution: akin to the reverse engineering of analog things in the nature. Simply put, as we have referred to in this book, Google's Waymo had also participated the autonomous vehicles' research as early as any other companies; however, Waymo ultimately concluded that their autonomous cars had not been ready for the street yet. On the other hand, Tesla model 3 cannot detect the street traffic lights so far, with all the fine prints nobody read, Tesla had been marketing their vehicles "auto pilot", a phrase that general customers would consider as autonomous driving.

Boeing Starliner glitch failed space station rendezvous; early landing ordered, as reported by CBS news and the software glitches are at the center, as we have touched base on this in the previous chapters.

§ 14.3 ASE/ AUTONOMOUS VEHICLES, THE OUTLOOK AND THE BOTTOM LINE

Back to the drawing board, even before the examples of practical failures of these deployments, we had revealed the intrinsic shortcomings of the original IAAD extracting process, as the building blocks for all the infrastructures, nature languages come the first; computer programming languages the second. These primary tokens and terms had never given a second thought on their validations of the matching and fitting for their described targets. As the butterfly effect runs deeper, the end products of the DAAI, goes easily off the track.

The quest for our journey here is, with all the aforementioned deep-dives for these events and developments of the current society, to shed light on the fundamental issues on the homo sapiens understanding, interacting, and navigating through the maze of the universe. Find the cadence and tune in the rhythm in the nature without resorting destructive approaches and brutal forces. Planting the seeds of nature and harmony in lieu of sophisticated engineering mandate or business greedy. Solving the AI challenge wisely and in its due development course: a successful trajectory of modus operandi.

Waymo CEO's John Krafcik doesn't think the industry will ever be able to make the autonomous vehicles to run at any time of year in any weather and any condition, "You don't know what you don't know until you're actually in there and trying to do things" even though driverless cars are "truly here." How we understand and perpetrate John's words? As the autonomous car company, Mr. Krafcik would normally be anticipated to speak like Elon Musk or the top executives in Boeing. Full of promise and encouragements, or have to be read between lines as the words from Michael Gilmore, the F-35 Director of Operational Test & Evaluation, "the F-35 mission systems software development and test is tending towards familiar historical patterns of extended development, discovery in flight test, and deferrals to later increments". In other words, blow up the balloon first, if it pops out ... actually, that was always the pattern of what the government agencies are doing. NASA, have traditionally come out with a moderate budget, then double, the best bet; triple, or even higher budget demanding to the congress with the program hung in air — even though, NASA does not get what they want sometimes. For autonomous vehicles, this pattern is bad, at the cost of human's life. And for a commercial airplane company like Boeing, it can be considered a most malicious intended nightmare, results have been already out there.

For a high-level homo sapiens, it is pretty pessimistic to picture that the autonomous vehicles pile up on the road. In the meantime, we respect and value John Krafcik's comments really high for his honest in his position. When I was talking with automobile industry executives and semiconductor chip design sector senior directors, I was drilling down for the desperations and the possibilities on these new emerging technology breeds. What I learned and intuited from our conversation is, quite dialectical balanced situation: in which, a process, here a phenomenal new technology, of evolution does not naturally fit within normal logic perspective. This process may rely on the evolution of ideas over long period in the real world. In simple terms, the sophisticated process to realize this new technology will be determined by the future developments with aggressive methodologies to address the emerging issues.

Autonomous vehicles, or self-driving cars, are a sophisticated system and post a beautiful challenge for the DAAI applications. The sheer degrees of accuracy to attain, the methodically complete modeling for the unstructured problem, the balanced checks both for technique safety and publicized social attention, plus many other elements, all drive this industry sector to a paramount maturity all at once, and once for all the needs. Never before in the history, military purposed projects apart, the density of software algorithms, the width of universally applications, the depth of social runs, and the enthusiasm of expectations, are so solely focused on one set of enginery. Not a sketch, not a bare metal, it is a matter of real test on the true integrity of an inorganic man-made organism: the life form of ASE.

§ 14.4 DIALOGUES WITH PIONEERING INDUSTRY BUSINESS EXECUTIVES

There are a lot of visionary ideas and proposals out there. Among these demand-based solutions, as my interviews with this industry pioneers, dynamic connectivity is one of the unique and greener spots across the whole desert landscape. Nothing less to emphasis the importance of the variety of all the sensors (radar, laser, motion, cameras etc.), GPS, and so on. The proposed mutual connectivity in a real time dynamic scenario adds another practical layer of situation fitness. Connectivity means that users of a certain digital technology can connect easily with other users, other applications or even other enterprises. In the case of autonomous vehicles, it is essential for them to connect with other 'devices' in order to function most effectively. Autonomous vehicles can be equipped with communication systems which allow them to communicate with other autonomous vehicles and roadside units to provide them, amongst other things, with information about road work or traffic congestion. In addition, scientists believe that in the future there will be computer programs that connect and manage each individual autonomous vehicle as it navigates through an intersection. This type of connectivity must add on top of the traditional traffic lights and stop signs. The autonomous vehicles will understand and cooperate this type of characteristic devices and other future products and services (such as intersection computer systems) brought in the autonomous vehicles field. This can lead all the autonomous vehicles to use the same network and share information across that network. Eventually, this can encourage more autonomous vehicles using the network because the information has been validated through the usage of other autonomous vehicles. Such movements will strengthen the value of the network and is called network externalities.

Actually, if we check the history of a new emerging technologies, all following the patterns: comes out with the existing infrastructure as the starting phase; with the demanding and protocol maturity, either improves (with back compatibility) or total redesigns (exploiting full potential) eventually followed.

The aforementioned connectivity and infrastructure additions, including but not limited to, e- traffic lights, e- stop signs, e- lane boundary marks, and may be the rules of priority, specialized lanes as far as 3D type layers of transportations like the New York grand central station. All these, currently, are just perspectives and some are imaginations; however, this may fundamentally change ways of human dwelling patterns in the future. If the invention of locomotive had stimulated the railway system, in which the US is currently far behind the other countries — and the first world automatic high apeed rail has just been in operation: to be utilized during the 2022 winter olympic games (https://www.railwaygazette.com/high-speed/bei-jing-zhangjiakou-pdl-inaugurated-with-national-timetable-change/55435.article) — thanks to the conservative and profit-driven big US automobile and oil businesses, and the invention of automobile (plus the second world war) had lead the construction of the national highways systems, it is not all elusive to conceive the idea that the demanding of the brand new hardware, software, and real-time information sharing, thus the DAAI, autonomous vehicles can stimulate the all new global scale transportation revolution.

Granted that delightful perspective, challenges and ground works remain ahead with all the obstacles from the unfitting and "You don't know what you don't know until you're actually in there and trying to do things." Once we are getting close touches with mother nature, all the imaginations are subject to reality test. You are not sitting in an oval office doing fantasy and twittering, or launching propaganda campaigns. If you said you can go across a river, you will have to find means for you to stay floating on top of the water, if you are not doing it right, you "wet your pants" and may be more, the least per se.

§ 14.5 CHECKING OUT BABY YODA (MEME) FROM THE STAR WARS: THE MANDALORIAN

As in the "epic" Disney+ launching failure, in which the most requests came from the new TV series premiere *the Star Wars: The Mandalorian*. Aside from the launching failure, here we talk about *The Mandalorian* and its content: in all fantasy and metallic grand, these flying objects never sinks even if the cartoon design algorithm was not properly applied. The weaponry always fires regardless the form factors of the barrel and the body. They may launch flame from normal rifle and so on, all depends on the screen writer's appetite. Anything can function or nothing can function regardless the bugs and worms in the software packages, which had caused one of the critical failures of the F-35 joint fighter because the software bug had caused the air pressure in the chamber fluctuation, which will never happen in *The Mandalorian* except purposely in screen writer's appetite. In virtual land, there is no hard core and stringent point to point checking and matching for the system to function, it just functions, regardless. The renowned baby Yoda, albeit in his 50s already, does not mentally perceiving a danger. Thus, baby Yoda radiates the innocence of cute and appeals moving affections. As, a result, the baby Yoda meme went viral overnight. Let's dissect this very meme for our theme purpose.

First let walk through the steps to save our research target the baby Yoda video, as it is happening/trading right now.

§ 14.6 ANATOMY
OF BABY YODA

- Google "Baby Yoda Meme" Most of them lead to a Twitter site, in which the animation is in MP4 format (Twitter converts all animation to MP4 to play, thus easy to shield from "save as"). If you right click the lovely meme from Twitter site, you cannot save as, instead, you can only "copy video address", so copy it. Got:
  - https://twitter.com/i/status/1200458953865326592
- Go to here:
  - https://ezgif.com
  - Choose "Video to GIF" now your led to:
  - https://ezgif.com /video-to-gif
  - Paste the above twitter address into the box below "OR paste video url:"
- After click the "upload video!", you can click the floppy disk icon "save" (will download) to your local computer.
  - ezgif.com-video-to-gif.mp4
  - with info:
  - 45.2 KB (46,333 bytes)
  - Now you can analysis the mp4 using any handy software and stop reading the following.
  - Should you be lazy or do not know

> how to analysis, you can keep reading...
>
> ○ However, the MP4 was converted from "GIF" when Twitter published it. This GIF was showed in Twitter site: if you paste the Twitter URL into any browser address bar, you will be led to Twitter site. Thus the original file is "GIF"

- Without input anything, scroll down and click the "Convert to GIF!" button you get as GIF formation animation file (with frame rate 10 fps), counting 3.2 seconds total, the GIF animation has total 32 pictures/frames.

- Scroll down and click the "floppy disk 'save'" below the image, it will download the animation GIF file into your local computer.

- For the purpose of easy analysis, let's perform on-site analysis by clicking "frames"-'view and edit frames' Now you have the full display of all the embedded pictures in the Baby Yoda animated movie.

The frame-by-frame layout for the baby Yoda meme from *The Mandalorian*. After this dissection, the sensational viral meme all but 32 pictures played out in certain time sequence. Extracting, saving, converting, processing the video have been detailed in the context.

You do not need to be a forensics expert for examine the scenes. One of the immediate evidences you may discover is that the 50-year-old Yoda's mouth-slit was close-shut the whole time: movements and expressions before and after the sipping action. Set aside the unproportional facial features and none-coordinated movements, for this of creation, if put in the rigorous scenarios like the self-driving car, baby Yoda is doomed to starve or facing all kind of jeopardies in life, not only because the retarded mentality but also because his mouth-slit has been "designed with erratic algorithm" which lacked "sipping" mechanism.

Last but not least, since there is no way to animate the

GIF on baby Yoda via Kindle Create, I host the animated GIF elsewhere:

https://1.bp.blogspot.com/-cYMABbb66Fc/Xg19hAI-kOOI/AAAAAAAAACA/y1T8eBW_8v4pdnUQqboDnD-vWvdyjlTofQCEwYBhgL/s1600/Baby%2BYoda%2BTakes%2BOver%2BKermit%2BFor%2BMost%2BLoved%2BMeme.gif

CHAPTER 15: AI BUILDING BLOCKS AND RESOURCES

§ 15.1 WHEN IN ROME, DO AS THE ROMANS DO

Since we are in the social platforms' era, we will talk like a pro: do as the social media does.

The "You don't know what you don't know until you're actually in there and trying to do things" tells the real difficulties these AI pioneers are facing. You are not knowing until it happens. In the first layer, that is directly linked the software program error handling. We are about to code for the demonstration purpose. As Python ranks the #1 on the list of the current programming languages, it is the proper language to set this on. First let's examine all the Python building blocks/resources as start.

Python has a set of keywords that are reserved words those cannot be used as variable names, function names, or any other identifiers. And here's a list of all keywords in Python Programming:

Full list of Python keywords:

```
and       A logical operator
as         To create an alias
assert  For debugging
break    To break out of a loop
class    To define a class
continue           To continue to the next iteration of a loop
def       To define a function
del       To delete an object
elif      Used in conditional statements, same as else if
else      Used in conditional statements
except  Used with exceptions, what to do when an exception occurs
False    Boolean value, result of comparison operations
finally Used with exceptions, a block of code that will be executed no
matter if there is an exception or not
for        To create a for loop
from      To import specific parts of a module
global  To declare a global variable
if          To make a conditional statement
import  To import a module
in          To check if a value is present in a list, tuple, etc.
is          To test if two variables are equal
lambda  To create an anonymous function
None      Represents a null value
nonlocal           To declare a nonlocal variable
not        A logical operator
or          A logical operator
pass      A null statement, a statement that will do nothing
raise    To raise an exception
return   To exit a function and return a value
True      Boolean value, result of comparison operations
try        To make a try...except statement
while    To create a while loop
with      Used to simplify exception handling
yield    To end a function, returns a generator
```

33 words in grand total.

Your options of creating the world have to be from these 33 building blocks, essentially.

Oops! This is the revelation on where and why are the "holes" in the "loop" of DAAI deployments. To address anything, you need for a specific scenario, your options are limited within the above 33 building blocks.

§ 15.2 WORKING LIKE A PRO WITH "ELITIST" LANGUAGE PYTHON

As we are trying to bring forward our sample code in Python, we have the first dilemma: after carefully examining, the "all things considered statement" keyword cannot be found in the list. If you have learned a little on the coding, you may have known that keyword is "switch" statement, which exists in C/C++, Java, R, JavaScript, and even in spread sheet MS excel; in the oldest language Fortran, it is "SELECT ... CASE", in Bill Gates & Paul Allen's BASIC, it is "ON ... GOTO/GOSUB", and in the AI coding language created by MIT John McCarthy Lisp (LIST Processor, second oldest computer language after Fortran), you have "CASE" construct, the very primitive language ASM (assembly language), can also implement switch case statement.

Good Lord! The switch statement does not exist in Python, which has been ranked the #1 programming language for the latest social media "networking" community and to process the big data of the things. If using this first ranked Python to write the AI-purposed software, the must-have all-situation considered launch pad cannot find a solid ground: this, and at least part of this very awkward schema, might be the smoking gun for the failed execution of the DAAI projects. Using a language that is short of all-round consideration (i.e. switch statement is one of them), how to build a real-world function system that is working in all "weather" scenarios! The biggest hole so far for in the whole loop of the eco, in terms of coding convenience, at the minimum.

Since Python language doesn't have a switch statement, as the consequence, for our programming purpose, we will have to create something that functions like the all things considered statement.

Here is the same code, for example to "AI" the traffic lights. Provided the color detecting sensors are functional and in place without the problems like the "sensor fusion software" in F-35 program (they all sensor handling, though). For the RGY coding: red light, green light, and yellow light, albeit no car now able to obey the traffic lights properly. The sloppy and lazy, or the great part of python is that you can write a code without the header and footer, just a line of code will work (with the expense of big background interpretation software engine), so the code will look like this (by defining a function):

```
function(RGY){
    switch(RGY) {
        case 0:
          return "Stop!";
        case 1:
          return "Continue moving";
        case 2:
          return "Wait! (not moving)";
        default:
          return "nothing";
    };
};
```

Of course, there are many other scenarios, red flashing (4 ways/2 ways), yellow flashing, then the "entity" will have to observe the surrounding and take actions.

§ 15.3 BKM 0.1

In the simplest scenario, a first version (In high-tech company, especially high-complexity fabrication process, the methodology to establish a acceptable platform is long — they can be called "BKM 0.1": best known method version 0.1, not there yet for Version 1.0) from a programmer would be dealing with these RGB situation BKM 0.1: Suppose PG&E decides to shut down the power again. The above code will not able to handle the situation of all lights out (of course, there is emergency power sources for traffic light, should there is a planned power outage). This is the simple bug that the programmer shall to debug. Even though, the above code has a basket for default: if we have set the default action is stop! Then there will be no traffic accident for this kind of unknow, to the least of safety. However, as the story told in Tesla and Uber cases, their vehicles had not stop. With an unknown case not in the code selection, they had chosen to speed head on and caused disastrous consequences, how they can let the vehicle run driverlessly! The bugs in this piece of code will need to be debugged: (traffic lights) all out, flashing, partially broken, police overriding, and many more. See! Writing a piece code is not that difficult, but the maturity is the biggest challenges.

Simply because there are so many missed links when the homo sapiens try to represent the natural events. And the digitalizing process of the first phase: IAAD, has tossed away the living essential: the integration mechanism, albeit with piles of discrete data points.

The above mocking code of Python for autonomous vehicles is an example, but from this extreme simple case, some obvious "holes" in the loop (IAAD -> DAAI)can be observed, in a similar analogical approach that we had partitioned the situations into IAAD vs DAAI, this specific case can be panned out and address our topic of interest.

CHAPTER 16: THE INSIDE-OUT OF THE AI: FROM IAAD TO DAAI

§ 16.1 THE DISCOURSE OF IAAD

§ 16.1.1 IAAD tSpace to enSpace: Natural Phenomena to English Language

Original thing representation (instead of using object, we use a hot word "thing," tailored from IOT "internet of things"). In the traffic light thing, the representation's first layer is the human language descriptions. Does English language, in words, phases, sentences, statements, and many more (in that Python RGY code, polices and citations might be also involved), has enough capacity to represent the event that is happening in the real tSpace domain?

Actually, we do not know? But conceptionally, we cannot think our way out in a domain (enSpace) that creates such conceptions. For now, as there is no better way out of this dead loop, we will leave it there, and jump to the next by assuming that the English languages is complete. Despite the fact that Shakespeare was able to complete all his conceptions and representations in 31,534 words, somehow, he had to invent 1,700 words for the proper description (that accounted 5.4% of insufficiency of English. With another assumption that 20% of these deficiency are fatal in traffic like AI projects, it would have resulted more than 1% fatality). This might tell us that English in deed is not sufficient to express all you want to express. Now, with more than 218,000 words (including more than 40,000 obsoleted) have been used in English, we just hope the pool is enough, no matter what, there is no option to complete the language pool quickly and easily. The universe, the tSpace of mother nature and everything inside it, are to be recreated and represented with these 218 K English words within the enSpace "universe".

§ 16.1.2 enSpace to iSpace: From English Language to Computer Programming Languages

Second round distillation. This time, it is the transcoding from English language to the computer languages, from which the computer or any electronic gadgets can pick up and carry out the task as loyalty as they can.

Now, things get awkward and obvious.

You have 33 options to select from for the creation based on the enSpace plots (with 218 k different building blocks) and this very creation will function in the unlimited tSpace domain (some of the tSpace phenomena have not been properly represented in the enSpace manifolds yet: the quantum entanglement, for the least example).

The theme thread of IAAD vs DAAI evolving has never been so explicitly articulated to the extent of artificial intelligence: the layers of difficulties and the awkwardness of representations. With the perseverance in dissection and patience in-depth mining, the innate flaws and looping holes have been evidently elucidated.

That's as simple as that.

No matter how almighty talent you have, with merely 33 words (we just use Python as example) to form a fabric to hold the whole structure of the universe, the net must be very sparse, that is 12,762 cubic billion light-years volume for each keyword to represent consider the current observable universe has a diameter of 93 billion light-years [(4/3) x PI x (93/2)^2=421,160 'cubic billion light-years', with PI=3.14].

With the example of the above coding sample. No further emphasis is necessary.

§ 16.2 THE DISCOURSE OF DAAI

§ 16.2.1 Natural Change from Red to Green Is not easy While <0|1> Transition Is

In the DAAI reverse engineering execution process, applications to the real-world scenarios are deployed and implemented. All the processed soul food from the whole civilization history and "things" can be referred and used to fulfil the tasks for the ultimate success. However, most of the cases, people create the end products predominantly based on the scopes and constrains in the iSpace, which is the IAAD depositories from the entire fabrication as explicated in the preceded sectons. As the F-35 director stated: the process had to be (forced) phased into a build-up and then step-by-step improving phases, at least for the military applications. With the limited representative tokens, i.e. 33 in Python (20 below the Google's owned D-wave quantum's computer qubits, 53, even with all sort of functions and subroutines), the prototypes could hardly escape an artist conception of the toy (as in the case of *the Star Wars: The Mandalorian*). Of course, we have specifically limited our scope within the Python, ironically, the tech crowds love it as their #1 choice.

The migration to Python (from C++, Java, etc.) loosens a lot of checks and restrictions in the code writing. In the meantime, the code, even runs, bears a lot of holes (bugs), it can be deployed on a grandma's chatting suites with these dismays. However, the fooling around business practices have to be kept at bay and never out of the bottle. Think about the Twitter, you still can understand your president's intention "**Despite the constant negative press covfefe [sic].**" Picture that apply this (the president's language skill) to the Green vs Red traffic light scenarios (from the view point of a computer, Green and Red can be interpreted as token "1" or "0". The slipping from "0" to "1" or vice versa, is not as difficult as to move the wavelength from 0.54 um, middle wavelength of red, to 0.67 um, middle wavelength of green. This has inherited from the step 2 of IAAD process, from the enSpace human languages to the iSpace computer languages transcoding process; paradoxically, starting from the human languages, the continue light spectra had been partitioned into and represented by a handful color names) that would be produce totally different consequences, none of them could be interpreted as pretty.

§ 16.2.2 With Heavily Human Engineered Entities, The DAAI Starts Awkwardly

For the DAAI phase of recreating of the real-world things, the topmost constrains are the starting set of building blocks. A tiger of paper does not carry Tiger's strength, and the traditional method of divide and conquer meets the intrinsic difficult by the method itself. In one of the align GYM classes, I've heard what the instructor said this, think the body as a whole entity and they work collectively; often a pain in one muscle is the consequence of the others. The connecting tissues, contrary to people think traditionally — only the muscles are the part to take care for the pain, are equally important because they form an integrity like a mesh and all the muscles are filling into their pockets. I was surprised to hear this from a lady on massage. So, I questioned her sources of her aforementioned knowledge. The answer from her did not embrace the "cognitive consciousness thinking" or "the mechanism of referral pain" (she did mention referral pain, but said, nobody knew why), the general conclusion for me to borrow here, is the requirement of her massage outcome matching to the reality in this tSpace: releasing pain or not. She had massaged a lot of people (had all kinds of pains and issues in their bodies), she had to match her practice (although massages, but most of the cases for these who had neck issues, back issues, knee issues, and so on) to the result that she brought to her customers. On one side, she had to be diligent to learn and read; at the end of the day, the ultimate sine qua non that has pushed her in such an understanding was the constant reality check: she has to be objective (from her point of view) to cure this often-called subjective symptoms (pain).

Unfortunately, the starting point of the DAAI, is from a very little subset of the intelligent resources. With the "benefit" of concise selection on the elements, the path to a successful representation of the versatile tSpace reality is an uphill path, "materials and resources" wise, at least an exponential expansion, to match the things. With a porous iSpace shaking infrastructure, the construction will never be a one-step thing, unless an all-considered comprehensive new infrastructure has been fully built.

§ 16.2.3 The Starting Kit
Had not Been for Real but
with a Game Mindset

Using Python as an example, the analogical narrative clearly portrays the insufficient accumulation on the IAAD elements, the multiple-step condensation processes. These inabilities and shortcomings had never loomed so large as the autonomous vehicles, which are real-world utilities with life or death concerns. In virtual games or current realities representations, a drifting white mass is a cloud, a green "floor-scape" can be a grass landscape, a linked 3-point moving object can be a bird, and so on. For the applications at these ends, not a lot of complaints because there are no hard boundaries to hold these and there is no obvious consequence for the designs. Here is the Screenshot of the Microsoft Donkey game in 1980s, from here, we can also get the simplified representation of the real things.

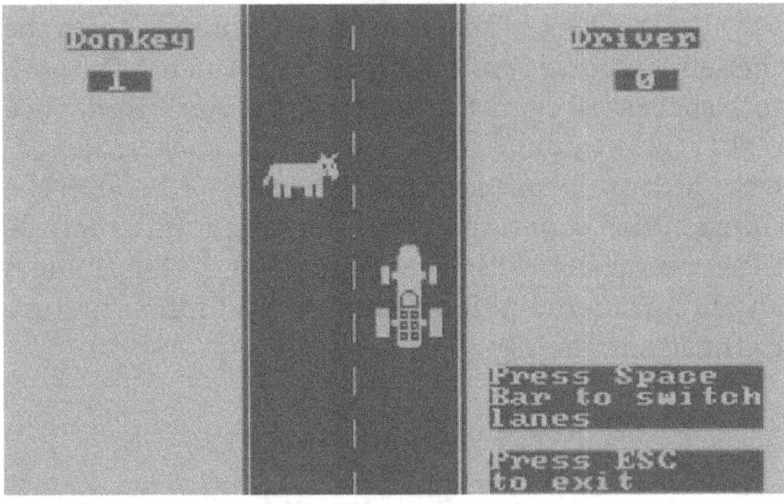

Actually, it was myself and Neil Konzen at four in the morning with this prototype IBM PC sitting in this small room. IBM insisted that we had to have a lock on the door and we only had this closet that had a lock on it, so we had to do all our development in there and it was always over 100 degrees, but we wrote late at night a little application to show what the Basic built into the IBM PC could do. And so that was Donkey. bas. It was at the time very thrilling.

——————Bill Gates

§ 16.3 LASER FOCUSING ON THE ASES FROM FRESH START

With all the issues from intrinsic flaws and limitations, what are the outlook on this self-driving car thing anyway? Although there are not as good as one may expected, they are still silver lines out there. As one of a kind ASE, the Autonomous Sentient Entity. Embracing great expectations, performing due diligence in all facets of layers and phases, employing real-time inter-communications, exhausting all the foreseen scenarios on debugging, preparing safety-baskets for all unknow events and many more. May be there is a possibility for the execution before the required infrastructure built up.

§ 16.3.1 Tabula Rasa

A total redesigned infrastructure. This is the fundamental artist's fantasy on this lane for now. However, as we have examined all the past emerging technological inventions, from automobile highway to information highway, they all have developed in a soft-revolution approach: in the first phase, restraining and holding while working hardly to fit into the old shoes, even with sharp aches in the toes; in the second phase, once grown up and strong enough, start flexing muscles and taking off, this time, the old foes finally realize that their days are numbered; with their desperate efforts of resisting and holding back, they are shipwrecking.

§ 16.3.2 Successful Story of Locomotives' Railroad

There is excellent story of born anew. The locomotive railway serves the best example in this category. Since the invention of the steam engine, the emerging technology was different from the moment of conceiving inside the cradle. That was simply because of that technology was not conceived inside any "thing" of the existing "things" (I found this is creepy for the "things" directly from internet of things and originally from, from a physicist point of view, starting from the "The theory of every 'thing'", article on PNAS by Bob Laughlin, Stanford University, and David Pines, Princeton University). The railroad was a success. In Europe, Japan, and China, the modern high-speed railway system is the major transport means to carry the passengers, cargos, and most of all, the economies. The so-called belt and road initiative in the framework of Eurasia continental is a highway, rail and high-speed rail integrity, eyes on "moving" the economy. From a practical and geographical perspective, this is the most exigent demand for the general population and enhances the largest continental overall economy with balanced local micro-societies (there are always cold-war minded dudes in different views like the parties in congress). Comparing with the Trans-Pacific Partnership (TPP), the belt and road initiative is more civilians and wholesome, while the TTP is more of a political brainchild from cold war dudes. Why, there are so much vacuum in terms of markets in the central American, south American, and Africa, why not just open their doors and form partnership and help them develop, in the meantime, the Made in American products will find an unlimited depth of markets. But the hawks do not want that, which only "helps" the poor while the surge of hawk hormones in their blood cannot be released. If you measure the distance, the distance to Japan, a big player and enthusiasm, is much bigger than the distance to Brazil, to just name one out of many.

§ 16.3.3 High-Speed Rail

The railroad came out of nowhere in similarity with anything before and it was a success across the continentals around the globe. Here is US as well. Only the oil and automobile industry, for the best of their interest, they literally choked the US railroad. For the past century, that was not a big deal. In the meantime, United States can convert the past infertility in railroad into huge opportunity now. The US still can bypass the total period of traditional railroad recession, absorb all the experience in Europe and Asia, reach the ultimate high-speed railway maturity in one-step, and jump to the modern railroads. The mostly noticeable feature of it is the matured high-speed railway system based on better tracks and better engines, a gradually developed system with the wheels still on the track, physically touched. Another emerging technology is the levitation train. The whole train, including engines and coaches, are out of touch by the rail, which is actually the foundation of guideway, can be totally different depending on the levitation mechanisms used. In maglev technology, there are no moving parts (no friction such like in sliding or rotating). The train travels along a guideway of magnets which control the train's stability and speed. Maglev trains are therefore quieter and smoother than conventional trains, and have the potential for much higher speeds (Japanese Maglev Train clocked at 375 MPH). On the matured high-speed rail system, across Europe and most part of Asia, here is a personal experience. Landed from a plane originated from New York, transferred to high speed railway hub via airport shuttle, reached a small city 300 miles away in less than 2 hours (The high-speed train runs close to 200 MPH), which is quicker than the transferring airplanes here in US with two major advantages among others. The first advantage is the proximity to home, because there are more train stations than the airports as the simple truth; the second advantage is the comfortableness of traveling: The latest hardware of the high-speed train equipped with refined seats and air conditional system. With all electric-powered system, the train is quiet and very smooth; at the normal travel speed of 200 MPH, the water level in the mug on the table almost "pacific". In these cases, the high-speed railway shows superior advantages over airplane: another transfer to regional airline connection. With the well-integrated airport vs train stations, passengers do not have to experience another round connection of final airport to end destination (home, office, etc.)

§ 16.3.4 BKM 2.0 Path Forward
US on High-Tech Railway

For the success of high-speed rails in all other developed countries across world except in the United States, the US can catch up by the powerful industrial capacity. In one hand, that will really bring the jobs back to US; on the other hand, with the successful and failure stories in Europe, in Asia, United States can redesign a "BKM" Version 2.0 highspeed railway system with autonomous driving and future 3-D transporting system as the demanding theme, retake the leading role in this high technology territory. Because the automobile industry and the oil company had almost annihilated the railway system in the United States, for the bad side - the current existing railway foundations are thin and weak; for the bright side - there are less barriers for the impeccable new technologies to take the roots in fresh soil. United States can convert the disadvantages into opportunities: a clean starter and full embracing geographic open space. Such as the mobile pay system growing fast in the markets of some emerging economies.

§ 16.3.5 High-Speed Rail as ASE

The network of these railways in the mission of autonomous vehicles cannot be in the old design pattern. The vehicle running model, or the road utilizations should be much higher, with really close distance from vehicle to vehicle. Instead of the current thin and long stereotype, the network can be more interconnected like a net, an all connected entity. Even can be 3D, scale up to the air.

If we really examine the current high-speed rail, which is 100% closed, either high in the air or in the tunnel, even underground. Total leveled elevation and flatness require a fine-tuned design. In reality, most of the part are on the elevated tracks like the bridges or the highway cross-section structures.

The modern high speed rail system, mostly can be considered as closed.

With these new-conception infrastructures, the autonomous vehicles driverless driving can be the easiest part: simple because all the current troubles regarding on the complicated control just eliminated from the beginning: intrinsically inclines to fully autonomous.

§ 16.3.6 HIGH-SPEED RAIL ASE INAUGURATION DAY HAS BECOME HISTORY: A PICTURE BOOK OF HIGH SPEED RAIL ASE

The world's first high-speed railway on which self-driving trains can reach speeds of up to 350 kilometers per hour.

"Now, the drivers only need to push a button and the system will automatically speed up, slow down, stop and open the passenger doors,"said a high-speed train driver. "Intelligent high-speed railway line," the line features not only self-driving, but also intelligent modules including automatic lights and the Navigation Satellite System.

There are also 2,718 detectors on a train's single carriage that can detect the train's operations comprehensively. "We want to integrate high-speed train with various new technologies, like cloud computing, internet of things, big data and artificial intelligence, and make passengers feel at home." All the stations are equipped with smart devices, robots and 5G networks for the convenience of passengers.

Does that sound familar?!: in our book.

This section, § 16.3.6, is a last minute add-on, after all other parts completed.

(C)   https://newsus.cgtn.com/news/2019-12-30/China-s-Winter-Olympic-high-speed-railway-to-open-on-Monday--MO5HfJim9q/index.html

In this section, pictures are the means to illustrate the world first high-speed train: ASE' Inauguration:

Speed: 350 kmh ~218 mph

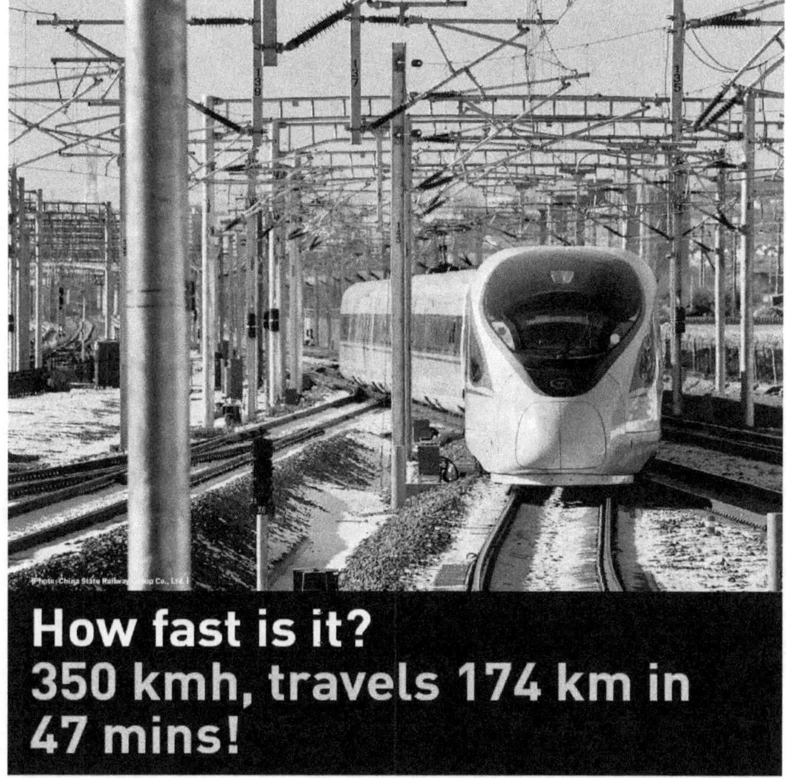

Mission: Welfare of 2022 Winter Olympics, a lot of people from all the world can experience and enjoy the riding (right).

The ASE takes off fully in high-speed rail on Dec 30, 2019. (below)

Locomotive of the autonomous high-speed train

§ 16.4 ASE GOES UP INTO THE AIR

Although Amazon lost the bid for the government project (JEDI), their idea using drones to deliver goods is a wonderful intention. Especially in the implementation of ASE. However, Amazon also lost to Google, who had firstly obtained the federal license for the drone delivery. Amazon has so far not been licenced.

(a) The air bound traffic throughput will be enormous, and the operation layers practically infinity.

(b) This design solves all the hard problems that the current self-driving cars have. Once again, it starts anew with all the troubles naturally non-existed.

(c) Autonomy is the backbone and foundation of the whole plot and no longer as a hard-achieved final goal.

(d) With the pioneer work of maturity of military applications, tons of "toy" drone products, and performance gaming/racing drones, the adopting and broadening processes are just a nature expansion.

(e) The integrity of the land, air, even the sea, can actually do away with the origins of all dilemmas, what is the point of put a human there inside. With all the goods smoothly conveyed and properly dispatched, the scenarios requiring a human being inside these vehicles greatly reduced.

(f) With all these in place, the human carrying vehicles can have priority and running on fast track, point-to-point, via a graph algorithm solution: in a 3D interconnected tSpace scope.

§ 16.5 FACING ALL THE CHALLENGES STEP-BY-STEP WITH DUE DILIGENCE

C lashing head-on for all the big and small hardware, systematic and particular software, as well as all sort of engineering integration due diligences.

Although no party claims explicitly, this is the state of current autonomous vehicles' development.

We have elucidated the intrinsic inadequacies, the original "sin" from the IAAD process with non-universally-represented DAAI precursor (the end result of IAAD), and twice "language-wise" processed "keywords", like the meat burned to a cinder, as well as the incompatible infrastructures for its developmental environment. Nonetheless, that does not warrant a total no-go blockage. Plenty successful stories out there, for the national priorities, we had the Apollo moon landing, Normandy landing, dust bowl management, to just name 3.

"We choose to go to the Moon in this decade and do the other things, not because they are easy, but because they are hard; because that goal will serve to organize and measure the best of our energies and skills, because that challenge is one that we are willing to accept, one we are unwilling to postpone, and one we intend to win, and the others, too.

"But why, some say, the Moon? Why choose this as our goal? And they may well ask, why climb the highest mountain? Why, 35 years ago, fly the Atlantic? Why does Rice play Texas? (a joke referring to the Rice–Texas football rivalry. In today's NBA, can be "Why everyone in NBA wants to beat the hell out of Warriors")

"We set sail on this new sea because there is new knowledge to be gained, and new rights to be won, and they must be won and used for the progress of all people."

Things were tough and elusive; however, with all the efforts and due diligences, the US had realized their national plan of "going to the Moon."

§ 16.5.1 Unstructured Problems of Catch-22

For these self-driving cars' tech companies, they have already at their wits' end for this catch-22 kind of unstructured problems. The 100% satisfied answer to bring them out of the woods does not exists and will likely never be, with the current automobiles' ground-work paved from the beginning of last century and for-tified for the WWII war model's German. Shying away from shaking up the traditional existing infrastructure universally keeps a tight rein on the autonomous ve-hicles albeit in their infancy. By going off at a tangent of the pivotal solutions as these illustrated brainchildren, due diligence in every developmental step and sector is a must; tedious work and endless effort on the refining processes for all these virtuous circles are their twin siblings. When the party's responsibility issues arise, lawsuits and new bills will storm all over, a trigger of society orthodoxy redefinitions.

§ 16.5.2 Applying AI is the Key

The centrepiece of the whole DAAI reconstruction is the AI deployment. The implementation of Self-driv-ing car, through AI, declares the full-scale matching between machines and homo sapiens for the first time in evolution history. As the humans themselves have not been fully equipped with the skill set and mental-ity to qualify all of them for the driving, a HI (human intelligence) selection procedure had already in place to ensure to screen off these unfit (failed to pass either writing test or road test). The emerging autonomous vehicles may need to follow the same suit to screen off the unfits. That will be an interesting development.

§ 16.5.3 Good Luck ASE with Brutal-Force approach

Finally, the brutal-force solution for the self-driving car, as our tech executives conversations has unveiled, might be the interconnections, namely among, vehicles vs satellites, vehicles vs uniform traffic control devices and signs, vehicles vs vehicles, vehicle situation manifest board vs human intervention, as well as the central traffic management hub, also autonomous or manned, to just name so many but still not all. This integrity is far more comprehensive than the current execution, in which only the first two categories have been employed.

§ 16.6 THERE THE INAUGURATION OF AUTONOMOUS HIGH-SPEED TRAIN IN ASIA HERE THE S*** HITS THE FAN: ANOTHER DEADLY SELF-DRIVING CAR ACCIDENT IN US

In § 16.3.6 High-Speed Rail ASE Inauguration Day Has Become History. Looking through the picture book of high speed rail ASE, the fast, dizzy, glamorous, and comfortable autonomous train has become a new breed of national luxury display, at this point, the technology has nothing to do with the United States, the US does not have anything on that level. The old school play book to fool the general population: ***You have this and I have this, so you must have copied from us!***

Which does not play out, as a result, all the news media just shut all these news out, and "shield" our tender public from these "toxic advancement" in technology, just like the first satellite from USSR.

But our media has at least one honest innate nature: to expose the ugly side of the s*** hits the fan, on the US turf.

In US News and World report:

Feds Will Investigate Deadly Tesla Crash in California

The National Highway Traffic Safety Administration is investigating the crash of a speeding Tesla that killed two people in a Los Angeles suburb.

The black Tesla Model S was on Autopilot when it crashed: had left a freeway and was moving at a high rate of speed when it ran a red light and slammed into a Honda Civic at an intersection on Dec. 29, 2019 in Gardena. A man and woman in the Civic died at the scene. A man and woman in the Tesla were hospitalized with non-life threatening injuries.

An NHTSA statement said the agency has assigned its special crash investigation team to inspect the car and the crash scene. That team has inspected a total of 13 crashes involving Tesla vehicles that the agency believed were operating on the Autopilot system.

Another Tesla crash killed a woman Sunday in Indiana and the Telsa driver was seriously injured after he rear-ended a fire truck parked along Interstate 70.

Earlier this month, a Tesla struck a police cruiser and a disabled vehicle in Connecticut.

the National Transportation Safety Board referred to it as **"automation complacency."**

For the best benefit for the US auto industry, albeit already left behind, and the "oil" business, the US will continue suppressing the high-speed rail and advocating freedom of automobile and boosting oil industry, such as the leaking Keystone Pipeline and the offshore oil spilling Deepwater Horizon thus to stimulate the endorphin secretion in the 1% population's nucleus accumbens.

ing freedom of automobile and boosting oil industry, such as the leaking Keystone Pipeline and the offshore oil spilling Deepwater Horizon thus to stimulate the endorphin secretion in the 1% population's nucleus accumbens.

CHAPTER 17: A BRIEF HISTORY OF MIND OF THE EARTH BRAIN

(Cover Story of Time Magazine on the golden jubilee of MOTEB)

When all said and done, it turned out these self-driving car business entities, the Tesla, Uber, Waymo, etc. had already been dancing inside "Thriller" floor. # Although they had opened the avenue for the technology; this avenue had been recognized akin to San Francisco's Lombard street, resulting from Russian meddling, road blocks piled up: Russian Hill; it was Jekyll and Hyde, from which it starts; only found worthless upon leaving: Leavenworth (leave-not-worth) street, to which never had been reached smoothly without both of human hands on the wheel with great precaution and constant manoeuvring. # Despite that they had laid their hands on the emerging technology and gotten a leg up on the public enthusiasm, at the same time, the majority of the people are still troubled by the tone of apologies for the never end inadequacies. # For all the due diligences they claimed they had done, they had not been able to deliver an all-round vehicle, to cope with full nature situation regarding on the temperature, icy, sleet, wind, and go off road for checking out the infrastructure to evaluate if the structure was strong enough to withstand the weight in an emergency situation, soft sand, thickness of ice on top of the river, everglade, Everest, and many more.

The homo sapiens have taken great challenges and prevailed many times in the history. The Dutch people traditionally created new land by filling the sea; the Egypt erected the great Pyramids; the Great Walls, Panama Canal, Tennessee Valley Projects (TVA), plus the recent Three Gorges Dam. All these large-scale projects were once and done, required no constant checks and go through loops. The Apollo moon landing was a different and technology concentrated project, same great with the first human satellite, which was from USSR so we do not want to talk about in US. The Apollo project was a typical unstructured problem with sophisticated threads, all depended on the forecasting, planning, testing and improving, for the whole period of the project and beyond. Was the system ready on the eve of launch? Not really, this was why there were so many delays, and there were so many trips. Granted that so many tests on the ground and in the air, still the project was not successful until Apollo 11, in which came the Nail Armstrong's "one small step". However, there were many missions before that first human stepping onto the moon surface.

NASA web site: https://www.nasa.gov/mission_pages/apollo/missions/index.html

This website lists some of the missions. Nevertheless, the most striking revelation of the Apollo missions was not how many tests or failures before the success. The most intriguing divulgence issue was, after Apollo 11 successful landing; howbeit, missed the marker of designated target location; after Apollo 12 successful landing, that time hit the target; then with matured "protocol" and experience, what was happened next was disappointed: The Apollo 13 disaster: the astronauts' lives hung in the balance. So, the success was still by chance. Recently Indian lost their module; same fate with Israel's one, which has dumped a lot of organisms from the earth, including tardigrades, the tough killed water bear, onto the moon. Concerns are these alien creatures could bring a biological disaster for eco system on moon: the USSR's camera left on the moon, picked up by one of the omitted Apollo missions. When the camera was brought down to the earth, examination found some "creatures" still alive, a shocking discovery. These are from my conversations with one of the coordinators of in NASA Ames research centre.

How the USSR landed on the moon is a no telling for the people on this planet, we do not have an accountable story for that, and no way to tell the events for their program.

For the Apollo program: with ample researches and resources, exhausting all the proper steps, sorting out all the possible roadblocks, and executing full spectra of due diligences; plus numerous flight tests, on top of these, the success missions of Apollo 11 and Apollo 12; be that as it may, they have not guaranteed another elaborate next Apollo 12 mission: precisely exposed the inadequacy and the bumping trajectory of the DAAI process, the unknow loop holes in the path of applying artificial intelligence. One of many aspects that we have learned from that is the success is not a once and done deal. The challenges of big technology program, such as, then Apollo program, now the big data vs autonomous vehicles, are extremely broad, deep, and profound; preparations and dry runs, can improve the outcomes; even so, the test missions are always limit, success or failure, it is elusive for human to have 100% confidence for reaching the target. As models of methodology tells, it takes infinite cycles to achieve a guaranteed outcome. And for this reason, with a "matured" recipe and success stories within the same NASA, the returning to the moon is no easy task. And for the full success deployment of autonomous vehicles in any kind of weather and conditions, there is a long way to go down the track if not take the alternative paths elucidated in our discussion in the context (§16.6) and the ART (Autonomous Rail Rapid Transit), a railless urban passenger transport, had been also unveiled outside the US soil. ART is a crossover between a train, a bus and a tram and has the flexibility to move around like a normal articulated bus. The business greedy sets in layers capitalist protections, which express in many and even in the format of the patents, had hold back the natural evaluation of civilization and only served a self-imposed delusion in their locked-in awkward mind-sets.

CHAPTER 18: A STROKE OF GENIUS

The incompetence of human languages

Summary & introduction on next volume on this book series

As elaborated in the book, it clearly reveals that the homo sapiens' enSpace representations of the external tSpace stratagems and events are limited and not in the good-willed loyalties. In a developing science manifold, we have the roman catholic church prohibition against the Copernican theory of the earth's motion; now more than 400 years later, in a political scheme, hopefully it is the case instead of ignorance, the group of US government executive branch, akin to Roman catholic church, is advocating against the candor of the climate change facts. In a general schema, the enSpace hierarchy is not in their full spectra: the limited tokens in the human language domain, the tinted views of the original nature. As seeing the colors, literally, the homo sapiens can only see the fraction of the full infinite spectra between 0.38 to 0.740 micrometres, besides missing all the other properties of them, including but not limited to, wave–particle duality, polarization (bee, ant, and the sharpest polarization vision is from cuttlefish), and so on. Every species hold the world in their specific color spectrum: while Dogs, cats, mice, rats and rabbits have very poor color visions and see mostly greys with some blues and yellows; bulls are color-blind and they charge the red cape because it is moving, not because it is red (A red-colored cape is used purely as a matter of tradition. Plus, the red color of the cape helps mask the blood of the bulls as they are fended off by the matadors. Still don't believe it? In staged experiments: bulls charge red, blue, and white objects equally and prefer moving none-red objects over still red objects). With the simple fact that humans and dogs dwell together pretty well under the same environment without issue, it is intriguing to admit those puppies can live happily without awareness of the different observations on the world between them and the English-speaking humans; vice versa.

The survival and observation-based languages had been created in the same circumstance and serve for purposes of inter-human communications; not for the communication to the environment, sort of. The early homo sapiens might have observed the nature events very differently. In the recorded past, humans viewed the thunderstorms as sort of responses from heaven for human's certain behaviours; they also made big fuss over tsunamis, earthquakes, and the solar eclipses and so on. Even now, the middle-east is still filled with religious conflictions rooting from the different interpretations of a few things. When the homo sapiens put their enSpace thoughts and observations "on the paper" in the formats of languages, the facts and events have been transcoded from the external tSpace original phenomena into the reconstructed hierarchies using building blocks within their language enclave. Members of the species who are lacking certain portions of languages will be incapable to understand, describe, and transliterate whatever they witness: suppose you carry your cell phone and descend in front of, say, the crowd who was constructing the Egypt pyramid. When you show all the basic Photo/Audio/Video/Recording functions, not mentioning the phone conversations, 5G lighting speed networks, video/texting chatting with s/he, you would be astonished by their descriptions on the magic thing you have. In the nature and the universe, we are constantly facing the same scenarios like the pyramid constructing crowd, albeit without even knowing how much we have missed because of the simple truth that these fall beyond any of our perceptions.

It is obviously, that the languages by themselves have the innate limitations.

The flawed computer languages

When the homo sapiens progress to the digital era, with all sort of computer-based hardware gadgets, software programming languages, and many a kind of interconnected social networks have been booming. Taken the most popular languages, Python, which has 33 keywords (as for now), other languages have more or less similar numbers. Starting from this limitation on the infrastructural building blocks, regardless, what they are doing out there, what all the tech firm crowds are doing is to use these (extremely limited) tokens to mingle with the infinite tSpace external world, for the AI applications.

As this has been fully dissected in the context of the book, from more than 200,000-word incompetence English language to 33-keywords Python, it goes without saying, is of a piece with ridiculous blows on the reduction in terms of the representing on the original universe, details and loyalties are in extreme jeopardy. Without further ado, it is self-evident that,

The languages toying in computer coding have their intrinsic inadequacies.

IDEA for the MOTEB
(rudiment mind of IoTs)

The IAAD (Information Artificiality : Analog to Digital) has introduced two lossy-transcoding operations in their blood. Inescapably, the launch pad of the DAAI (Digital to Analog : Artificial Intelligence) has consequently constructed on a porous fragile ground.

The major tasks of all the AI or DAAI recreations are using machine automations and decision-making in lieu of human operations. In an overhaul, they can be broken down in several compartments; in which the top two on the list are precise actions (hardware actions) and truthful assessments (iSpace AI software cognitively executes the intended functionalities originated from enSpace). In the first layer: the instructions to hardware movements, mostly rotations or/plus step-motor-based linear sliding along guiders and their combinations, had been well developed for centuries. Now just those machineries have been deployed in a total manless situation: in the past, human operated machines; now machines (either software powered virtual things or robotics) are operating machines. Charlie Chaplin's work to "screw up" the big "nuts" in the movie *Modern Time* can now be implemented by machine. The software coded instructions to hardware motions are periodical and repetitive, put in the quantum supremacy of the Shor's algorithm — easily expressed with Fourier transforms as outlined in the book, and consequently, very small number of basic blocks are required to complete the tasks (a finite-term math formula in Fourier transform). This is one of best successful demonstrative showcases on the applications of the condensed computer languages: in merely 33 keywords in Python; 32 keywords in C; 51 keywords in Java, and so on; nevertheless, they can perform tasks.

When we go to the second layer of DAAI, the truthful assessing on "all weather" situations in a computer thinking space, iSpace as we denoted, has been on a stern bumpy path from the beginning. Again, in this territory, repetitive activities can sometimes be achieved in demonstrative performances, but the full nature events have always been challenging. In the chess game or the Go game, as enumerated in the context, they essentially repetitive motions: chess is with a smaller iteration upper boundary (400 possible board setups after both initial moves and the 197,742 possible configuration, and so on), thus the IBM Deep Blue sorted it out in 1990s; Go has a higher limit — first ~130,000 possible moves — thus 20 years later with Google's Alpha Go! These limited successes are within the sufficient math formulas and the capacities for iSpace depictions to represent the little tricks in enSpace; these situations are not applied in the case of IBM Watson's Jeopardy quiz game, which employed more bandwidth to implement the tangled dimensions spans between iSpace and enSpace, a more revolutionary breakthrough than the first two board games in terms of DAAI development. The Watson Jeopardy even was happened in 2011.

Beyond these games, which perform iSpace acrobats and some of them deeply "BackRubing" into the enSpace, be that as it may, they have not extended into the tSpace, the reality in nature. From the fragile iSpace tokens — a few dozens of keywords, to enSpace languages domain — armed with more than 200,000 words in English and growing, the manifolds in iSpace domain have already exhausted their expressing capacity to match the objects, ergo the full-controlled automation evolves into dimension-reduced AI, which cuts off the higher order of factors for results to convergent. Moving further into the real tSpace: from enSpace design to deploy in real tSpace via iSpace resources, the whole process called AI events in human eyes, has just embarked the cruise at the base of the journey. NASA's Apollo moon landing program had provided the best "role model" of prototype of hybrid DAAI, artificial intelligence with all means of resources collectively.

As we had examined in detail, for such high degree of complexity, with ample learning, extensive training, and many flight-tests, plus, successfully landing, a guaranteed positive outcome was still elusive, failures had followed (Apollo 13 failed after half-successful Apollo 11 and successful Apollo 12). Furthermore, the new failures of moon landing programs from Indian and Israel are the fresh wounds, and the US returning to the moon from the same agent NASA is no easy task, currently set years down the road.

Autonomous vehicle, is one of the touchstones for a comprehensive and recreative engineering for homo sapiens to plant the ASE (a broad conception of self-drive car, Autonomous Sentient Entity) properly and seamlessly in the surrounding environment. So far, they have not very successfully: in Waymo CEO's view, a full weathered car may always elusive because "—you don't know what you don't know until you're actually in there and trying to do things", which exactly tells the truths and the facts of the limitations of human's acquired information (the IAAD harvest) and the challenges of recreations based on the reduced construction blocks of resources. Borrowing experiences of Apollo program, with loops of redesign, training, and test-drives, plus great efforts of all considered due diligences, the ASEs have been engineered to see the sunlight some day in the future. Even though, a guaranteed positive result will be still difficult to warrant from the fact of pure math that infinite cycles of refinements are required to achieve 100% accuracy.

We had explored the alternative approaches to achieve the same goal of ASE in a broad spectrum: from the basic infrastructure-based railway examples, including high-speed rails and levitation trains (both magnetic levitation and superconducting levitation) to 3-D transportation system, one of which was a conception from Amazon's propaganda, all seem the doors can be open anywhere if the stubborn mindset can be relaxed a little, retreating from the compatibility requirements to build on the current transportation foundation, which was a war-based civil infrastructure, designed and implemented last century for the original emerging basic automobiles.

While US House and Senate could not find a common ground on almost anything, on Dec 30, 2019, an AI role model was set on the ASE with High-speed rail and it has been commerically running: trade war and tariffs plus hawky attitude have not help. Diligence and hard work are always paied off.

If going back to the drawing board, without aborting the existing classic automobile infrastructure, big leap might be still achieved by the integrity of real-time communications, the on-demand point-to-point interconnections. The nodes (points) will include but not limited to human portable devices, ASEs, road structure indicators, centralized district exchangers, general hubs serving for weathering and routing the traffic and so on. The refining process for the hybrid system, which mixing manned and unmanned vehicles, will be a long way; the totally elimination of the traffic accidents will never happen, based on the discrepancies between the AI and the cognitive human thinking.

A lot of ground works and researches have to be in place for the aforementioned system to function smoothly: communicating and manoeuvring in real time plus dynamic and on-demand point-to-point executing. The installations of AI traffic "markers", new elements inside the ASEs, decisions based on the real-time information collecting and position broadcasting from and to other ASEs and systems, plus all the expected and unprepared events handlings. Hardware-wise challenges are much less than the software-wise DAAI deployments, on top of that, the real-time non-delay network information exchanging and sharing are the back bone: this makes the 5G, 6G, ... the must-have elements, and new network protocols these are capable of no-delay AI layers' transcoding are of paramount importance. Once of the advanced phenomenon in quantum entanglement can achieve none delayed communication, albeit there is a long way to make it useful for human, as for now.

When everything done and fitted into their roles, an integrity of DAAI, the global scale artificial intelligent entity collectively forms. That is what we called rudiment mind of the earth brain (MOTEB) takes into form in the heat of culminating big data processing power, increasingly distributed artificial intelligence, and seamlessly interconnected global network information highway channelling. The flow of information creates communications; the competing and gating of these streams are representations of the natural selections of survival of the fittest; finally, global consciousness comes into existence in the form of the integrity of the distributed entire assembly (IDEA).

Take the human's pain and consciousness as the prototype framework: the tiresome pain has always been related to one of the indistinguishable natures for a conscious mind. Pain may indicate real life threat events or an exaggerated cry wolf: a stroke readily kills without any symptom of pain while unbearable sharp pulses of pain under the nail or on the eyelid put people in deep agitations--upon checking often hardly to detect a blood spot if from mild piercing. Thus, they are not proportional, at the least. As elucidated in the context of the book with the example of the pain mechanism vs align class instructor, who had to heed the realities on the effectiveness and the response during her course of massage practices with the customers. Pain has ultimately helped the animals on the planet to steer their acting and planning directions constantly to a comfortable and safe development trajectory.

If pain is an inseparable element for a high intelligent species, the "pain" detecting and pain-based designing might be a good-to-have essential add-on for the DAAI based human made machinery "organisms". The most outstanding bursts of phenomena both in the nature and homo sapiens' domains are normally in forms of resonant. Not only which is the case in the quantum computing (the phenomenon the quantum computing and state are either in resonant, the superconducting case, or coherence, an alternative of resonant in laser), but also in a lot of brain storm type activities, plus many more. With Resonant Entity of All Components: REAC, IDEA, "pain", the MOTEB comes into life. The essential of the aforenoted hardware, software, protocols, together with conceptions of DAAI, REAC, IDEA, and MOTEB will be the topic and elucidated in out next volume of this book series.

ACRONYMS & NEW_{LY-COINED} WORDS:

AI: artificial intelligence

AMU: atomic machinery unit, isolated computing entity.

IDEA: integrity of the distributed entire assembly

IAAD: Information-Artificiality : Analog-Digital

DAAI: Digital-Analog : Artificiality-Intelligence

MOTEB: mind of the earth brain

QM: quantum mechanics

REAC: resonant entity of all components

enSpace: **en**closure **Space** within the skull

iSpace: denoting **i**nformation **Spac**e **e**ntity

tSpace: **t**ime-**space** of the external physical world

nosenet: tiny "transparent" pantie, to dress is for naked purpose

WFS university: worker-farmer-solider university (mocking)

BackRub: Coined by Larry Page on his original methodology

PageRank: Coined by Larry Page and Sergey Brin on their original algorithm, on which the unsuccessfully selling for $1 million had caused Google to erect as a independent company.